Political Campaigning, Elections and the Internet

The Internet first played a minor role in the 1992 US Presidential Election, and has gradually increased in importance so that it is central to election campaign strategy. However, election campaigners have, until very recently, focused on Web 1.0: websites and email.

Political Campaigning, Elections and the Internet contextualises the US Presidential Campaign of 2008 within three other contests: France 2007; Germany 2009; and the UK 2010. In offering a comparative history of the use of the Internet as an election tool, the authors are able to test the optimistic view that the Internet is transforming elections while also mapping the role the Internet plays and performs for parties and candidates. Lilleker and Jackson offer in-depth analysis demonstrating how interactive Web 2.0 online tools, including weblogs, social networking sites and file-sharing sites, are utilised and evaluate the role of these tools in the marketing and branding of parties and candidates.

Examining the interactivity between candidate, party and voter, this important book will be of strong interest to students and scholars of political science, elections, international relations and political communication. It will be of value to those within public relations, marketing and related communication and media programmes.

Darren G. Lilleker is Senior Reader, The Media School, Bournemouth University, UK.

Nigel A. Jackson is Lecturer, Plymouth Business School, University of Plymouth, UK.

Routledge research in political communication

1 **Political Campaigning in Referendums**
Framing the referendum issue
Claes H. de Vreese and Holli A. Semetko

2 **The Internet and National Elections**
A comparative study of web campaigning
Edited by Nicholas W. Jankowski, Randolph Kluver, Kirsten A. Foot and Steven M. Schneider

3 **Global Political Marketing**
Edited by Jennifer Lees-Marshment, Jesper Strömbäck and Chris Rudd

4 **Political Campaigning, Elections and the Internet**
Comparing the US, UK, France and Germany
Darren G. Lilleker and Nigel A. Jackson

Political Campaigning, Elections and the Internet

Comparing the US, UK, France and Germany

Darren G. Lilleker and Nigel A. Jackson

Routledge
Taylor & Francis Group
LONDON AND NEW YORK

First published 2011
by Routledge
2 Park Square, Milton Park, Abingdon, Oxon OX14 4RN

Simultaneously published in the USA and Canada
by Routledge
711 Third Avenue, New York, NY 10017

Routledge is an imprint of the Taylor & Francis Group, an informa business

Typeset in Times by Wearset Ltd, Boldon, Tyne and Wear

British Library Cataloguing in Publication Data
A catalogue record for this book is available from the British Library

Library of Congress Cataloging-in-Publication Data
Lilleker, Darren G.
Political campaigning, elections, and the internet : US, UK, Germany, and France / Darren G. Lilleker and Nigel A. Jackson.
p. cm. – (Routledge research in political communication ; 4)
1. Internet in political campaigns. 2. Elections–Computer network resources. 3. Comparative government. I. Jackson, Nigel A. II. Title.
JF1001.L55 2011
324.70285'4678–dc22 2010037473

ISBN: 978-0-415-57218-7 (hbk)
ISBN: 978-0-203-82943-1 (ebk)

To those whose support has made this book possible, and to the future – Eliot, Toby, Mark, Kayleigh and Yazmine.

Contents

Illustrations

Figures

Tables

Contributors

Preliminary work which shaped the conceptual framework and methodology was contributed by Casilda Malagon Ibanez in the process of research on the MA Corporate Communication (Bournemouth University) under the supervision of Dr Lilleker, and a pilot study conducted into the French Presidential candidate website which was published in the European Journal of Communication (Lilleker and Malagon 2010).

Chapter 7 was commissioned, and was produced by Eva Schweitzer, University of Mainz, Germany.

Preface

We suggest that elections can be best understood by understanding different aspects. Campaigns can be seen as consisting of several discrete but interconnected elements, as well as the sum of all elements. Audiences, potential voters perhaps, can accidentally or intentionally be exposed to all elements, or one small aspect of the campaign. Elections are part of a competitive process between political actors such as political parties and individual candidates, at national, regional and local level. These actors seek to gain competitive advantage, and this drives them to consider using and mastering a range of new and long-standing techniques and tools. Yet, at the same time elections play a key role in liberal democracies, as they are very often the main way individual citizens participate in politics. Therefore, winning is not alone all that matters. Elections may have an obvious short-term goal of maximising support at the voting booth, but there are also longer-term impacts that the conduct of campaigns can have on attitudes towards, and trust in, the political and democratic process. Thus, it is argued that how political actors interact with citizens in chasing the quick sell, can have a key bearing on the long-term health of each individual country's democracy. Elections are health checks of the body politic, telling us how strong individual political actors are vis-à-vis their competitors, but also the overall heartbeat of the political system.

In the past ten years or so there has been increasing interest in the potential impact of the Internet on the body politic, by and large outside of election campaigns. At the same time, there has also been growing interest in the impact of the Internet on the techniques used by professional campaigners during the short election period. This book has arisen because we were interested in assessing both of these drivers of interest in election campaigns. Thus far it seems we have to either look at the impact of the Internet on democracy between elections, or how the Internet is utilised as a tool for potentiating the maximisation of vote winning. We seek, however, to see if the study of online election campaigns has to be an either/or situation. In short, we are seeking to assess whether we can now identify a discrete Elections 2.0 which combines the practical needs of the permanent campaign with those of encouraging greater elector-elected dialogue between voters and the elected.

The ideas contained within this book have been several years in incubation prior to their reaching maturity. We had previously focused essentially on the use of e-campaigns in one country, the UK, and that mostly in 'peacetime' between elections. However, we felt that this provided only a partial insight, a sense which was magnified by the fact that the Internet has no national boundaries. Moreover, we felt that the development of the Internet was potentially changing political discourse. From the very outset, debates have centred on the extent to which the Internet and associated technologies would enhance democracy, but the debates have primarily concerned their possible impact on governance and democracy. We feel that, potentially, Web 2.0 might move on this debate so that within election campaigns, political participation is not limited to voting. This book seeks to test whether there is some substance to this view, or whether it is naïve 'pie in the sky' thinking.

In raising these big questions regarding participation, we considered two different lines of enquiry. The first direction of research relates to the nature of campaigning and the use of technology for campaigning purposes. Campaigning within corporate, pressure group, not-for-profit and political contexts, constantly seeks an edge and over time has adapted to a range of communication tools. Equally, our context of practice, political communication, has itself adapted to the challenges of new tools and technologies; the impact of television for example had profound impacts upon the prioritisation of the visual over the rhetorical. The latest technologies have been used to enhance the online environment. The Internet is now firmly embedded as a tool of political communication, but largely has played a peripheral function, having historically a limited role and so little tangible impact upon the behaviour of political actors. Web 2.0 tools are significantly different to those of the Web 1.0 era and the early days of the static web page focused Web presences. We thus sought to assess whether the social uses of Web 2.0, and the associated big ideas, will lead to a change in political communication, as the online user appears to have learned to expect a qualitatively and quantitatively different, more participatory, experience.

Our second line of enquiry focuses on the more incremental and evolutionary shifts in political communication which are driven by lesson learning between campaigns and nations. Specifically, we seek to capture evidence to test the notion that political campaigns do learn from one another and that the diffusion of innovations can, therefore, be mapped. This line of enquiry began as an MA student charged into the office of Darren Lilleker with the idea that elections must now be interactive, and the question of how interactivity could be measured. The conceptual framework developed for this, published elsewhere and revised, was extended and the data collection process expanded from selecting a sample to analysing whole websites. However, it was the overall idea that raised a number of empirical questions regarding both the strategic thinking underpinning the use of the Internet with political campaigns and so the experience that campaigns potentiated for visitors to their online presences. As the ideas for measurement developed, the need for comparative work became apparent to test for the embeddedness of Web 2.0 within the professional or marketised model of political election campaigning. Comparing the presidential election in France and the US was not uncontroversial due to the differing extents of Internet penetration and traditions of campaigning, but broadening the comparison to parliamentary systems raised further problematics. Germany and the UK were included as test cases to test the Americanisation thesis to an extent, and given the interest in both countries that followed the innovative techniques employed by Obama, this appeared highly fertile territory. Thus, over numerous debates, some accompanied by a pint of good English real ale, and the helpful comments of reviews of our original proposal, the plan for research came together. The journey since has been an interesting one. Obama appeared to tear up the campaigning rule book, while European parties paid only lip service to ideas of Web 2.0: but this is only a fragment of the story we will be telling.

Acknowledgements

This book would not have happened without the help of a number of people. In both instances our family provided the support and love, not to mention coffee, that we needed. Our students and colleagues at both Bournemouth University and the University of Plymouth have helped stimulate us with ideas and comments about online political communication in general. Given that this book is about the Internet, some of our ideas have been tested out in our blogs (http://darrenlilleker.blogspot.com and http://politicalpr.blogspot.com), and we thank those people who have provided comments. We owe a very particular debt to Eva Schweitzer, whose expertise, forbearance and professionalism were key to enabling us to compare four different countries. In addition to help from our family and colleagues, we would like to state our debt of gratitude to our Commissioning Editor, Hannah Shakespeare, and Editorial Assistant, Harriet Frammingham, at Routledge who saw something in our original idea, and have both helped us take an idea from the drawing board to being published. The biggest debt, however, is to Casilda Malagon Ibanez; her initial questions and analysis of the websites of candidates participating in the 2007 French Presidential Election kick-started our thoughts for what became this book. While it is difficult to acknowledge how discussions and idea development contribute to the overall shape of a project as many of these take place with numerous individuals, Casilda played a pivotal role in drawing our thinking to a range of questions that were beyond our usual focus on developments in the UK system alone. Thus, we recognise her significant contribution and in doing so congratulate her on the 2010 marriage to Anees Al Qudaihi, and wish them both all the happiness in the world.

On a more personal note, we would both like to thank the restorative powers of real ale, which always helped when our creative minds were flagging.

Although we have many people to thank, any errors are of course our own. Though the advantage of having two authors is that if there are any mistakes, you can rest assured that we shall each blame the other; or collectively blame the real ale.

1 Introduction

On Thursday 6 November 2008, Brian Eno, the musician and music producer, stated on the BBC's flagship current affairs discussion programme *Question Time*, that the 2008 US Presidential Election was the first to be won on the Internet. The relevance of Eno's observation is not that it demonstrates a unique insight he alone has, rather that an interested 'amateur' has come to this conclusion. This suggests that this impression of the impact of the Internet in 2008 is widespread. However, we do not need to take the view of just individuals such as Eno, as professionals also take a similar view. For example, *Wired* magazine (Stirland 2008) noted that Obama's victory was 'propelled by the Internet', suggesting that without Web technologies as a fundraising and organising tool he would not have won. Similarly, Greengard (2009) agrees that the Internet was central to Obama's electoral success, and moreover he concludes that how politicians and the public interact will never be the same again. That the Internet 'won' the election for Obama, and as a consequence other elections will never be the same again, is fast becoming a popular axiom. The purpose of this book is to contextualise the US Presidential Campaign of 2008 within three other contests: France 2007; Germany 2009; and the UK 2010. In offering a comparative history of the use of the Internet as an election tool, we are able to test the optimistic view that the Internet is transforming elections while also mapping the role the Internet plays and performs for parties and candidates.

The optimistic view of the Internet as a revolutionary tool is not one limited to either the US or Obama. It is argued that in 2005 the Internet, and so its use as a communication tool within society, for corporate communication and in our context of the election campaign, changed forever. It did so not because of a technological 'big bang', but because of a conceptual idea: Web 2.0. Up to this time, the Internet had gradually increased in use, importance and possibly impact during Western election campaigns. The Internet first played a role (albeit very minor) in an election in 1992, and this has increased at each subsequent series of elections. However, few commentators stuck their neck out and stated that this technology would transform election campaigning. Many commentators had suggested that the Internet might transform democracy, but far less credence was given to its importance on the process of how citizens decided to choose their representatives. The focus was on the impact of the Internet on governmental decision making, not how the Internet shaped individual voters' decision making. However, the first few years of the twenty-first century saw a 'cranking up' in the use of the Internet within the body politic. In particular, as a number of new communication channels became socially popular, such as Facebook, YouTube and Twitter, created in 2004, 2005 and 2006 respectively, pioneering political actors began to adopt these new technological developments. Taken alone, as technological improvements, these developments would have had a marginal impact on elections. However, if Web 2.0 cumulatively heralds a revolution in online communication, this may be driving changes in how organisations communicate in general, and so collectively transform the societal impact these technologies may have.

In 2005 O'Reilly published an article where he suggested that the nature and use of the Internet was radically changing. The era of Web 1.0, that of static content-driven websites was, he believed, being enhanced by a radically different phase in the Internet's short history. He suggested that Web 2.0 represented a fundamental change in how the Internet would be used. O'Reilly identified seven key themes,[1] the sum of which suggested that not only did new Web technologies offer increasingly interactive possibilities, but perhaps more importantly, the attitude of users towards the Internet was changing. This bottom-up approach that O'Reilly highlighted implied significant change for political actors in 'peacetime' between elections, but also the 'wartime' of election campaigns.

In the era of Web 1.0, the Internet played a secondary campaigning role in the four countries we will study. Probably the most advanced was in America, and certainly the experience of Howard Dean in the primaries did increase interest in the Internet (Chadwick 2006). Although the leading candidates did mobilise support and raise funds online (Cornfield 2004; Kim and Margolis 2005; Vaccari 2008), the Internet was still a second-order campaigning channel in the 2004 US Presidential Elections, lagging way behind the advertising and public relations use of mass communication channels. Probably next in importance was the UK, where during the 2005 General Election, the Internet became a mainstream campaigning channel for the first time, but its real impact was limited to the use of email lists to mobilise support offline (Coleman and Ward 2005; Jackson 2006a). At the German 2005 National Elections, use of the Internet was evolving but it was also a secondary communication tool (Albrecht 2007; Schweitzer 2008a, 2008b). Some way behind the other three countries was the experience of the 2002 French Presidential Election, where the Internet was a novelty. The inherent logic of O'Reilly's thesis is that the electoral world has changed forever, and that with the force for change from below, political actors cannot ignore the Internet; rather, they should embrace it in their election campaigns. If O'Reilly's analysis is correct, at the next tranche of elections the Internet would become a primary campaigning channel. We will explore the meaning of Web 2.0, and what impact this concept has had on elections. In short, we shall consider whether we have now entered the era of Elections 2.0. This book seeks to identify whether academics and practitioners can identify common lessons to be learnt from the four elections we will study. Therefore, the rest of this chapter will help set up the key debates that this book will explore. First, we will explore the evolution and professionalisation of election campaigning in general, as this underpins our approach to understanding and assessing online election campaigns. This will lead on to a contextualisation of Web 2.0, its social implications and the potential impact that new technologies may have on the conduct of election campaigns.

Modern election campaigns

Textbooks on elections typically focus on their evolution, purpose, the electoral system applied and the type of government they result in (Katz 1997; Farrell 1997; Powell 2000). Whilst these factors are part of the contextual background of the four elections we study, and we will return to them in Chapter 2, our focus here is narrower. We are interested in how parties and candidates campaign during an election period. The Colombia School (Lazarsfeld *et al.* 1944) focused on the importance of communication and campaigning. This was, however, soon replaced by the Michigan School in America (Campbell *et al.* 1960), and the Nuffield studies in the UK (Butler and Rose 1960; Butler and Stokes 1971). The received wisdom at this historical juncture was that the campaign itself had little effect, but that the principal actors undertook campaigning techniques such as giving speeches, holding meetings and talking to the media because it was expected of them and it might have some minor impact. This view was the dominant academic view until the 1980s. However, this approach is now challenged, and increasingly, the view that election campaigns matter has support (Holbrook 1996; Farrell and Schmitt-Beck 2002).

The growing importance of election campaigns is not something that has happened by accident; a range of social and political factors have led to increased numbers of voters that need convincing of who to support at the ballot box. The received wisdom is thus to target these median voters, terms such as 'Average Joe', Middle England or in Germany the *ungebunden*, literally translated as the unattached (Zelle 1995; Lilleker 2003). The perceived importance of the floating or swing voter (*Wechselwähler*), who has little loyalty to any party and so may vote differently between elections, has increased since the late 1970s/early 1980s, which means that political actors now put greater emphasis on campaigning. We shall discuss three interrelated concepts which we believe are shaping the nature of election campaigns, and hence why, how and with what effect the Internet in general, and Web 2.0 applications in particular, may have: postmodern campaigning; the permanent campaign; and professional campaigning.

A number of commentators have suggested that the evolution of communication technologies has had an effect on political campaigning (Wring 1996; Blumler and Gurevitch 1995). We feel that this approach is best presented by Norris (2000), who suggests that campaigning in the past 100 years or so can be divided into three different ages dependent upon the communication channels and techniques used. In pre-modern campaigning, from the nineteenth century through to the Second World War, the dominant political communication technique was direct communication, such as face-to-face meetings and public events (Maarek 1995; Norris 2000). Election campaigning was characterised by three features: a partisan press; reliance on local volunteers; and a short national campaign (Norris *et al.* 1999). The second, or modern era has been dominated by television (Harrop 1986; Kavanagh 1995; Denver and Hands 1998). Although mass communication had existed for some years with a national print media and radio, it was television which gradually became the mass communication tool of choice for politicians. From the late 1950s/early 1960s, political communication was essentially mediated (Swanson and Mancini 1996).

If the modern era of political campaigning has been dominant since the 1950s, a number of commentators (Wring 1996; Norris 2000) have suggested that from the early 1990s it has been challenged by a third era, the postmodern. Whilst not yet dominant, postmodern political campaigning has encouraged greater use of unmediated communication between citizen and politician. The postmodern era has been driven by three factors. First, television has become more fragmented, with significant increases in the number of terrestrial and satellite television stations (Norris *et al.* 1999). Second, to maintain market share the national press has had to become less partisan in nature (Norris *et al.* 1999), so political parties can no longer rely on communicating their messages through a few national newspapers. The third factor, the introduction of ICTs such as the fax, the Internet and text messaging, enables politicians to directly communicate with targeted groups of voters. The postmodern campaign uses a much wider range of techniques and tools. Norris's approach suggests that campaigning was originally based on direct communication between politicians and electors. This, then, was largely replaced by indirect communication via the mass media, and now direct communication is possible again. In postmodern campaigning, political actors will use both direct and indirect communication channels, building what Howard (2006) describes as a hypermedia campaign.

The second concept that we will consider is the 'permanent campaign', a phrase coined in 1980 by Blumenthal. There is significant support for the view that a permanent campaign is now a fact of American political life (Nimmo 1999; Ornstein and Mann 2000; Thurber 2002). Bill Clinton is credited with being the first permanently campaigning president (Jones 2000), and George W. Bush continued this process (Thurber 2002). The essence of permanent campaigning is that the clear separation between campaigning and governing is blurred, so that political actors seek to campaign every day and dominate the political agenda, not just during a formal election campaign (Orstein and Mann 2000; Heclo 2000).

Although Nimmo (1999) believes that permanent campaigning has taken several centuries to develop, most commentators see its history as much more recent and fuelled by particular political factors. Blumenthal (1980) believed that the existence of a professional political consultant class was vital in altering the nature of election campaigning. Steger (1999) adds a more simplistic motive, namely that candidates turned to the permanent campaign as a means of ensuring incumbency. But it could be argued that politicians have always sought re-election; what, therefore, is so different about the past thirty years? Peters (2002) provides an answer by identifying four changes to American politics: realignment of the political parties; changes to the electorate; new communications technology; and the ever-growing demand for funding. Two further trends help link the Internet with the permanent campaign. First, in recent years the influence of marketers within the political consultant class has grown. Second, Thurber (2002) adds that the tragedy of 9/11 highlighted the importance of coordinated communication within a 24/7 news cycle. Therefore, the nature of the permanent campaign will be influenced by developments in the Internet, such as Web 2.0 applications. Permanent campaigning is, according to Ornstein and Mann (2000), a zero sum game with one winner. Therefore, the techniques used are constantly evolving as the competitors seek an advantage. Because the permanent campaign has no end, participants are always striving for new means of dominating the political agenda. As a result, Web 2.0 applications have attracted great interest from those looking for an edge.

The third concept is the increasing professionalisation of political campaigning. In the era post the 1992 and 1996 campaigns of Bill Clinton in the USA and of Blair in the UK in 1997, phrases such as 'campaign professionalisation' (Gibson and Rommele 2001: 40) and descriptions epitomised by 'the smoothness, slickness and all-too-evident professionalism of recent campaigning' (Watts 1997: 142) have become common in academic parlance. For some this is related to the increased employment of professional strategists and consultants who have, in the words of Wring (1997), colonised political campaign headquarters (see also Farrell *et al.* 2001; Scammell 1995). Equally, such developments have given rise to discussion of the marketisation of politics, both in terms of its reliance on marketing communications and public relations (Jamieson 1996; Kavanagh 1995; Maarek 1997; Newman 1999) as well as debates surrounding the introduction of a marketing philosophy into politics more generally (Newman 1994; Lees-Marshment 2001, 2008). What is common to most works on campaigning is the sense that political campaigning is in a constant state of flux, adapting a variety of strategic and tactical tools in order to gain electoral advantage.

Professionalisation has been criticised as a blanket term which obscures many of the specifics of the evolution of political campaigning. Indeed, a call has been made to use instead phrases such as specialisation of tasks, the increased use of experts and the management or centralisation of the campaign (Lilleker and Negrine 2002). However, there is one aspect of this professionalisation that is important for this study. That is the notion of campaigning evolving: 'The introduction of national newspapers, of radio and later of television as forms of mass communication altered the ways politicians sought to communicate with the public, in the same way that the Internet will alter practices in the future' (Lilleker and Negrine 2002: 101) This implicitly argues that rather than categorising change within eras (Norris 2000) or stages (Blumler and Kavanagh, 1999), we should focus on the way in which campaigns adapt, and adapt to, new techniques of communication.

The design of the style and content of messages is equally consistent with the marketisation of political campaigning. Though some argue that political marketing as a study should centre on the prescription of the market-oriented party – one that designs its policies as well as communication as a result of market research among voters (Lees-Marshment 2001; 2008) – there is little evidence of the existence of such a party (Lilleker and Negrine 2006). At best, the evidence to suggest parties or candidates have any adherence to a market orientation is patchy across various aspects of the design of the brand and its messages (Lilleker and Lees-Marshment 2005), and the one study that discussed all aspects of a campaign, albeit in a single nation, found marketing was a tool mainly used in the context of the design of communication (Lilleker *et al.* 2006). Thus, we would expect that professionalisation and marketisation would drive parties to use the most up-to-date communication devices available via the Internet. One study of UK elections described political strategists as being akin to magpies (Lilleker *et al.* 2006), borrowing tools and ideas from marketing, social communication and any other realm in order to improve the sophistication of their campaign. We build on this to suggest that this process of lesson learning is not just related to the use of tools, but also techniques of usage; and lessons will not simply be learned within a domestic context, but from other campaigns around the world. In particular, the lessons of recent online elections may encourage the targeting of voters in a way that will draw them to the campaign.

Comparing online election campaigns

The use of the Internet in America has probably generated more research than any other single country. This may, in part, be explained by the Americanisation hypothesis, which suggests that as the dominant world economy, American political actors are also the first to develop and master new technologies and techniques. As a consequence, this hypothesis suggests that all other countries learn their lessons from American practice. If this is the case, this book would simply identify the use of Web 2.0 applications in the 2008 US Presidential election, and see where and how they have been used or adapted by our other elections. We suggest that the Internet in general, and Web 2.0 specifically, does not recognise national boundaries. Developments in one country are as likely as another to influence the use of Web 2.0 as are those in the US. This book will seek to identify what lessons different campaigns learn from one another. Rather than suggesting an inherent Americanisation, we suspect that there are other structural factors which shape how and why political actors use Web 2.0.

Existing comparative studies of the Internet have primarily taken two different forms. First, a number of individual articles have compared the use of the Internet in two or more countries (Gibson *et al.* 2003a; Gibson and McAllister 2003). Second, a number of books have introduced an overall framework with a range of individual case study chapters written by different authors. Gibson *et al.* (2003a) focused on three factors: campaigning and style of politics; electoral outcomes and the balance of power between parties; and internal organisation and democracy. Kluver *et al.* (2007) applied the concept of the Web sphere (Foot and Schneider 2002) to understand the impact of technological, cultural and political factors on Internet use by a range of political actors (not just parties and candidates). Ward *et al.* (2008) applied to twelve national case studies an assessment of whether four factors influenced Internet use in elections: nature of the party system; election process rules; the role of conventional media; and access to the Internet. Learning lessons from these studies, our approach will consider the following factors as possibly shaping the use of the Internet in election campaigns:

1 Political system. In presidential systems the focus is on the individual who holds Executive power. In parliamentary systems the focus is more complex. Yes, it may well be on the person who as party leader may lead the government, but it can also focus on the desired party. Equally, as electors are choosing, technically if not in practice, their locally elected representative, there may be a multi-layered approach to campaigning.
2 Electoral system. Each of our four countries uses a slightly different electoral system. The two presidential systems have some form of selection to whittle the process down to two main candidates. In the US there is an internal party process of primaries, which selects one candidate to represent either the Democrat or Republican Party. Whilst third-party candidates may enter the actual presidential election, they are usually largely ignored. In France, the parties select their candidate and then voters have two rounds of votes. The first round is based on the whole slate of candidates. The second round two weeks later is of the top two candidates. In the UK, a first-past-the-post system for single member constituencies operates, where the candidate who generates the most votes in a constituency is elected (they don't need to secure more than 50 per cent). The Prime Minister is the leader of the party with the most seats. This system nearly always delivers one party or another with a majority of seats, and so is able to form a single party government. In contrast, Germany uses a mixed member proportional representation system. Half of the seats in parliament (Bundestag) are elected as in the UK in single member constituencies, the other half based on party lists. Voters have two votes, one for the constituency and one for the party. Whilst there are two main political parties, there are a number of minor parties, and hence coalitions are a common outcome of elections.
3 Party or candidate. In strong party systems, such as the UK and Germany election strategy, resources and campaigning messages are controlled largely by the party (Klingemann *et al.* 1994). Whereas in candidate-based elections such as in the US, the candidates have to build up their organisation and resources, and hence there is a stronger individualist model (Miller and Stokes 1963). Anstead and Chadwick (2008) suggest that this creates an incentive for candidates to use the Internet to generate funds, mobilise supporters and promote their messages. Although French Presidential elections are clearly based on a candidate, there is a much stronger party emphasis than in the US.

4 Party size. One of the key debates about the Internet is whether it maintains 'politics as usual' (Margolis and Resnick 2000), so that inequalities offline are maintained online. Or, if the Internet will help level the playing field (Gibson and Ward 1997), by allowing smaller political actors to bypass traditional communication channels such as the media and have their voice heard. This has been referred to as the normalisation versus equalisation hypothesis. In essence, this argument is over whether the Internet is merely another communication channel, dominated by larger political actors, or whether smaller political actors can be equally successful online. The politics-as-usual hypothesis suggests that the larger political actors dominate cyberspace because they have both the financial and staffing resources to do so, and their advantages offline (such as access to the media) support their online activities (Margolis and Resnick 2000). Conversely, the level playing field approach suggests that smaller actors are likely to utilise the Internet as effectively as the major players, and the media can be bypassed so lessening the disadvantages they have offline (Jackson 2006b). As with any approach, there is a third way which suggests that the picture is more complex than an either/or approach, that the Internet can be used to both maintain the status quo, but also to help undermine it at the same time; in other words, there is an 'ebb and flow' (Gibson *et al.* 2003). The evidence, thus far, suggests that the use of the Internet in the US and Germany is nearer to normalisation, the UK is a more mixed picture and in France there is limited data for a conclusion.
5 Ideology. Ideology is the party's position on a left–right continuum on the socio-economic axis, according to EUprofiler (www.euprofiler.eu/). Sudulich (2009) used expert views to assess a party, while we will apply the EUprofiler approach. Whilst Sudulich concluded that it was left-wing parties who were more likely to use the Internet, there is also evidence that smaller right-wing parties seek to utilise the Internet (Copsey 2003; Jackson and Lilleker 2009a). We seek to assess whether there are any relationships between approaches to the Internet, in particular, the use of interactive tools and the ideology of the party, its ethos or political tradition and its political stance on democratic participation.

Conceptualising Web 2.0

When conceptualising the Internet, it is important to note the division between the nature of the infrastructure (such as IP protocols) and actual uses of that infrastructure (such as email) (DiMaggio *et al.* 2001; Bohman 2004). Researchers in IT and computers tend to concentrate on the former, whereas our focus is on the latter. Due to the permanent development of the technology that supports the Internet, it is also a constantly evolving medium. The first phase of the Internet is now referred to as Web 1.0, but as we noted above, since 2005 there has been talk of Web 2.0, and already some media commentators are discussing Web 3.0 (Richards 2007). Web 1.0 was the iteration of online communication that hinged upon the page metaphor – as with a book, a website was seen as offering a linear experience where user behaviour was largely limited to moving between pages to gain information. More interactive features existed, however usage was limited by website designers; thus initially, the Internet user was presented with very limited interactive opportunities. These gave way to a range of tools that allowed users to interact with the architecture of a website, what Stromer-Galley (2004) refers to as interactivity as a product of the technology. However, it is suggested that Web 1.0 has now been overshadowed by Web 2.0 (O'Reilly 2005; Barsky 2006; Barsky and Purdon 2006), where online communication can be an interactive process that replicates and contributes to a global conversation. Arguably, we can suggest that there are no such concepts as Web 1.0 or Web 2.0, but in fact they are simply stages in a process of evolution in the technology and social use of the Internet. However, it is a useful way of delineating stages of technological development and their attendant effects on online communication.

Since the late 1980s, technologies for browsing and creating online content have improved and so usage has become more widespread, reaching an almost critical mass. The first uses of the Internet situated it as an elite communication tool, where only a small minority had the necessary software skills to create sites, and as Java and other software applications developed these offered more and more sophisticated experiences for visitors. The Web 1.0 phase was largely understood from the site creator's perspective, and studies focused on how organisational objectives could be met through adapting to the online environment. Developers would request feedback from site or application users, and academics reviewed how functions of websites matched with users' expected and actual gratification (Jackson and Lilleker 2007). However, there was a gulf between those who saw the Internet as a way of increasing corporate profits, and developers producing shareware and freeware and working in a non-hierarchical way with the online community, if albeit a small group of users: techno-geeks, perhaps (Chadwick 2007). The adaptation of the Internet by those involved in file sharing appears to have had a wider impact on the uses of the Internet. Hence, we now have two parallel, but competing approaches; the organisation-oriented perspective still exists, but it is increasingly challenged by an array of users who use the Internet as a collaboratory, non-hierarchical communication environment.

Although the Internet remains fundamentally based around websites with specific addresses, the potentially revolutionary aspect of recent developments, particularly with the launch of online blogging software and social networking sites (boyd and Ellison 2007; Phillips 2007; Haspells 2008), is that it is becoming easier for the ordinary Web visitor to not only browse, but also contribute to websites. For example, file sharing sites such as YouTube allow anyone with a video camera, which now includes most mobile phone users, and a fast Internet connection to upload any of their own videos to the site. Links can then be forwarded to friends across the globe and can be embedded within other online presences. Profiles on the myriad social networking sites are easy to create and can be as simple or as complex as the user desires; updates to Facebook or Twitter can be sent from the majority of mobile phones. Collectively, such sites fit the definition of

> Web-based services that allow individuals to (1) construct a public or semi-public profile within a bounded system (2) articulate a list of other users with whom they share a connection and (3) view and traverse their list of connections and those made by others within the system.
>
> (boyd and Ellison 2007)

Such changes imply that the 'techno geeks' are shaping the Internet into a more anarchic and user-led platform, yet this may not be the case for political campaign communication.

Websites, and thus Web 1.0, were associated with a philosophy of build it and they will come. It has become de rigueur for any serious organisation to have a website and is as crucial a way to talk to audiences as a shop window, magazine or press release. However, within the environment associated with Web 2.0 this philosophy is turned on its head. Blogger, Facebook, LinkedIn, as well as more specialist sites such as PROpenMic or MyRagan, work on the philosophy that they will come and build it (Barsky 2006). The content built by the users of Web 2.0 tools can be on any subject: personal lives, concerns and issues; music and popular culture; or indeed politics. Whilst media commentators and satirists have always intervened in the political communication process, it is now possible for any citizen to express their support or opposition to any aspect of a party or candidate's platform. This presents a danger, in terms of the public leading the agenda and undermining a campaign, but also potentiates a range of opportunities. Web 2.0 technologies allow parties to meet and interact with Internet users in public forums. Issues can be discussed, opponents won over and supporters converted into advocates. This suggests that election campaigns may well be events which will include a broader range of actors, each playing a more significant role, some independently and others in tandem with parties and candidates. This vision begs the question of how this fits within the professionalised model of campaigning.

Professionalised campaigning conceptually suggests a centralisation of strategic thinking and control over all messages and communication (Lilleker and Negrine 2002); however, Web 2.0 challenges these notions that are at the heart of accounts of professionalisation. Hence, the use of Web 2.0 raises the issue of whether major political actors can control campaign communication any more. The normalisation hypothesis implies that online political campaigning is largely a one-way vertical communication channel. The equalisation hypothesis suggests that, rather than controlling political communication, the Internet forces political actors to respond to bottom-up developments. Therefore, online political communication should adhere to the norms of broader online communication and adopt a bottom-up two-way vertical and horizontal mode and style. This book assesses which of these positions is tenable within a Web 2.0 environment.

As these technologies produce communication tools that are embedded within the lives of the masses, can politics maintain its top-down monologic style or will there be a noticeable shift towards a dialogue? The advertising industry is told to adapt to Web 2.0 and social media via the Internet or die (McStay 2009); marketing and public relations professionals are instructed to embrace interactivity and adapt to it (Scott 2010); society meanwhile seems to be already enthralled with such technologies (Van Dijk 2007) as more and more individual members of Western societies join Facebook, learn how to tweet, and share photographs on Flickr, videos on YouTube and their thoughts on weblogs. Whether this constitutes a social revolution is a moot question, but what it does suggest is that social interaction is changing, that barriers between public and private are eroding, and that these trends not only affect social behaviour but also organisational communication.

Conclusion

Web 2.0 opens up the possibility of a social pressure for political communicators to enter into a dialogue with their supporters and potential voters. This impetus is at no time more pressing than during an election. At these times the electorate require information and are increasingly going online to receive a diet of political news and gossip. While information seeking does not suggest a desire to interact with the party per se, if the option is available it may provide a richer political experience than simply reading content. Equally, some members of the electorate, as well as media commentators, may well be participating online themselves. The online users are, in increasing numbers, creating commentary, images and videos, some of which can go viral and have greater reach and influence than any official communication. Election campaigns allow political parties and candidates to experiment, and they can become catalysts for new forms of political communication (Albrecht *et al.* 2007). However, are parties and candidates harnessing this power in any way during elections? Do parties and candidates attempt to persuade voters to support them by entering into conversations and allowing visitors to their various Web presences to post material, comment and develop a dialogue?

Such behaviours are argued to have become the norm within a Web 2.0 environment, but is there any suggestion that the behaviour of electoral parties and candidates is going to fall in line with this trend in communication? We propose that there are two potential options party leaders, candidates and their strategists may consider when assessing how to implement a Web 2.0 campaigning strategy. They may conceptualise Web 2.0 as merely a persuasive resource generation tool, or embrace the more social aspects of Web 2.0 and seek to interact with their Internet-using audience. Whilst distinct philosophical approaches, we would also enquire if in practical terms these offer the distinction they appear to possess, or whether political strategists are attempting to create a set of hybrid communication tools that bridge both Web 1.0 and 2.0 and what impact can be detected on their engagement with the Web 2.0 savvy user?

2 E-campaigning and e-elections

The comparative study of electioneering began with Butler and Ranney (1992), who noted that in the elections they studied from 1950 to 1990, there was no fundamental change in the electoral systems, but that there was in the campaigning practices used. As a result, they suggested that 'Elections, once oddly amateur and intuitive, have become an increasingly technical and self-conscious operation' (Butler and Ranney 1992: 4). This statement is consistent with a plethora of research emerging on the subject of the professionalisation of political communication and campaigning (see Lilleker and Negrine 2003), which collectively adheres to the assumption that what political actors do during election campaigns matters. However, this view has been contested, particularly in the context of election campaigning. The traditional view of psephologists was that what parties and candidates did during an election had little, or no, impact on the result (see Lazarsfeld *et al.* 1944; Converse 1966; Zaller 2002). There are a number of different explanations for this approach. It is suggested that individual voting behaviour is primarily influenced by long-term factors which shape an individual's political outlook, such as education, occupation and their network of family and friends, the latter of which are argued to have some potential impact on preference shaping (O'Keefe and Atwood 1981). Within such an orthodoxy little or no room was available for shorter-term influences such as what politicians themselves said or campaign events. Another argument for sidelining campaigns is the belief that it is the economic and possibly political context of an election which determines the outcome (Heath *et al.* 2001). If the economy is doing well, the incumbent may benefit, but if there is a recession, the incumbent may be blamed and reap an electoral whirlwind as a result. One variation of the minimal effects approach to the study of election campaigning is permanent campaigning (Ornstein and Mann 2000), the belief that it is campaigning outside of an election which matters most. Therefore, if campaigning has any impact, it is in slowly changing individual and public opinion in the years running up to the election, rather than the finite period of the formal campaign. However, in the past twenty years the minimal effects school has been increasingly challenged.

One school of thought that has dominated the recent study of American presidential elections is that campaigns do have an effect, even if they may not be the prime factor. Although Holbrook (1996) and Campbell (2000) disagree slightly in their analysis, they both essentially suggest that what happens in the campaign, as well as what happens before it, has an impact. Holbrook (1996) suggests that what happens during a campaign shapes public opinion, and therefore, he suggests that the outcomes of US presidential elections are shaped by a combination of two factors: what happens during the campaign; and prior national conditions. Campbell (2000) takes a similar predictive effects approach and suggests a combination of political competition, incumbency and economic conditions shapes the result. Within the UK, there has also been a growing body of thought which has suggested that general election campaign activity can have an effect (Denver and Hands 1992, 1997; Denver 1998). In part, this greater interest in an election campaign reflects the enhanced use of professional communicators. The inherent, but empirically untested, logic of this development is that if well-paid and experienced professionals are spending a lot of effort during campaigns, then they must believe it has an effect. Studies from the US suggest that spend has an impact, as the more that candidates spend, the more voters have recall of their name, can offer positive evaluations of the candidate and so have greater propensity to vote for them (see Jacobsen 1978, 1990). A link has also been suggested between campaign effort, a function of spend and resource utilisation, and vote share in constituency-based contests in the UK (Denver and Hands 1997). However, and perhaps more fundamentally, the growing attention given to campaigns reflects long-term changes in voting behaviour. In the countries we are studying there has been greater volatility in voting behaviour over the past twenty to thirty years. Where once voting behaviour could be fairly predictable, this is less so now (Schmitt-Beck and Farrell 2002). Therefore, at the beginning of an election campaign there appear to be more undecided or floating voters who might be persuaded by parties' arguments. We argue that, potentially, the Internet could play a key role in providing political parties and their candidates with an opportunity to speak directly to voters (Morris 1999), rather than relying on two-step or multi-step flow models of communication (Lazarsfeld *et al.* 1944). This direct communication, if it adopts more interactive models, may also replicate the effects found within peer-to-peer communication, which is argued to promote learning and recall, within an array of contexts from purchase behaviour to healthy living (Thomas 2005). Furthermore, within a political context, online interaction may lead to offline discussions, so deepening and enhancing participatory culture (Barber 1984; Chadwick 2006).

Arguably, one would expect the Internet to now be embedded within the professional model of political campaigning. It is suggested that, within a postmodern era of political communication, voters will be ruthlessly targeted using every possible appropriate medium (Norris 2001a). Furthermore, if we adopt the description of the process of professionalisation as one that is evolutionary (Lilleker and Negrine 2003), adapting new technologies and innovations to improve outputs, again the Internet should be a key feature within political campaigning as much as it is within the spheres of public relations and marketing. As the Internet has become a mainstream political tool, a set of specialist skills has come into demand across politics, both in government departments, parties, local administrative centres and campaign teams. Equally, as noted by Negrine (2007: 196), professionalisation is also driven by 'the accumulation of knowledge, in part as experiences spread and new techniques become possible'. This links to the notion of political marketers and strategists as magpies (Lilleker *et al.* 2006), adopting anything that appears to offer some form of communicational advantage. In particular, strategists attempt to design campaigns using myriad examples gathered from elections around the world, extrapolate evidence for success and the means by which these were achieved, and then adapt for the context in which they are working. It is this observation that underpins our comparative study, and suggests that development will be incremental across nations, with the campaign being assumed to have clear effects on the electorate.

If we also assume that election campaigns do have an effect, then Farrell and Schmitt-Beck (2002) provide a model which may be relevant to Web 2.0. They suggest that campaign effects can be divided into micro and macro effects. The micro effects are the immediate effects influencing a campaign, such as events and policy statements. This largely has been the focus of most election effects studies. However, macro effects are long-term effects that the campaign has on society or the political process. We would suggest that if the use of Web 2.0 applications during our four elections has had a long-term effect, then potentially this could be on the level of voter participation both during the election and possibly continuing after the conclusion of the contest; though we are not directly seeking to detect the latter. Shifts towards a participatory e-democracy were predicted in the late 1990s prior to the bursting of the dot.com bubble (Morris 1999), however it is argued that due to social demands, there is increasing pressure placed upon political organisations to provide richer and deeper participatory opportunities (Stoker 2006; Coleman and Blumler 2009).

Any current study of comparative electioneering would likewise need to be aware of the art and techniques used by political parties, and their candidates, to fight an election campaign. Given the possible importance of campaigning, Schmitt-Beck and Faas (2006) suggest that parties seek to control all aspects of their campaign, but they also note that the wider political environment, what opponents do and events, will shape each party's abilities to keep to its own campaign plan. Indeed, Iyengar and Simon (2000) suggest that campaign effects are not restricted to voter choice, but also include influencing learning and agenda-setting control. The importance to political parties of orchestrating a professional election campaign raises interesting questions for an election where Web 2.0 technologies may play a role. As noted in Chapter 1, and we return to this point in more depth in Chapter 3, Web 2.0 could help parties be more persuasive, but it could equally open up space for voters to participate and interact with the party and with each other. This chapter will briefly introduce the historical development of the Internet to set the scene for the use of Web technologies in the modern, competitive, election campaign. We will then explore the strategies available to parties and candidates in election campaigns. Finally, we shall consider the key functions of the Internet during elections, which will shape our understanding of how Web 2.0 might be used in our four elections.

The development of the Internet

What is now known as the Internet has taken over forty years to evolve. The driving force behind the creation of the Internet was the Cold War between the US and the Soviet Union. The launch of Sputnik 1 in 1957 and the Bay of Pigs crisis in 1962 led US military planners to ask how their armed forces and government would communicate during a nuclear war (Winston 1998; Abbate 1999; Slevin 2000; Castells 2002; Hassan 2004). The ability of one computer to 'talk' to another was considered a vital solution to issues of national security. The 1960s saw the development by military scientists of the ARPANET, launched in 1969, whereby military bases could communicate with one another in the event of a nuclear holocaust (Abbate 1999; Chadwick 2006).

The military had been the driving force behind this nascent computer network, but during the 1970s and 1980s the academic community was increasingly involved. US academics could share information between one another, but also use their skills and experience to help improve the communication process. However, of crucial importance was the fact that the development of the Internet was not restricted to this official community. From the late 1960s, a computer network operating outside of ARPANET grew up around the US counterculture movement (Castells 1996; Chadwick 2006). In 1970 email was developed, and this was fundamentally different from the ARPANET because it enabled person-to-person communication (Joinson 2003). With the invention of the modem in 1978 and the creation of an online forum, Usenet, in 1979, another element of the Internet was in place (Davis 2005). Therefore, by the 1980s the development of software and various protocols meant that the Internet, in effect, existed as we now know it. However, it was still the preserve of a small community of experts.

The creation in 1989 of the World Wide Web by Tim Berners-Lee and Robert Cailliau, who brought together a range of technological innovations to create HTML and HTTP codes, led to a rapid change in the use of the Internet. Up to this point the Internet was peripheral in use and importance, but with HTML and HTTP, coupled with in 1993 the free availability of a browser, Mosaic, the Internet was transformed and became increasingly open to wider social, commercial and political usage (Joinson 2003; Chadwick 2009). Although the term Web 2.0 was not coined until 2005, the interactive basis for this term can be traced back to the 1990s. For example, Figure 2.1 shows a timeline for the development of Web 2.0 applications, where three components of the concept, Wikis, weblogs and social networking sites, were created in the mid-1990s. Weblogs were first published in 1996 (Kumar *et al.* 2005), but up until 1999 they could only be developed by those who had the right technological skills (Kennedy 2004; Drezner and Farrell 2004). The introduction of free easy-to-use software saw the number of weblogs rapidly increase (Blood 2000). Where weblogs were a fast fuse, social networking sites (SNS) have, despite recent hype, been a slow burn, with the first SNS created in 1997 (boyd and Ellison 2007), and they really only took off after the introduction of Facebook in 2004. Ten years after the first tranche of Web 2.0 applications came a second series of file sharing sites, more

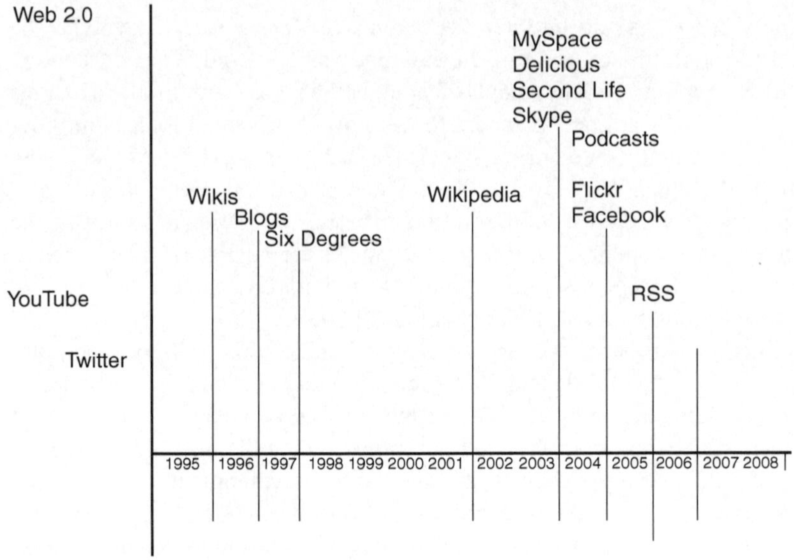

Figure 2.1 Web 2.0 timeline.

popular social networking sites (in particular Facebook) and microblogs such as Twitter. Each year sees the introduction of new components of the Internet; some are rapidly adopted, some take time and some do not take off at all. What seems clear is that technology can provide the tools that underpin communication innovations; however, usage appears to be driven by the users themselves. This could be particularly the case as online tools for social communication are adapted to suit the objectives of political election communication.

Contesting elections

The goals that any political party or candidate has in entering an election might appear to be fairly simple, as Schmitt-Beck and Faas (2006) state: to win elections and gain votes. Largely, it appears that Internet use has linked to these simple objectives, given that most party, candidate or campaign websites have tended to be used for broadcasting persuasive messages directly to as wide an audience as possible. Certainly, parties and candidates want to win elections, and if it is unrealistic that they will win, then they want to do as well as they can. In addition, as Butler and Ranney (1992) suggest, parties want at the very least to have been seen to have fought a 'good campaign'. However, parties and candidates are faced with a range of subtle variations within this overall aim; largely this is down to the electoral environment in which each is located. In France and the US the final stage of the contest is a winner-takes-all contest between two competitors; however, this is not the case with multi-party systems such as

Germany and the UK. Here the larger, established parties may aim for political power at the end of the election, while smaller parties may be looking to establish themselves vis-à-vis their competitors as well as gain a degree of political influence and increase their credibility as a political force, and newer parties may seek to launch themselves, and therefore their focus is on gaining publicity. However, there is scope for manoeuvre; for example, a party might wish to maximise its national vote across all of a country, or to focus its efforts on select geographical areas. In first-past-the-post electoral systems like the UK, probably only two or three parties can realistically expect to have any hold on power, whereas with proportional systems like Germany, more parties could realistically expect to be part of a coalition government. Moreover, the electoral system also has an impact, for example, the use of the winner-takes-all electoral college system in US presidential elections suggests that candidates seek to maximise the electoral college vote and not necessarily their total population vote, as is the case in France (Brams and Davis 1974). In this way, political parties and candidates seek to make rational decisions in electioneering.

Candidates and parties usually take a strategic approach to election campaigns (Shaw 1999; Schmitt-Beck and Faas 2006), but there is a range of strategy options open to them. Rohrschneider (2002) suggests that when determining their strategy, a party or presidential candidate addresses five questions, or what he refers to as 'trade-offs': policy or vote maximisation; core or unaligned voters; rely on party ideology or use of polls to determine election appeal; focus on the leader or constituencies; and determine whether the purpose of the party organisation is merely to reach voters or to encourage participation. The answer to each of these trade-offs influences the exact details of the final strategy a party/candidate employs. Rohrschneider adds that a party or candidate may seek to enhance their electoral attractiveness through innovation. Such an overall strategy will, in turn, shape how each party/candidate seeks to utilise the Internet.

We have identified at least five different strategic approaches that parties might take: rational choice; targeting voters by characteristics; mobilisation of core voters; geographic targeting; and game theory. The first two focus on the behaviour of voters, the remaining three on the use of resources required to reach voters. The Downesian approach of rational choice has influenced strategy since the 1950s, and suggests that issues influence voters' choice. Therefore, parties and candidates seek to differentiate themselves from their competitors on the key policy issues, which it is believed in turn can determine voting behaviour (Key 1966; Clarke *et al.* 2004). For example, Wright and Berkham (1986) found that Congressional candidates' policies were important to voters. Following a rational choice strategy implies an attempt to maximise votes. A strategy based on voter characteristics recognises that voting behaviour is influenced not so much by the party's policy stance, but by the individual characteristics of voters. Therefore, parties and candidates seek to represent large sections of society and identify groups through aggregations of characteristics, both demographic and ideological. Mobilisation seeks to focus on reaching only certain voters. The party can choose whether this is those who have a close association with them, or those that do not. Rosenstone and Hansen (1993) found that mobilisation strategies were more likely to be successful at reaching party activists, whereas Kenny and McBurnett (1994) suggested that parties were more likely to reach the less politically interested through such strategies and the choice of strategy can be contingent upon the political system, or the party and the situation in which they find themselves. For example, Criado (2008) found evidence in the 1996 Spanish elections for both approaches being dependent upon the nature of the party. Targeting is a more sophisticated variation of mobilisation, where parties and candidates seek to reach key audiences because they have a disproportionate effect on the election result. As Schultz *et al.* (2005: 58) note, 'Election campaigns have turned into target group campaigning'. Such targeting may take two forms: targeting voters by demographic factors or specific geographic areas. Drawing upon lessons from commercial marketing, Webber (2006) suggests that UK political parties are increasingly profiling to identify their 'nearest neighbours' to target as well. This means that they draw up a profile of seats where they do well, and then try to identify other seats with a similar profile and then target them.

A more scientific approach for parties to use their resources efficiently and effectively is game-theory (Brams and Davis 1974; Colantoni *et al.* 1975; Belenky 2005). This approach encourages strategists to use mathematical formulae to identify how best to use resources. The research for this approach has all been in the US, and has primarily focused on the minimal resources needed by presidential candidates to win in each state, the so-called Boolean Knapsack problem (Belenky 2005). Given the electoral importance of some larger states, Brams and Davis suggested the 3/2 rule, suggesting that presidential candidates should focus more resources in terms of money and time on the bigger seats on a ratio of 3/2. Common to all these strategies is the need to communicate goals, messages and activities to volunteers, the media and citizens.

Campaign communication

Communication is central to a party's ability to deliver its strategy. Norris (2001b) notes that the role of communication during an election is to inform, persuade and mobilise. The consideration of the meaning, process and techniques of political communication is a relatively new field of study. Although books were written on public opinion and propaganda in the 1920s (Lippmann 1922; Bernays 1923; Lasswell 1927), its origins as a discrete discipline are usually associated with research projects considering the role of mass communications during the US presidential elections (Lazarsfeld *et al.* 1944; Berelson *et al.* 1954). Political communication theory was initially dominated by American scholars (Klapper 1960; Chaffee 1975; Nimmo and Sanders 1981; Chaffee and Hocheimer 1985; Trent and Friedenberg 1991), and led some to suggest an Americanisation hypothesis (Maarek 1995; Swanson and Mancini 1996; Blumler and Gurevitch 2001). As noted in Chapter 1, this hypothesis implies that America alone is the test-bed for new campaigning ideas by virtue of its global economic position. These new advanced campaigning ideas, wrapped up as a scientific approach, are then 'exported' to other countries. However, another body of thought suggests political culture and structures in other countries will influence whether innovative techniques will be appropriate or successful. As a result, Gurevitch (1999) suggests that a European culture of campaigning exists; supporting this, Plasser (2002) argued that campaigning may well develop as a hybrid resulting from a mixture of influences.

In the UK, any significant body of work that addressed the communication process within the political sphere did not really emerge until the 1990s (Franklin 1994; McNair 1995; Blumler and Gurevitch 1995; Negrine 1996; Watts 1997; Street 2001). The focus of this research was primarily on the impact on public opinion of the relationship between journalists and politicians. Similarly, Neven (1998) suggests that political communication started to develop in France amongst younger researchers also from the 1990s (Maarek 1995; Cayrol 1997; Maarek 1997, 2002; Chalaby 2005). However, the focus of such a body of work is slightly different from that in the US and UK, being more sociological in nature (Neven 1998). Kuhn (2005) notes that whilst French political actors look to the US for innovative political communication techniques, this does not equate to an Americanisation; rather, they cherry-pick and adapt those they believe are best suited to their political culture. Therefore, whilst French political communication has become more professional, for example emphasising the use of 'sound bites' (Moscovici 2003), there exist a number of indigenous features such as the importance given to books written by commentators and politicians (Neven 1998) that imply a more French approach. Similarly, political communication research in Germany starts in the 1990s. For example, Schoenbach (1996) considers whether a process of Americanisation is influencing German political communication, and concludes that it is not, an argument reinforced by the work of Holtz-Bacha (see for example Holtz-Bacha *et al.* 1994). It is suggested that the American model is inappropriate due to the level of spending by candidates, the partisan nature of the main broadcasters and the lack of regulations on paid-for advertising (Pfetsch 2001). However, it is noted that there has been a steady professionalisation of election campaigning in Germany, drawing on public relations and marketing techniques (Esser *et al.* 2001; Holtz-Bacha 2002; Lees 2005). The one clear difference noted is that such techniques are less intrusive within German politics, due to the media performing the role of informer as opposed to offering a focus on process and strategy news which offers a more cynical account; thus suggesting the political communication process is more straightforward, lacking the hyper-critical or hostile media seen as predominating across all four countries, if to varying extents (Esser *et al.* 2001: 38; see also Müller 1999; Pfetsch 1998). Therefore, whilst there is evidence of local variations, political communication in the US, the UK, France and Germany follow advances in international practice.

The style and mode of delivery of political communication is shaped by a number of factors. Within the context of elections, election legislation creates some of the parameters within which campaigning communication takes place.

In the US, the use of primaries before the actual presidential election means that the campaign season can last for nearly a year. Candidates are allowed to use political advertising, especially on television, which necessitates financial support to pay for such costly adverts. The election law encourages candidates to seek a large number of smaller individual and corporate donors, and prevents one or two supporters bankrolling the campaign (Anstead 2008). Moreover, given the weak party system, in a candidate-centred election, each team needs to build up its organisation and supporter network from scratch. In the UK, a party-centric system encourages the party apparatus to take the lead in political communication. As the exact date of a general election is invariably selected by the Prime Minister, the campaign usually lasts formally for only three to four weeks.[1] There are only limits to funding of the central machine based upon transparency of the identity of those who donate over £5,000 nationally (or £1,000 locally) (Grant 2005). Moreover, UK parties are more reliant on membership for funding (Grant 2005). Neither candidates nor parties can advertise on television (though they can in newspapers and billboards), but parties with a minimum number of candidates contesting an election are eligible for free Party Election Broadcasts.

In France, up to the 1988 Presidential Election 'affiches' (posters) were the dominant means of communication by presidential candidates during the election campaign (Haiman 1989). However, changes to election law in 1990 banned any form of advertising in the three months prior to the First Round of the presidential election (Maarek 1997; Michel 2001). Instead, all registered candidates are guaranteed equal time on national television, so in 2002 all sixteen candidates had the same access to television in the three weeks prior to the First Round (Cole 2002). At the same time, the amount which could be spent on the campaigns was reduced by a quarter from the 1988 to the 1995 Presidential Election (Cayrol 1997). As with America and the UK, television is the prime source of political information; however, unlike America and the UK, more traditional, or pre-modern (Norris 2000), channels such as rallies and meetings also play an important role (Maarek 1997).

In Germany, the mixed-member proportional system means each voter has two votes, one for the representative of a particular district and the second for a political party. The former is based on the first-past-the-post majority system, and the second is a proportional system where seats are allocated using the Sainte-Laguë/Schepers method. To gain any additional members from the party list vote, a party must have at least five per cent of the total national vote or win three constituencies. The Constitution, the Basic Law, suggests that the Bundestag elections must be held no less than forty-six months and no more than forty-eight months after the beginning of the legislative term. After the dissolution of the Bundestag, an election must be held within sixty days, and the date of the election is chosen by the president. Elections at the federal, land and local levels are not held at the same time, and as a result there is often an election campaign under-way. Moreover, the result of land and local elections may have a bearing on national government policy. Esser *et al.* (2001) suggest that German campaigns are similar to those in the UK because election campaigns in both are party centred, legislation restricts paid political advertising and in both countries parties have restricted access to television. Moreover, Schoenbach (1996) suggests that television is not the supreme communication channel, and that town meetings, canvassing, information stalls at local markets, posters and billboards, magazines and newspapers play an important role. This view is supported by Korte (2006), who suggests that televised debates have limited impact on the results of a campaign. In short, Schoenbach is suggesting that pre-modern techniques still play an important role. As with the UK, the main print media are linked to particular parties (Pfetsch 2001). Under the Political Parties Act (1967), the political parties receive public funding on the basis of their performance in European, Bundestag and Landtag elections. Therefore, whilst television may be the dominant political communication channel in the US, UK and France, and to a much lesser degree Germany, each country has its own unique way of approaching political communication.

The role of elections within liberal democracies is to legitimise the system, and they provide an opportunity for there to be popular influence on government (Anderson *et al.* 2007). Elections are key to representative democracy, where citizens are able to express their opinion not so much on individual policies, but on the system as a whole and their representatives (both individually and collectively). This implies that the role of the electorate is limited to one activity: the vote. As Butler and Ranney (1992: 1) note, 'For all but a handful of citizens, voting in national elections is the most important form of political participation; for most it is the only form'. Parties and candidates want to attract as many votes as possible, but they do this through persuasive messages, rather than by expanding the level of citizen participation. Whilst before election campaigns parties may listen to opinion on their policies, personalities and activities, during the campaign participation is very narrowly defined. Parties expect this to be limited to voting, and for those interested in politics possibly getting involved in some way as a volunteer, donating money or simply seeking to persuade their friends. However, given the nature of democracy, perhaps participation should be of a greater depth and significance?

Online election campaigns

The conventional view is that election campaigns are dominated by traditional media. For example, Schulz *et al.* (2005) suggest this is due to the fact that Western democracies have become mediated societies. This view is essentially supporting that of Blumler and Kavanagh's (1999) 'mediatization of campaigning'. Such reliance on mass communication to promote their message also implies a media logic dominates strategy, whereby parties and candidates seek to influence the messages which citizens receive via mass communication channels. Hence, in the era of modern campaigning, the most effective means for parties to communicate to voters is indirectly via a third party, the media. However, the Internet, be it Web 1.0 or Web 2.0, provides parties with a direct and alternative communication channel; and one, it is argued, that cannot be ignored but must be integrated into campaigning to balance and enhance offline activities (Panagopoulos 2009).

Both the practice and study of elections in our four countries have evolved. By and large, America is considered the most likely to be the first to develop new techniques, and to perfect their use sooner. Similarly, American commentators have frequently been at the forefront of developing conceptual and methodological advances in psephology. Certainly, as early as the 1959 UK General Election, David Butler (1970: 3) noted that American academics were 'far ahead' of their British counterparts in utilising techniques from sociology and psychology in studying elections. Although French elections may have been studied since 1913 (Lewis-Beck 2004), and those in Germany began with the Bundestagswahl in 1953 (Hirsch-Weber/Schutz 1953), the level of sophistication of the techniques of both practitioners and academics has tended to be behind that of the US and the UK. However, the nature of the Internet creates rapid technological change, which means that one technique, or communication tool, can quickly be outdated by another. Ideas which work at one election may have been superseded at the next. Consequently, online campaign managers will seek to learn not just from practice in their own country's elections, but also the most recent developments in other countries. Equally, the academic study of elections cannot give precedence to models which can no longer serve to explain any aspect of the design, or implementation of the campaign or its reception by national audiences.

The first use of the Internet in an election was the 1992 US Presidential Election, where the Clinton–Gore campaign offered just the very basic information about the candidates to the inhabitants of cyberspace (Davis 1999). However, the first coherent use of the Internet was in 1996, when the presidential candidates and their parties created simple, content-led, websites. By the 2000 congressional and presidential elections, the Web had become an accepted, although not a dominant, election campaign tool. However, it was not until the 2004 campaigns that the Internet came of age in the US (Institute for Politics, Democracy and the Internet 2004; Chadwick 2006). UK political actors were a little slower to utilise the electioneering potential of the Internet. Ward and Gibson (1998) suggested that the 1997 General Election was the UK's first Internet election, but they also noted that it had virtually no impact. By 2001 the use of party, candidate and commentators websites had become more common (Coleman 2001), but again, the use was fairly unsophisticated and remained a marginal communication channel. In 2005 there was much more widespread use of websites, and some use of email, but commentators were still questioning the impact of the Internet (Ward 2005; Jackson 2006b). Use of the Internet within election campaigns in Germany started in 1998, when all parliamentary parties had websites. Though it remained a secondary communication channel, innovations were observed when the websites were relaunched in 2002, when twenty-seven out of the twenty-eight competing parties developed a professional online campaign (Schweitzer 2008a). The incremental innovation continued in 2005 with the home pages of parliamentary parties displaying a greater level of information, interactivity and sophistication; though Schweitzer's overall findings suggest only a partial professionalisation took place across the 2002–5 period. That point aside, it is clear that all German parties were taking the Internet seriously as a communication channel by the 2005 contest. The first use of the Internet in France was in the mid-1990s where the National Front and the Greens took the lead (Villalba 2003), but although by the 2002 Presidential Election candidates provided websites, these were essentially content based (Kuhn 2004; Footitt 2004). Footitt explains that the impact of the Internet on election campaigns is explained by country access levels. She notes that at the time of the 2002 elections, 26 per cent of the French population were online, compared with 55 per cent in the UK and 58 per cent in the US. This brief history suggests that American political actors were the most likely to use the Internet in an election, followed by the UK and Germany, with France some way behind.

In all four of our countries, online election campaigns have become progressively more sophisticated and integral to the overall campaign. To varying degrees, the Internet in these countries has moved from being a tactical gimmick to becoming an important, though not the most important, component of how parties and candidates communicate. Where initially the use of the Internet merely equated to a content-driven website, by the 2004 US Presidential Elections, the 2005 UK General Election and the 2005 German National Elections, this had moved on. First, there was increased use of a wider range of Internet modalities such as email lists, e-newsletters and weblogs. Second, the nature of such modalities implied a slow move from the content-based one-way dialogue consistent with Web 1.0 websites to greater use of interactive dialogue. Such a trend towards interaction has gained momentum since the last round of elections, with the creation of the Web 2.0 concept and the growing popularity of SNS.

While specific differences in developments in the use of the Internet pervade across the four nations we cover in this book, it remains possible to identify some general functions the Internet plays within election campaigns. Gibson *et al.* (2000) suggest that there are five major functions of a party website: information provision; campaigning; resource generation; networking; and participation. These five functions were refined by Gibson *et al.* (2003b), who suggested that there are six: information provision; campaigning; targeting the youth audience; symbolic significance; efficiency gains; and soliciting participation/feedback. We feel that some of these categories are quite broad, and that a more specific set, with more narrowly defined purposes, offers a better way of understanding the role of the Internet within election campaigns. Our framework for understanding the use of the Internet by political parties and candidates identified six roles, each of which is discussed below.

1 Information provision

The Internet provides another means by which political parties, and their candidates, can provide information on their policies and activities. Focusing on the provision of content is a largely unsophisticated use of ICT, a one-way form of an electronic brochure (Bimber 1998; Bimber and Davis 2003; Jackson 2003). Some of the early research was relatively dismissive of this approach, suggesting that it was a missed opportunity (D'Alessio 1997; Auty and Nicholas 1998; Sednow 1998; Ward and Gibson 1998; Sadow and James 1999). However, it is now recognised that whilst a limited use of the Internet, it is perfectly legitimate to provide information (Ward and Gibson 2000). Indeed, there is even some evidence that electors actually want primarily to access political information (Ward *et al.* 2005; Jackson 2008a). Within an election contest, detail on the party history, candidate or leader biography, as well as policy stances, is likely to be information that is actively sought by many of those who visit party or candidate websites.

2 Campaigning

Particular characteristics of the Internet offer political campaigners new opportunities to reach voters (Gibson and Rommele 2001). For example, the Internet can be quickly and easily updated to facilitate regular updating of news, and rebut instantly opponents' claims (Gibson and Ward 2002). The increased bandwidth, coupled with the ability to identify the interests of visitors and the range of applications, allows political campaigners to narrowcast their messages to key targeted audiences (Gibson *et al.* 2000; Gibson and Ward 2002). It is also suggested that because younger people are disproportionately likely to access the Internet, Web technologies offer a means of encouraging youth political participation. We suggest that campaigning also includes the desire to win votes. In terms of winning votes, the focus is on whether the Internet can shore up the support of existing supporters, or reach undecided voters (Vaccari 2008). The evidence suggests that, so far, for political parties the Internet does not help reach and persuade 'floating voters', but it can help reach existing supporters (Jackson and Lilleker 2007). However, as part of the representative function, e-newsletters have helped MPs convert some voters (Jackson 2008a).

There is limited evidence that US politicians believe that the Internet helps them win votes; a study by the E-Voter Institute (Jagoda 2002) found that political consultants believed the Web was more effective at motivating existing supporters than acquiring new ones. Interviews of the staff of the thirty-three most marginal Congressional seats by the Institute for Politics, Democracy and the Internet (2002), found that respondents were evenly divided as to whether they would put more effort into Web campaigning next time. However, the lessons drawn from Howard Dean's 2003–4 campaign in the US suggests that the Internet can be used to develop a grassroots organisation which may attract active supporters if not voters (Chadwick 2006), and we could expect this function to be increasingly employed, as well as increased targeting of non-aligned, floating voters who need convincing.

3 Negative campaigning

Trent and Friedenberg (1991) identify three negative campaigning strategies: attacking opponents; taking the offensive on issues; and calling for changes; whereas positive campaigning strategies stress self-promotion and emphasise past accomplishments. It might be assumed that the Internet will encourage more negative campaigning because of its uncontrolled nature. However, the early empirical research suggested that in fact, parties and candidates promoted positive messages through their websites (Klotz 1998; Kamarck 1999; Tedesco *et al.* 1999; Carlson and Djupsund 2001). Yet, later research suggested that as election campaigners became more comfortable with the technology, negative messages would be used to a greater extent, though not that they necessarily dominated a candidate's online campaign communication strategy (Klotz 2004). For example, Trammell (2006) studied the weblogs of the 2004 US presidential candidates and found that as the campaign progressed towards election day, negative posts became more common. Similarly, Schweitzer (2005) found that both the incumbent governing coalition and their opponent parties used negative messages on their websites.

4 Resource generation

In the US, the Internet has become, particularly since the 2003–4 Howard Dean campaign, viewed as a tool for delivering resources in the form of fundraising and building a volunteer base for offline activities (Foot and Schneider 2002; Williams *et al.* 2005). In a party-centric system like the UK, fundraising and creating an organisational structure play less of a role (Anstead and Chadwick 2008), though there is evidence that the Internet can help attract new members, raise some funds and mobilise activists (Jackson 2006b). The area which from the outset probably engendered greatest interest was whether the Internet would enhance participation through greater interactivity. It is surrounding this element of resource generation that the Dean campaign offered particularly innovative lessons, and this may be an increasingly evident function of party and candidate websites.

5 Networking

Castells (2002) suggests that the Internet in general encourages the development of networks. While the social units may be fragmented and dispersed over space and time, they operate within an ecosystem that relies upon participation and connectedness (Van Dijk 2006). Specifically in regard to political campaigns, it has been suggested that the ability of a website to link to others enhances the potential for networking (Gibson *et al.* 2000; Gibson and Ward 2002). Arguably, the use of the Internet can encourage linkages both between political actors, and between them and wider publics, as well as intra-communication within political organisations. Such pronouncements were offered during the era of Web 1.0.

Web 2.0 applications, especially social networking sites, might be expected to further enhance the political networking capabilities of the Internet.

6 Promoting participation

Since the early 1990s, there has been disagreement over the potential impact of the Internet on political participation. The inherent logic behind the argument that the Internet can enhance participation is that it lowers barriers to entry, and is a more efficient and effective means of sharing information, which in turn influences whether and how citizens participate (Bimber 2003; Shah *et al.* 2005). However, there is disagreement as to whether or not the Internet has increased participation. A number of commentators suggest that as a campaigning and communication channel, it merely reinforces existing levels of participation (Norris 2001a; Bimber and Davis 2003), and so helps the most politically engaged to expand and deepen their range of participatory activities (Weber *et al.* 2003; Gibson *et al.* 2003c; Lusoli and Ward 2004). However, there is some evidence that this reinforcement view is being challenged. The specific areas of activity which the Internet facilitates include donating money (Bimber 2003), increasing the likelihood of voting (Tolbert and McNeal 2003) and supporting voluntary organisations (Quan-Haase *et al.* 2002). In America, the Institute for Politics, Democracy and the Internet (2004) identified a separate body of online political activists, while in the UK, research suggests that a very different group is becoming politically active online for the first time. Gibson *et al.* (2002) identified a very small subset of 15–24 year olds engaging in online politics, but who have not been involved in traditional offline political activity. Online participation during elections appears to include giving money and being mobilised to get involved as an activist, but possibly the key question is whether Web 2.0 participation means more than this in terms of political actor–voter interaction.

Conclusion

The empirical research up to 2005/6, both during and outside of elections, very much describes the use of the Internet by political actors using what we might now describe as Web 1.0 applications. Due to the speed of development, and uptake, of Web 2.0 applications, few previous texts have had the opportunity to focus beyond the website. It is hinted at as part of the hypermedia campaign (Howard 2006), but the Internet and Elections project found little use for forums and captured many of the other features of websites that may come under a Web 2.0 heading as e-paraphernalia, again a feature that was underused across fourteen countries included in the study (Kluver *et al.* 2007). Whilst interactivity has been studied as a feature of websites, and one study (Foot and Schneider 2006) talks of the joint production of Web objects by site host and visitors, and so of Web spheres, within the context of their study of elections this was limited to 'the provision of forums to which site visitors can contribute and through appropriating materials produced by others' (112). This reflects the extent to which joint production and interactivity was possible prior to 2005, after which the explosion of Web 2.0 and the technologies that enabled social networking to go mainstream was witnessed. The elections that we are studying potentially represent a new era of the Internet, one which gives birth to interactive electoral websites, replacing the static websites of earlier election campaigns. It is this, alongside the traditional uses of the Internet, that this study intends to capture.

3 Web 2.0

Interactivity and the potential for democracy

The elements we refer to as Web 2.0 are essentially technological developments that have allowed websites to evolve. Initially from online brochures, through a phase where links and click-throughs enabled the user to shape their own experience of a site or browsing session, to the users being able to shape many or even all the contours of the site. The ability of users to shape the online experiences, and with Web 2.0 to also shape the experiences of others, has led scholars to suggest that there are also social impacts and consequences that have emerged with this new co-productive online environment (Kanuka and Anderson 1998; Van Dijk 2007; Castells 2007). Political communication, in particular in the context of reaching out directly to voters, is not immune to technological developments. Strategists have to adapt to the norms of societal communication and so political communication evolves in line with society; albeit, as Downes and Mui (2000) suggest, often behind the curve. Thus, we would expect to see political communication online increasingly embrace Web 2.0 and its norms of communication behaviour.

Paul Anderson (2007) talks of there being six big ideas,[1] as derived from concepts outlined by Tim O'Reilly (2005), which explain Web 2.0 as not simply a technological innovation but also a social phenomenon. These are the capacity for individual production and user-generated content; the ability to harness the power of the crowd; access to data on an epic scale; the architecture of participation; a network effect; and openness. It is to these big ideas this chapter will turn prior to considering their potential contribution to a political public sphere.

More than a technology: the big ideas of Web 2.0

The notion of the user or audience member as co-producer or even produser, an entity that combines the roles of producer and user equally, is perhaps not a completely new concept. BBC children's television programmes such as Take Hart in the 1970s featured a gallery of art produced by the audience, which the show's host, Tony Hart, would showcase each week. Equally, one could argue that Talk Radio in the US is a platform where there is a blurring between audience and content creator, as without members of the public contributing there would be no content. The notion of the produser was introduced to explain collaborative software development (James 1991); however, it is now inextricably linked to Web 2.0 and the fact that anyone can produce and edit content on sites such as Wikipedia, YouTube or Facebook. Obviously not everyone will contribute, however within Web 2.0 there is a lack of hierarchy and all contributors have equal levels of opportunity as well as credibility (Bruns 2005; Burgess *et al.* 2006; Cammaerts 2008). Whilst well-known websites may be able to attract more visitors than the unknown amateur, this is no longer a given. Equally, it is the user that selects where to place their contribution, and there is less of a sense of selectivity by the host. Whether they are innovative bands whose work can be listened to on, and downloaded from, their MySpace profile; or bloggers who offer their own perspective on public affairs, celebrity gossip or popular culture; or citizen journalists who contribute experiences and viewpoints that traditional media are unable to access or to publish, any individual within any niche area of interest has the capacity to create an audience within the long tail of distribution that characterises the online ideas economy (Anderson 2006). It can be suggested that the produser has two aims: to earn money (Anderson 2006), or to gain exposure and reputation (Wu 2006); this links to notions of individual enhancement within a promotional culture, where fame is a currency. However, within a political context, it could alternatively be argued that the produser seeks to influence others, or to play a more active role in civic society. Civic activities may well offer the by-product of enhancing the produser's individual reputation, however there may be broader aims than simply individual self-aggrandisement.

This notion is part of the big idea of harnessing the power of the crowd, and is linked to more overtly political objectives. O'Reilly (2005) talks of harnessing not just the power, but the wisdom of crowds through collaborative spam filtering. This links neatly to notions of 'asking the audience' (Suroweiki and Silverman 2007), and can be an objective in itself of writing weblogs in which personal, social or philosophical questions can be asked that require a response from readers. Equally, the sharing of information can bring individuals closer together, whether it is asking about political beliefs, interests, musical tastes or the favourite films of visitors to online platforms. However, whilst this may create communities, one should not confuse communities of interest with communities that act. Evidence suggests (Canetti 1978) that the power of crowds is a powerful political tool, and that crowds can be mobilised more easily through interactive environments such as forums (Cox 1999), which are facilitated to a far greater extent by Web 2.0 technologies. For example, anti-capitalist protestors, environmental groups and anti-nuclear protestors have all employed the Internet to mobilise activists and centralise their resources on key publics to maximise impact (Rodgers 2005). Facebook, and a range of social networking sites, for example, have provided a further platform for extending the reach of such organisations, in particular the use of the Cause application, which allows users to recruit contacts and, once recruited, for the Cause to communicate its messages to a broad cross-section of the user community. Thus, there is potential to harness Web users in a multitude of ways, each of which is enhanced by the fact that more people can contribute than simply those within the leadership of organised pressure groups, political parties or organisations; and equally, that a broader base of individuals are able to access the crowd to make an impact. This new bottom-up capacity is potentially a threat to political parties, as it implies an alternative mobilising source. However, parties and candidates may also be able to create spaces to which they can draw supporters, and mobilise them into online and offline activism.

Perhaps what may mitigate against these bold notions is that all Web users have access to epic amounts of data, and that the amount of information placed online is increasing infinitesimally through the activities of produsers. The positive outcome is that as the amount of information increases, there will be a trickle-down effect (Von Baeyer 2003). While it is noted that there are voracious media consumers who will turn to online resources as much as, or more than, traditional outlets (Ketchum 2008), these are distinct from the general public: those with an appetite for information who pass on links through their social networks. Thus, ten readers of a weblog post on current affairs by an independent produser can save the link to Delicious, post it to their Facebook profile, re-blog it or email it to friends. These individuals may also choose to create mash-ups that relay complex information and messages to a wider, perhaps less educated or less engaged, audience to increase their influence. While this was also possible within the Web 1.0 phase of Internet development, Web 2.0 makes sharing increasingly easy to a wider audience using a range of differing modes of communication that can be interlinked.

While this suggests the creation of an informed active public sphere (Papachrissi 2002; Dahlgren 2005), it should also be noted that there is an alternative perspective. The Web user may be faced with potential information overload, and so focus purely on their own interests and block out extraneous information, creating a series of filters to ensure they get no material that is not of interest or offers views that contrast their own (Sunstein 2007). Web tools such as RSS (Really Simple Syndication) specifically allow the individual to filter information that arrives to their desktop or palm-held device; other information could be simply ignored, as it is lost in the morass of background noise. Therefore, whilst for some Web users there is a wealth of information available to them, the majority can be filtered out within social networks. However, the fact that information sharing is made possible means the produser is able to exert power and influence within their social groups, enhancing their reputation as influential, and giving them the ability to shape their contacts' agenda. Certainly, this may mean that some individuals have greater influence than they should have, yet conversely, it also suggests that influence is spread disparately and no longer vested in media owners or established information-rich elites (Johnson and Kaye 2004).

All this is facilitated through the architecture of participation (O'Reilly 2005), and it is within this concept that the notions of technology and the social dimension of Web 2.0 meet. The technology provides the architecture, just as any building facilitates the activity which transpires within. However, it is the participation that is crucial for Web 2.0. Participation is facilitated by offering few barriers to taking part, and must be targeted at those with an average level of skills and access to technology, hence not just permitting the critical mass of Web users to browse but to also become produsers. Whilst some Web 2.0 communities, such as those created to develop open source software such as Linux, may be reliant on the technological skills of participants, the majority of social networking sites, weblog host sites or forums must ensure that almost any regular Web user is able to familiarise themselves with the procedures for logging in and contributing. Equally, those who offer commenting or posting facilities within their sites, weblogs or social networking profiles must ensure they are accessible to a critical mass of online users.

The notion of 'openness', expressed above in terms of permitting access to all, is key to the fifth big idea associated with Web 2.0: the network effect. While it would be inaccurate to talk of a singular Web 2.0 network, one can view the Internet as now offering a series of networks which interact and overlap, but to which membership is the crucial element. Internet users can join these networks or attempt to create their own; however, often the important aspect is to link into existing networks in order to build a sub-network. Moreover, using Web 2.0 applications makes it easier to create a network than within a Web 1.0 environment. For example, a weblogger may wish to build a network of participants, but does so by publicising their posting via a social networking site. Currently, Facebook has the greatest global reach, though its popularity in France and Germany was lower than the US or UK; however, the popularity of social networking has grown exponentially, and across all nations, citizens have access to a combination of nation-specific and global networks. Equally, despite a slow take-up, the micro-blogging tool Twitter allows organisations and individuals to communicate and so engage with a broader community. Hence, the interconnectedness and embeddedness of any individual can be vital to reaching the Internet user community and its networks. It is argued that networks are essentially products of their members, and that as each new member joins the network it is enhanced due to the fact that all members of the network have one more person they can communicate with (Klemperer 2006). Robert Metcalfe, reflecting on the development of his invention, the Ethernet, suggested that the value of such a network is n^2, basically the number of members squared (Anderson 2007: 21). Whilst this equation is beyond measurement and open to question (Briscoe *et al.* 2006), what it allows is a sense that the technology that can create a network is only useful if it permits participation by the greatest number of users. Furthermore, the open access nature of the networks, in theory at least, is the factor that facilitates the creation of 'interest-based clusters' (Benkler 2006). Each cluster acts as a focus for the voracious produser and consumer of information, but also allows members to be drawn into the network because of their common interest and filter information out to the wider community of Web users. Hence, the network grows in both size and value, and contributes to educating and informing wider society, so fulfilling to some extent the notion of a network society, which in 1996 Castells suggested would be a social outcome of the development of the Internet.

While all these big ideas may be open to debate, what they represent is an ideal that may be present to some extent and in some places on the Internet, but elsewhere may be absent or in their infancy. Because Web 2.0 technologies are constantly in a state of evolutionary flux, it may be too early to tell to what extent the production of user-generated content may be democratising society, or even the Internet user community itself. One could suggest that the Internet may actually be creating an elite of produsers who are constantly providing information for consumption by the networks within which they exist. Rather than encouraging participation and mobilising other users, all this may achieve is reaching anonymous browsing consumers who do not commit to any form of participatory activity. The power of the crowd may be harnessed at key points within interest-based clusters, but as marketers try to also harness crowds to purchase their products there may be a counter-reaction, and the Web user may well retreat from open access sites where anyone can post and contribute. Equally, it is reasonable to question whether networks will reach overload, where too many members and users become locked into small communities that protect them from information overload, but also isolate them from the wider community. In other words, these big ideas that underpin predictions may actually be unrealistic, and rather than becoming one huge open access network of participants, the Internet may become a series of pockets of interest or online issue ghettos, what Sunstein (2007) refers to as cyberghettoes, where members of small communities access information only from familiar and reliable sources and so end up as, or at least no less, impoverished than if they relied on a single newspaper for their window on the world. Clearly, these future reflections are purely speculative, and it is too soon to tell what impact Web 2.0 will have on society and its relations with government and politics; indeed, this book cannot supply definitive answers to these questions. However, we intend to try to draw inferences based on a study of four years of use by political actors during election campaigns. What we suggest is that currently, the big ideas offered by O'Reilly are present within many of the sites that use Web 2.0 technology, and therefore they represent a useful starting place from which to consider what role these could play, and did play over the last four years. The question is whether political communicators would want to embrace the big ideas of Web 2.0; this may largely depend on what benefits are perceived to be attainable from developing an interactive communication strategy. It is to the definition and components of the latter that this chapter now turns.

Interacting within an architecture of participation

Interactivity is an implicit thread that underpins many of the big ideas that are associated with Web 2.0. Just as one can contest the meaning of Web 2.0 and link it to technology or usage, the same is true for interactivity. Essentially, notions of interactivity and interaction, and the implications of the enhanced features of Web user experiences, emerge from two distinct disciplines. A significant body of work draws on research into interaction with technology. This work has particular significance when considering how to ensure technology, tools and interfaces are open to anyone (Card *et al.* 1986). Interactivity is stressed as experiential and perceptual (Bucy 2004), and in the following fairly stark terms: 'If I am skilled enough to ably use a given interface, I would rate it as quite interactive. It's simply self-fulfilling. If not I would rate it poorly' (Sundar 2004: 386). However, locking interactivity to being an attribute of technology is problematic. While hot debates in the 1980s could perhaps rightly distinguish between non-interactive static texts that could be opened and closed and those that contained a variety of alternative paths between start and finish, in the twenty-first century it is difficult to imagine any website not containing some element of interactivity, given that some sophisticated interactive elements were found to exist even on political websites as early as 1999 (de Landtsheer *et al.* 1999). It is now simply a product of the technology that is used to create websites and is an embedded, but perhaps now taken for granted, feature of our online user experience.

Thus we look backwards for better definitions of interactivity online that go beyond locking interaction to being a product of technology. Rafaeli used, as a starting point, human interaction and conversation. In what is now a classic definition of interactivity, he posited that 'interactivity is an expression of the extent that in a given series of communication exchanges, any third (or later) transmission (or message) is related to the degree to which previous exchanges referred to even earlier transmissions' (1988: 111). What is suggested here is that whilst face-to-face communication may be the highest level of interaction, this could also take place via the telephone, via email or via various personal communication technologies such as MSN Messenger, Skype or I-Chat. However, the technology behind developments such as Web-based forums, Walls and message spaces across global social networking sites such as Facebook or MySpace, which are popular across all four countries, or national-based sites such as the German sites openBC and spreadshirt (MacManus 2006), or the UK's Bebo, provides a new space for conversation. Furthermore, the existence and widespread use of open forums, bulletin boards and message spaces mean that conversation is now facilitated between any number of participants. Yet, one could argue that if only the conversation is deemed to be interaction, this could exclude a range of other features that allow users to participate and interact through the platform with other users. Within SNS, while not conversational in the traditional sense, the sharing of photographs, links, invitations to events or the giving of gifts all present opportunities to not simply interact with technological features but require the presence of a human element. Cumulatively, these can all be tools for building and maintaining relationships between users.

Thus, we find two polar opposite definitions of interactivity. On the one hand, interactivity is a product of technology; but this definition seems to have no boundaries, and so it can be argued that any click-through link is an interaction.

Alternatively, the conversation becomes the benchmark. Only if two or more people are exchanging messages and meanings which relate to previous messages can we define something as interaction. Technology certainly acts as the facilitator, but the key aspect is the role of human agency. Sundar can rightly claim that if he is unable to use something it is not interactive, but would it also be true to argue that if something is not deemed to be interactive by the user then it is also non-interactive? It would be more valuable to suggest that there are degrees of interactivity that may at the most simplistic level be clicking the mouse to follow a link, and at the most advanced level be participating in a conversation or in activities that are part of the maintenance of human-to-human rather than human-to-site relationships.

Sally McMillan (2002a) recognised differing variants of interactivity, and made a link between behaviour online and the experience of users. Her typology (see Table 3.1) offers three levels of interactivity; the most basic is the user's ability to interact with the document. This can be simply the choice of accessing a file, reading, listening or watching, or it can involve choosing which links to follow, which can offer each user a unique experience. However, while allowing a form of interaction, this is a long way from the ideals of interactivity. The second level of interactivity for McMillan is an ability to interact with the system. Here, the user is able to choose what to access and how to access it; for example, news is delivered to the desktop via RSS feeds, and equally, users can take part in file sharing activities and have access to a wide variety of information and material. The highest form of interactivity is user-to-user, where file sharing can be accompanied by conversation and co-production of music, video and other users' experiences. This latter style of interactivity fits well with the 'big ideas' of Web 2.0, yet it also facilitates a range of other lesser versions of interactivity. Thus, we return to an observation made by McMillan (2000a) two years prior to the development of her typology, that interactivity is contested because we know when we see it, or we name it when we see it, but are not certain precisely what is not interactivity.

McMillan's (2002b) typology importantly builds on the notion of user control over their environment, which appears central to Web 2.0. The focus of Web 2.0 on a 'they will come and build it' philosophy (Barsky 2006) means that any user of Web 2.0 tools should, theoretically at least, offer high user control. Content on demand, such as RSS feeds, makes Internet users' lives easier, however this simple tool only allows a degree of choice over reception and not transmission. McMillan suggests that as interactivity moves towards a user-to-user style, the interface will become almost transparent to allow real-time conversation and simulated contact. It is perhaps such ideals that link well to notions of representative democracy and so, while recognising not all interactivity is conversational and user-to-user, we suggest that some elements perhaps should be within the context of political communication and election campaigning.

It has long been argued for the need for greater connections to be made between represented and representative, and the online environment is frequently viewed as a place for these connections to be made. Reflecting on research

Table 3.1 McMillan's typology of interactivity

Type of interactivity	*Dimension included*	*Communication model*	*Description/examples*
	Level of receiver control	Monologue	One-way, sender controlled communication, i.e. biographical details and brochure-like shovelware Webstyles
User to user	Low or high	Feedback	One-way communication with high-receiver control, i.e. email links, letters to editor
	Direction of communication	Responsive dialogue	Two-way communication with low receiver control, i.e. e-commerce feedback, customer service or some weblog posts
	One-way or two-way	Mutual discourse	Two-way communication with high receiver control, i.e. chatrooms, instant messaging conversations
	Nature of	Packaged content	Low level of receiver control, passive audience, i.e. text-based information, newspapers, magazines
User to document	Audience active or passive	Content-on-demand	Low level of receiver control with an active audience, i.e. personalised news aggregators like Google news, RSS feeds, pay-per-view
	Level of	Content exchange	Low level of receiver control with an active audience, i.e. weblogs, YouTube
	Receiver control low or high	Co-created content	High level of receiver control with an active audience, i.e. interactive fiction, multi-user domain games
	Centre of control	Computer-based interaction	Information is presented to the user, i.e. online poll results
User to system	Human of computer	Human-based interaction	Humans use interfaces to obtain information, i.e. database searching, RSS feeds
	Interface	Flow	The interface adapts to the needs of the user, i.e. adaptive sites, games
	Apparent or transparent	Adaptive interaction	High user activity with a transparent, adaptive interface, i.e. virtual reality

conducted when online political communication was still firmly locked into an era of static brochureware (Sadow and James 1999; Jackson 2003; de Landtsheer *et al.* 1999), Stoker argues that 'offering them [citizens] a "web space" where they can publish content easily can foster their engagement on- and offline' (2006: 333). Web 2.0 certainly offers tools for facilitating that as well as for measuring the extent of participation. Thus, conceptualising variants of interactivity has evolved alongside developments in technology and their social application. McMillan and Downes (2000) combined the Information Traffic Model (Bordewijk and van Kaam 1986) with Grunig and Grunig's (1992) model of Public Relations practice to develop the four-part model of interactivity. This was in turn built upon by Ferber *et al.* (2007). In recognition of developments in technology, they enriched the model by adding three-way communication (Figure 3.1); this now encompasses communication where any number of participants can interact via comments boards on SNS or within forums or chat rooms, and similar areas that facilitate public conversation.

A further concept that is useful to draw upon is the difference between interactivity as a product of technologies, and interactivity as a process of communication (Stromer-Galley 2004). Critical of much of the work that attempts to provide definitions of interactivity, Jennifer Stromer-Galley argues that there are two distinct ways of studying interactivity:

> By asking what opportunities are made available by elites and whether and how citizens use those opportunities, this line of investigation focuses on interactivity-as-product. Asking what transpires when citizens interact with elites is an interactivity-as-process question.
>
> (Stromer-Galley 2004: 393)

Essentially, Web 2.0 and the studies that have focused on interactivity online focus on the product, such as campaign sites providing forums for visitors (Foot and Schneider 2006). However, Web 2.0 also opens up the real possibility of product and process becoming synonymous, due to the public way in which

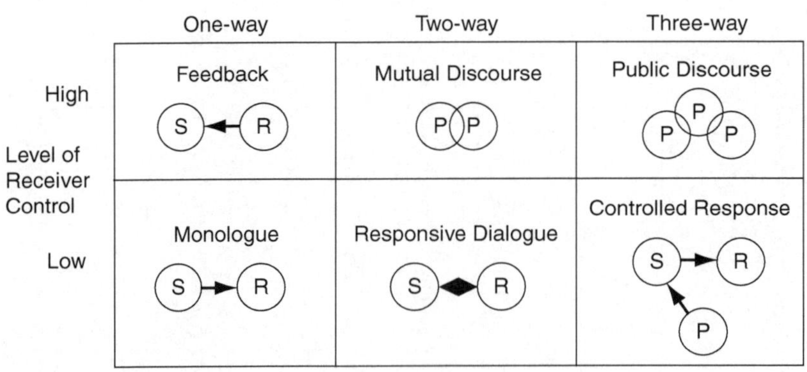

Figure 3.1 Ferber *et al.*, six-part model of cyber-interactivity.

communication can take form. Therefore, what is needed when focusing on political communication is an understanding of the product available, but also the process, whether a conversation is encouraged, whether questions are answered or comments gain responses. These behaviours are becoming norms for Web 2.0 users, and so we consider whether interactivity is not simply a matter of perception, but is now defined by the behaviour of one or many communities of users who enjoy the rich user experience provided by Web 2.0 technologies and tools.

Web 2.0 as a community

As Web 2.0 becomes embedded within the online environment, organisations, both corporate and political, attempt to harness the potential of these tools to reach new audiences and bolster their loyal support base (Reichheld and Schefter 2000). Advice for adopting Web 2.0 technologies suggests organisations need to appear everywhere online, what Chadwick (2009) refers to as 'granular', a tactic picked up successfully by US Presidential Candidate Barack Obama (Kiss 2008): that an effective Web presence can deliver reach, so increasing the organisation's audience; the richness of experience for the user; the speed of communication, a particular strength in a crisis communication context; high visibility to a range of audiences; and delivers the power to create and maintain relationships. However, arguably, such benefits are contingent upon the use of such tools, and the nature of the experience offered to these audiences. O'Grady (2007) suggests the trajectory is towards a phenomenological experience online, where learning, which can be interpreted as not just educational, but also finding and locating information as well as how online communities communicate, is experiential.

We suggest that Web 2.0 communities and users are by nature communities of practice, and can be viewed as such in two ways. First, those who have embraced Web 2.0 tools and modes of communication are familiar with them and so are comfortable with using them, and perhaps have some role in developing those tools further, but most importantly, they enjoy the style of communication offered by these tools. Quite simply, frequent Web 2.0 users will enjoy the rich user experience of interactivity and co-production, and so will gravitate towards websites that offer this experience. Second, each individual site is a community of practice. There are norms of behaviour, some constrained or even enabled by the site features, which have become norms due to the activities of users (Sharratt and Usoro 2003). For example, one can argue that within the Facebook community, common practice would include using the 'poke' function to interact very simply with friends. However, communication within SNS tends to happen across the Wall spaces on profiles, and users are encouraged to share applications. Contravention of the rules of the site, such as spamming all friends, can lead to profiles being blocked; however, the site members can also campaign against these rules when particular campaigners are blocked. Such features dovetail with Wenger's (1999) definition of a community of practice as being identified by a shared purpose enacted through relationships of mutual engagement that bind members to the community, which produces a shared repertoire of resources at the communities' disposal. For Wenger, these are created to face specific problems, and are consistent with issue groups that coalesce to campaign for or against a specific event, a school or hospital closure perhaps. We broaden this definition to develop an understanding of how the community can govern practice and so decide what behaviour is acceptable, and by whom (Jackson and Lilleker 2009a).

Key to understanding Web 2.0 communities is the notion of joint ownership. Wenger *et al.* (2005) note that social software offers the potential for a feeling of not only shared ownership, but also belonging. Wenger *et al.* talk of a weblog as something that can act as a bridge between individuals and communities; the creator may lead to discussion, but those who offer comments not only enrich future visitors' experiences but regular readers and comment makers can feel a common identity and shared responsibility for the weblog. For example, Jackson (2008b) suggests that this happens with some MPs' weblogs. Jansen (2006) proposes that this enhances the learning of all members of the community, as they become more aware of the issues raised within the community as well as becoming cognitively involved with the community and its raison d'être. This neatly links to the big ideas at the heart of Web 2.0, and thus we contend that the online environment is now made up of a range of communities, which are members with active or passive roles, but who expect certain types of experience and behaviour. Importantly, they also expect no hierarchy to exist, and there to be equal opportunities for all to take a leading role within a community; even when commenting on a weblog post there is no right or wrong opinion but all opinions are equal, and none should be constrained from contributing (Cocciolo *et al.* 2007). As Charles Leadbeater (2008) notes on the front cover of *We Think*, 'The generation growing up with the web will not be content to remain spectators. They want to be players'. While not all choose to be players, for example around only 1 per cent of the total number of Wikipedia users have ever contributed anything to an entry (Leadbeater 2008), the opportunity to do so has social meaning. Thus, any organisation wishing to enter into and interact with the Web 2.0 user community, and any sub-community, that exists online cannot simply join, but must also join with the community by adopting, sharing and shaping its practice.

Web 2.0, electioneering and the political marketing mix

In the case of a political organisation, there are clear advantages for entering into Web 2.0 communities. In fact, perhaps more so than many commercial organisations given low voter loyalty and party identification, high voter volatility and highly commercialised and often cynical, if not hostile, media all act as barriers to communication, demanding new routes be found to reach audiences (Jackson, D. 2008). However, the practice of Web 2.0 communities is based around a flattened hierarchy of co-production and interactivity; this is in sharp contrast to the traditions of top-down persuasion associated with political communication

(Lilleker 2006). Electioneering, and the related literature within the field of political marketing, has focused on the ways that tools from commercial marketing have been introduced to inform the behaviour of parties and candidates competing for electoral success (Steger *et al.* 2006). While academic study has largely been driven by practice, models of party or candidate behaviour have been developed as benchmarks for measuring the embeddedness of market forces within party thinking and behaviour. The notion of a market-orientation was introduced by Shama (1976) and further developed by Lees-Marshment (2001, 2008), Lilleker and Lees-Marshment (2005) and Lees-Marshment *et al.* (2009). Central to this is that a market-orientation does not simply equate to the use of various marketing techniques or attempts to professionalise the campaigning, but to gather data to discover the wants and needs of selected groups in order to meet and satisfy them. Such a concept links neatly with notions of a marketing philosophy where the consumer is placed at the heart of all decision making (Ulrich and Eppinger 1999; for debate see Kumar *et al.* 2000), and again moves significantly away from the traditional modes of political communication towards models that suggest the development of a less-hierarchical version of politics that fits more with the notion of MPs and parties acting as delegates than trustees (Jackson and Lilleker 2009b). Therefore, it is useful to assess how interactivity, and the big ideas associated with Web 2.0, hypothetically at the very least, can play a role within a marketised election campaign.

The ability of Web 2.0 technologies to facilitate individual production and user-generated content, and to post this on any site that enables this function, has at the most basic level a promotional function. If individuals can publicly comment or post ideas, and enter into conversation with other visitors and users, then it offers the impression of a party or candidate that is inclusive and willing to engage the public. However, and linking to the notion of harnessing the power of the crowd, parties and candidates can also use public input to their sites to refine their policies or communication in line with visitors' expectations and ideals. This may present a greater opportunity for parties or candidates to be more market-oriented as well as presenting themselves as responsive to the public, so meeting both the openness criteria of Web 2.0 as well as an increased demand for responsive and in-touch government from the public (Stoker 2006). This is predicated on election strategists building an architecture of participation in which visitors, as well as party leaders, key members and strategists, can communicate. What this may facilitate is a network effect that can bring more individuals to the campaign, so enhancing the information received to feed into the campaign, as well as securing the loyalty of those drawn into the network. However, an alternative perspective would be that parties and candidates may offer the impression of interactivity and build an architecture where participation was permitted, while also being controlled and censored; consequently, Jackson and Lilleker (2009a) identify the existence of Web 1.5. The final big idea of Web 2.0, access to data on an epic scale, can permit both inclusivity and exclusivity. While it may appear to make information available, it can also privilege certain information by promoting it. Equally, images of participation, collections of comments or references to user input can be used as a promotional tool in the same way as a photograph with 'real voters' can. Hence, these big ideas may fit comfortably with some aspects of the professionalised and marketised campaign, but may run counter to the ethos of Web 2.0.

Hence, we can offer a radical perspective on political marketing, and how Web 2.0 can realise an optimum or ideal model of political marketisation, that enhances democracy and the link between the public and their elected representative. Alternatively, we can also say that it can equally facilitate politics as usual, and be used as a tool of impression management (Jackson and Lilleker 2011) rather than to facilitate two-way, non-hierarchical conversation. History points towards the latter and not the former; however, there are positive indicators in recent practice. Attempts at drawing the public and stakeholder groups together, such as Labour's *Big Conversation*, have been criticised (Lilleker and Lees-Marshment 2005) as a sales technique as opposed to a mechanism for gaining data. However, developments such as the UK Conservative's *Stand Up Speak Out* initiative created a discussion agenda, and so represented more sophisticated ways of opening up, to varying extents, decision making to the public.

Promotional or participatory

Web 2.0, it is argued, can encourage engagement in politics (Stoker 2006). Citizens should, and this is very much an ideal, be drawn into the political architecture of participation, enjoy the rich experience, engage with a community of interest around politics generally, and be able to interact with other visitors and the party or candidate. In turn, parties gain from relationships built with voters and a network effect, which draws in a wider community of Internet users to their online presences.

In the context of an election it is the fate of a party or a candidate that strategists want voters to become interested about, and so emotionally involved in at the very least. To date, evidence is lacking that this is the case; rather it is a case of potential offered. Yet bold claims are made with significant certainty. While noting that the Internet was able to redress resource imbalances between contenders and so provide more informed citizens, the key predictions resulting from a more online campaign offered by Corrado and Firestone (1996) are that new media reconnects citizens, re-establishing the voter–candidate link, while expanding voter alternatives and increasing civic participation. Such predictions are predicated upon the idea that interactivity encourages participation and engagement, and that campaign communication must evolve to incorporate interactivity and so change the nature of campaign involvement.

However, we argue that political communication is currently at a crossroads; the course seems to be moving towards a more interactive model, but there is no evidence to suggest this signals a long-term shift, or if we will return to a phase of 'politics as usual', incorporating the Internet as another tool of top-down communication. This is, as Agre noted, a direction determined purely by the political candidates and their strategists:

> The Internet has its effect only in the ways that it is appropriated, and it is appropriated in so many different ways that nobody has enough information to add them up. Some of the changes will take the form of 'the same, only more so'; others will be qualitative, as the existing accommodations become untenable.
>
> (Agre 2002: 316)

What we propose is that society has appropriated the Internet as a tool of conversation, as well as information and entertainment seeking. Based on that appropriation, we suggest parties and candidates should be thus providing the Internet audience with a rich tapestry of information provision and features that facilitate interaction, as well as opportunities to shape future visitors' experiences: in other words, they need to harness the produser to the campaign. As campaigns learn from one another, this study offers a four-year history of the use of the Internet within election campaigning; not just a description of a period, but a study that focuses on the uses of the latest technologies as well as online social trends. Hence, we posit that the important question is to investigate to what extent interactivity is being potentiated by political actors during their campaigns.

4 Measuring for a new style of campaigning

Researching interactivity: a tale of three methods

While there has been a range of studies on political campaigning using the Internet that have asked similar questions, most approach the topic from a distinct methodological perspective. Schneider and Foot (2004) identified three ways of analysing political parties' and candidates' websites and categorised the studies they found according to the methodology used. The three methods, content analysis, discourse analysis and Web sphere analysis, all offer a range of advantages and disadvantages which are useful to acknowledge prior to discussing and rationalising our mixed method approach. Prior to outlining these methods, it is worth noting a fourth way to understand the role of the Internet within a political campaign. We could have approached the question of discovering the Internet campaign strategy deployed by asking party strategists and consultants, but this was quickly rejected. While the practical, access-related issues are one hurdle to this approach, the main problem is that interviewees close to a project can engage in post hoc rationalisation and, in the case of consultants, can overplay their own role in successes while shifting blame for failures (Lilleker 2003). While any insights from key players, drawn from media reports or their own publicly available accounts, will be brought in where relevant, the actual artefacts themselves, the way they are used by the organisation and the Web population, provide a safer basis for analysis and can be used to capture the site content as well as to make assumptions about the strategy behind its creation (Xenos and Foot 2005). The process of capturing an entire website means that the sites are frozen at the point of download and so cannot be changed, and so the research provides an objective and in-depth description and analysis of the user interface, including detecting evidence of how users actually did engage with the content, as opposed to an intended or ideal set of functions. Thus, we return to the three methodological approaches discussed previously, which we combine to form our approach.

Content analysis is a quantitative technique that consists of developing a series of categories that can later be tested for their presence or absence, and counted within a specific website. The advantage is that categories can be applied to a number of websites, and the method is one that is highly objective and transparent and can easily cope with a large sample. It cannot, however, deal with the issue of whether the presence of a Web 2.0 feature is a necessary and sufficient condition for interaction to be perceived, or to actually take place. Rather, it can be used to map the terrain of a website, and the user experiences potentiated by the micro-elements included within its architecture.

Content analysis has been widely used to assess the adoption of Internet tools and technologies. It has helped create a rich picture of the role that the Internet has played within election campaigning (Ward and Gibson 2003; Coleman and Ward 2005; Foot and Schneider 2006; Stanyer 2006; Kluver *et al.* 2007; Ward *et al.* 2008) and political communication (de Landtsheer *et al.* 1999; Jackson 2003; Gibson *et al.* 2003a; Ward and Lusoli 2005). For example, a study of features promoting Web-based activism (Hill and Hughes 1998), using a content analysis schematic to determine the political affiliation of 100 political websites, offered significant insights into the Internet's role in mobilisation. Similarly, content analysis was used to provide an in-depth analysis of the user-friendliness, including levels of interactivity, of the websites of all parties across the European Union (de Landtsheer *et al.* 1999, 2005).

Content analysis as a method of enquiry and analysis, in fact, provides the basis of much academic understanding of Internet use in politics. Norris (2003) used the results of the European Eurobarometer to apply a content analysis to 134 web pages in 15 countries of the European Union. She used a supply-and-demand research design to test Margolis and Resnick's (2000) normalisation theory that politics online were 'politics as usual'. She found that the Web was especially useful to smaller parties, but that the mainstream political actors continued to receive the majority of attention, coverage and visits. Such studies allow the development of measurable benchmarks and for predictions to be derived and then empirically tested through longitudinal research projects (for example Corrado and Firestone 1996).

Excellent examples of studies that have employed content analysis for the purposes of testing benchmarks and predictions include Williams *et al.* (2005), who conducted research into the online agendas of presidential candidates in the US 2004 Presidential Elections. They found that the online agendas rarely varied from their offline agendas, thus showing a coordinated use of websites to disseminate the campaign message, but there was a predominance of 'shovelware' (Jackson 2003). Equally, the content of websites of all 1998 US House and Senate candidates was analysed, focusing on their mechanisms for fundraising (Dulio *et al.* 1999). Through content analysis, they found that most candidates used their websites to deliver information and ask for donations, but only 30 per cent of the websites studied offered the possibility of donating online; during that election cycle, 72 per cent of candidates had a website (Kamarck 1999). In addition, content analysis has been used to study the influence of Web campaigning in Japan (Tkach-Kawasaki 2003), Finland (Strandberg 2006) and in the UK for measuring the online presence of British political parties (Gibson and Ward 1999; Jackson 2003; Jackson and Lilleker 2004; Stanyer 2006; Jackson 2007) and to assess the evolution of campaigning due to the directly comparable nature of the data (for example see Schweitzer 2008), all of which provided key insights into the role the Internet has played and has the potential to play within politics.

An alternative application of content analysis methodology is the webstyle method, a direct adaptation of videostyle. This was developed by Banwart to analyse the candidate's self-representation in advertisements (Trammel *et al.* 2005). Trammel *et al.* also used this method to study the levels of interactivity in websites and weblogs of ten Democratic contenders in the 2004 US Presidential Primaries. They concluded that interactivity was present; however, their study was limited to the websites' front pages and the candidates' weblog posts, with no reference to users' responses. Due to the concentration on features that allow a conversation, and not the physical presence of conversations or any sense of the extent to which interactivity could be achieved, the Webstyle method proved to be limited when trying to define levels of interactivity, as it cannot be applied to all aspects of the candidates' online presence.

The most influential work featuring content analysis within online political communication has been that of Rachel Gibson and Stephen Ward. They also set out to test the normalisation/equalisation hypothesis (Margolis and Resnick 2000), later explored by Lusoli (2005), in which they posited that the power struggle and presence of online political movements would duplicate those in the offline political sphere. Their creation of a schematic that categorises features as informational or communicative has become the key tool for testing for interactivity, though not the only method (de Landtsheer *et al.* 1999). This schematic has been employed in studies of candidates' websites in Germany (Gibson *et al.* 2003b), Australia (Gibson and Ward 2002), Italy (Newell *et al.* 2000), the UK (Gibson and Ward 2003) and comparative studies between the US and the UK (Gibson *et al.* 2003a), UK, US, Australia and Germany (Gibson 2002; Gibson *et al.* 2003a), New Zealand (Conway and Dorner 2004) and to study the German Parties' websites during the 2002 National Elections (Schweitzer 2005).

The schematic's importance and wide use for measuring the extent of interactivity is due to the two-dimensional categorisation of communication as either vertical (top-down) or horizontal (non-hierarchical), as well as the level of synchronous or asynchronous conversation (Gibson and Ward 2000b). It thus represents a flexible schematic for the analysis of political websites. Whilst Gibson and Ward's methodology is useful, and will represent one part of our methodology, we recognise the key criticism of content analysis that the data produced is limited, as it focuses purely on the presence of technological features and not the extent of their use. Thus, content analysis can test potential impact to an extent, but can be limited in evaluating the usage of features or their actual effects.

Discourse analysis is a qualitative technique that treats any Web-based communication as a text (Stein 2006a, 2006b; Davis and Brewer 1997). Text, taken to mean all features and layout (Fairclough 2003), is analysed using concepts borrowed from linguistics (Lemke 1999; Crystal 2006; Bergs 2006). The advantage of this approach is that it does not simply involve a counting of the appearance of technological features, but focuses upon the actual message offered by the hosting individual or organisation and the uses and characteristics of language in new media technologies from varying perspectives: for example, social psychology (Walther 2004); semiotics (Mayer 1998); and stylistics (Boardman 2005). While it tends to have a high level of subjectivity, so making it difficult to compare results with other studies, it allows some insight to be offered as to how Web 2.0 technologies and features are employed as opposed to simply recording their presence. Logically, there would appear to be a fit between a method based on looking at conversations, and a concept based on encouraging dialogue. While content analysis counts and categorises, discourse analysis focuses on words and their usage, but has been underused within studies of political websites. However, when it has been employed its effectiveness is demonstrated; for example, Benoit and Benoit (2000) ranked nine US 2000 Presidential Primary websites in order of efficiency and level of interactivity. Although their approach was closer to content analysis since it used a list of characteristics to rate the websites, it has, however, been employed successfully to test for interactivity on government portals (Negroponte 1995; Boardman 2005). Despite the importance of language in shaping reader perceptions, the notion of discourse is often in the background of studies of the Internet as an enabler of discussion and participation, for example, covering topics on and related to e-democracy (Chadwick and May 2003).

While usage in a political communication context is limited, this method has been used widely for corporate and commercial sites. For example, Irene Pollach (2003) used discourse analysis to explore the ethical stance of six corporations focusing on 'the ideational, the interpersonal, and the textual function of discourse' (Pollach 2003: 277). Equally, and from a public sphere perspective, Susan Herring (2004, 2007) combined information science and linguistics to analyse user-to-user interaction in social chat rooms within virtual communities. These studies demonstrate the ability of discourse analysis to provide richness in data that is lacking from the simple counting of content; our methodology links the two to gain both valid and rich data.

The final methodology, Web sphere analysis (Schneider and Foot 2002; Kluver *et al.* 2007), is an attempt to develop a grounded theory of website analysis. Through a process of compiling over 50,000 different websites and interviewing fifty Web producers to examine the political actions on, and among, websites in the 2000 election, Web sphere analysis became an established method. The results of these studies contradicted the normalisation hypothesis, for they found that the presence of websites was in fact transforming the way campaigns were conducted. They also predicted the impact of user-generated content, ones we are only beginning to recognise. The definition of the Web sphere as 'not simply as a collection of websites, but as a hyperlinked set of dynamically defined digital resources spanning multiple websites deemed relevant or related to a central theme or object' (Schneider and Foot 2000: 4), is also highly significant in broadening the understanding of user experiences of websites. This provides an understanding of how links, and the use of links, connect together parts of one site or different sites while recognising the nonlinear nature of the Web. Whilst a time-consuming methodology that relies heavily on testing and following links, it provides a snapshot of a site and its connectedness to the wider community.

Web sphere analysis has been used to explore the structure and linkages of the websites of candidates to the European Parliament in eleven countries (Jankowski *et al.* 2005). Their main question was to explore how website structures fostered engagement, election-related information and online discussion. However, due to the low level of engagement in such an election, the results were deemed exploratory and limited (Jankowski *et al.* 2005). This must not undermine the achievement of being able to compare the use of websites in such different contexts in order to paint a novel, albeit limited, picture of political websites. This study also resulted in scholars publishing the results of the exercise in their specific countries such as the UK (Lusoli and Ward 2004) and Finland (Strandberg and Carlson 2005), as well as producing a series of papers for the *Information Polity* journal.

What we find in mapping current research and findings is a lack of examination into how features are used by political parties and candidates when building a Web presence; what they are saying through the images and text in their websites; and how the site is structured to enable both internal and external navigation. There has been a significant amount of research employing content analysis; less has taken a critical discourse analysis approach; while Web sphere analysis is underused. In developing a methodological approach that combines elements of all three methods, this research is able to provide a much richer sense of what interactivity means in the context of a political website, and give indications of the direction in which e-political communication is heading. Equally, only content analysis has been used to study election campaigning, and specifically the content of websites, hence this offers a more comprehensive method of exploring interactivity and its role within election campaigning and voter engagement.

Elections and the Internet: searching for elections 2.0

This study focuses on four elections: the 2007 French Presidential Election, the 2008 US Presidential Election, the 2009 German Uber-Wahl or super election of members to the Bundestag and the 2010 UK General Election of Members of Parliament. Both latter elections determine the composition of parliament and who the ruling party or potential coalition members might be; the former two determine only the president and national leader, though other elections to Congress can take place concurrently. The study will first map the websites as an interconnected network, and then analyse the presence of Web 2.0 features across all pages of the sites to assess the extent of interactivity. The process of mapping will identify external links to other aspects of the candidate or party campaign, such as weblogs, presences across SNS or other Web-based innovations as well as links to other external sites. The second stage represents a count of features, all of which are categorised according to the direction of communication potentiated (top-down to horizontal); this categorisation adheres to the schematic adapted from the work of McMillan (2002a, 2002b) and the operationalisation of Ferber *et al.*'s model of interactivity which is outlined in detail in this chapter and has been used in published studies, one being a pilot study of interactivity within the French presidential candidates' websites (Lilleker and Malagon 2010) as well as UK party websites between elections (Jackson and Lilleker 2009a). Additionally, an assessment of the language used when delivering information and soliciting visitor inputs will be made to determine the extent to which the language is inclusive and encourages participation. The methodology used is based on a moderate constructivist perspective of reality (Fairclough 2003) and a mixed method research methodology offering an overview of the Web sphere within the specific website, and then combines quantitative content analysis and qualitative discourse analysis to assess interactivity. The methods complement each other to produce a richer analysis of a media product (Gillespie and Toynbee 2006), and are a recommended measure to study websites (Herring 2004).

The first step was to archive the websites so they could be analysed later in the research. For this purpose, the content of the websites was converted through PDF Professional and Web Dumper Software at a key point towards the end of the campaign when the sites were fully mature. The official websites of Presidential Candidates Ségolène Royal (www.desirsdavenir.org) and Nicolas Sarkozy (www.sarkozy.fr) were archived on 1 May 2007, those of Barack Obama and John McCain on 1 November 2008, the sites of the six major German parties on 27 September 2009 and the sites of the six UK parties on 1 May 2010. The six German parties selected all have representation in the Bundestag and had realistic opportunities of inclusion into a coalition depending on the result of the election. These parties are CDU: Christlich Demokratische Union Deutschlands; CSU: Christlich-Soziale Union; SPD: Sozialdemokratische Partei Deutschlands; FDP: Freie Demokratische Partei; Greens: Bündnis 90/Die Grünen; Left: Die Linke. Due to the UK's first-past-the-post voting system, less parties are able to gain seats in parliament, and thus the results are skewed towards three national parties, with the others represented in the House being parties that stand in one region only. Thus, for comparative purposes, selection was based upon identifying parties with some form of elected representation and who stand for election within more than 50 per cent of the country: British National (BNP), Conservative, Green, Labour, Liberal Democrat and UK Independence Parties (UKIP) on 1 May 2010. In addition, where appropriate, we also included in our sample the profiles of the presidential candidates within social networks such as Facebook and MySpace, their use of YouTube and Twitter for the month preceding the election, and a sample of any officially branded candidate, party or party leader weblog. These were only included if there was a link from the candidate or party home page; however, as this suggests, they are an integral and strategic part of the campaign. The result of this procedure delivered over 150,000 pages of content that would later be purposively sampled for the purposes of discourse analysis; the content of the entire website and any related or linked presences belonging to the candidate or party were included within the overall counting of features procedure. The sampling aimed to offer a cross section of pages of the site based on its design and structure; the front page of all sites was included, the rest were selected to be representative of the average user experience. These representative pages, detailed in each chapter, were identified to analyse the use of discourse and rhetorical techniques.

A sequential procedure

The research project consisted of three consecutive steps: (1) Web mapping, (2) content analysis and (3) discourse analysis, the latter in effect occurring concurrently with the content analysis, where screenshots were taken using Zotero software for the Mozilla Firefox Web browser,[1] and notes attached to highlight particular uses of language by the site creators. In order to better understand the focus of the study, the websites were mapped according to web page, site and purpose. Content was then analysed in relation to the categories proposed by Gibson and Ward (2000b), as used in the two most recent similar studies (Conway and Dorner 2004; Schweitzer 2005). The list of features measured was adapted for analysis of the US and French contests to eliminate those that were not applicable (such as information about party leaders), and include those that were not considered by Gibson and Ward, such as social networking, blogs and video tools. Indicators related to site delivery (such as 'flashiness') were not considered relevant for assessing interactivity and were eliminated. In addition, we have added categories relating to resource generation such as fundraising and encouraging volunteers (Jackson 2006b, 2007; Anstead and Chadwick 2008). Applying this methodology reduced the level of subjective coding, enhancing reliability and the validity of the content analysis (Gibson and Ward 2000b) and replicability of this study for future longitudinal or comparative analysis.

During the second phase of the data analysis, Critical Discourse Analysis (CDA) was applied to a sample of both websites. The analysis was based on the elements of the web page, when referring to it as a text. Images and videos were included within the definition of text (Wetherell *et al.*,2001). CDA can produce three levels of analysis: (a) the actual text; (b) the discursive practices (that is, the process involved in creating, writing, speaking, reading and hearing); and (c) the larger social context that bears upon the text and the discursive practices (Fairclough 2000). CDA examines the link between social action and language (Fairclough 2000, 2001). In a broader perspective, discourse analysis can approach language either as a topic or as a resource (Taylor 2001); in this case, the language in the text was approached as a resource; a product, feature or item that is accessed by the user for a purpose (to gain information, respond to questions or to affirm their support publicly perhaps) and which elicits a cognitive response.

The relationship between the Critical Discourse Analysis perspective and new media was established by Susan Herring in 2004 by examining three critical assumptions. First, CDA looks for patterns that might not be evident to the observer at first glance, or to those who participate in the discourse. Second,

Table 4.1 Coding categories used for content analysis (adapted from Gibson and Ward 2000b)

Categories	*Measures (where appropriate)*
Downward information flows	
Documents (e.g. manifesto)	present (1), absent (0)
Policies summed	present (1), absent (0)
Issues examined	present (1), absent (0); number of specific issues
Statement of values/ideology	present (1), absent (0)
Newsletters	number available (including archived copies)
Media releases	present (1), absent (0); number of specific releases
Candidate profile	present (1), absent (0)
Election information	present (1), absent (0)
Event calendar	present (1), absent (0)
Frequently asked questions	present (1), absent (0); number offered
Negative campaigning	present (1), absent (0); overall percentage
Videos	present (1), absent (0); number of videos
Targeted pages	number of groups targeted, download form: present (1), absent (0), online inquiry form: present (1), absent (0), online transaction: present (1), absent (0).
Upward information flows	
Volunteer	download form: present (1), absent (0), online enquiry form: present (1), absent (0)
Donation	why Donate: present (1), absent (0), give online: present (1), absent (0).
Merchandise	download form: present (1), absent (0), online enquiry form: present (1), absent (0), online transaction: present (1), absent (0)
Cookies	present (1), absent (0)
Lateral/horizontal information flows	
Partisan links	number of groups supportive of organisation
Reference links	number of general information sites
Internal links	number of sub-organisational groups
Interactive information flows: Asynchronous	
Download logos/posters	number of opportunities
Site search	present (1), absent (0)
Enmeshing	present (1), absent (0)
Navigation aids	present (1), absent (0)
Online games/gimmicks	present (1), absent (0)
Email contact	present (1), absent (0)
Email feedback	present (1), absent (0)
	online enquiry form: present (1), absent (0)
Join email list	present (1), absent (0)
Questionnaires	present (1), absent (0)
Visitor-initiated questionnaires	present (1), absent (0)
Polls	present (1), absent (0)
Visitor-initiated polls	present (1), absent (0)
Petitions	present (1), absent (0)
Visitor-initiated petitions	present (1), absent (0)
Join online campaign	present (1), absent (0)

continued

Table 4.1 continued

Categories	*Measures (where appropriate)*
Subscribe to e-newsletter	present (1), absent (0)
Membership	download form: present (1), absent (0) online enquiry form: present (1), absent (0), online transaction: present (1), absent (0)
Bulletin board	present (1), absent (0)
Blog tools	present (1), absent (0)
Ability to share videos/pics (embed code)	present (1), absent (0)
Podcasts	present (1), absent (0)
Social networking links	present (1), absent (0)
Twitter	present (1), absent (0)
RSS	present (1), absent (0)
Interactive information flows: Synchronous	
Ability of visitors to upload content/comments	present (1), absent (0), number of opportunities
Ability of visitors to share information	present (1), absent (0), number of opportunities
Ability of visitors to update information	present (1), absent (0), number of opportunities
Public conversations allowed via comments or wall posting	present (1), absent (0), number of opportunities
Forum	present (1), absent (0)
Chat room	present (1), absent (0)
Online debate	present (1), absent (0), number of opportunities to debate with candidates/leaders

discourse is a product of a speaker's choices, and these choices involve more than 'linguistic considerations', as choices come from cognitive and social elements (Herring 2004: 4). Finally, online communication 'may be, but is not inevitably, shaped by the technological features of computer-mediated communication systems' (Herring 2004: 4–5). Therefore, the patterns of language and choices made by the speaker, and the cognitive response they are likely to elicit, are as important as the ability to interact via technology.

Even though CDA belongs to a branch of linguistics, it is concerned with more than just language for the sake of language. CDA sees discourse 'as a form of social practice' and as 'socially influential' (Fairclough and Wodak 1997: 258), with the objective of analysing 'linguistic and semiotic aspects of social processes and problems' (Fairclough and Wodak 1997: 271). CDA is particularly appropriate for testing for interactivity given that the 'major priorities of CDA … converge and are instantiated in a variety of ways' (Mautner 2005: 283). That is, there is a social problem (citizen participation and new media) that can be analysed through the products of language (artefacts embedded within a website). CDA can be used to analyse websites at both the micro (semantic, sintactic and grammatical analysis) and macro level (genres, voices and orders of discourse) (Herring 2004).

This study focused on a macro-level analysis of the genres and voices present in the sample, and used these findings to describe the order of discourse found in the text and the categories of analysis: the order of discourse, the genre and the voices present. Genre provides the context for the conversation, and can be abstract or concrete. Concrete examples include biography, autobiography, interview and TV interview. The voices in a text are the different presences that can be found. Each voice has a different texture and style. The multiplicity of voices is related to the 'dialogicality' of a text (Fairclough 2003), which in turn is directly related to the Habermasian notion of the public sphere. The definitions of the genre and voices found in the text were not defined a priori, even though 'political discourse' may be the obvious choice. The study follows Mautner's recommendation to avoid premature judgments of the selection of voices and genres. The sum of voices, genres, styles and discourses found in a text result in the order of discourse. The order of discourse is the 'discoursal aspect of a network of social practice' that has 'relative stability and durability' (Fairclough 2003: 230). The text was analysed to find the number of participants present, and the extent to which information was delivered in a style that was rhetorical, negative towards opponents, or was presented in a factual way; while all political communication can be deemed persuasive to some extent, the aim of noting the overall style of communication assesses the extent to which parties and candidates adhere to Habermasian definitions of ideal speech. Any interactive debate must also be held in an open participative forum with a commitment to freedom and equality in the speech action. These aspects were analysed in the sampled website pages.

The revised user-to-user and user-to-document interactivity model

The last section of the analysis was concerned with discerning the level and type of interactivity, enabled both by the technological features and language present in each text. These were tested against the elements of the different categories present in the McMillan model of interactivity, as revised by Ferber *et al.* (Figure 4.1), and operationalised for the analysis of website content (Jackson and Lilleker 2009b; Lilleker and Malagon 2010). Each features as initially classified according to the kind of dialogue they enabled: simple one-way communication with some feedback; two-way asymmetrical dialogue or open participation. For the latter we sought to identify those tools that enabled public dialogue between the host and visitors, as well as between visitors. A proof of concept exercise was conducted by assessing our classifications and categorisation against those determined by expert website designers and online technology developers. This procedure involved asking a panel of experts to judge the initial classifications in terms of their consistency with expected usage by designers and end users. This added an additional measure of reliability to the coding and classification process, and reduces criticisms of subjectivity. The panel's agreement with the initial categories ascribed to features, and their subsequent agreement with a

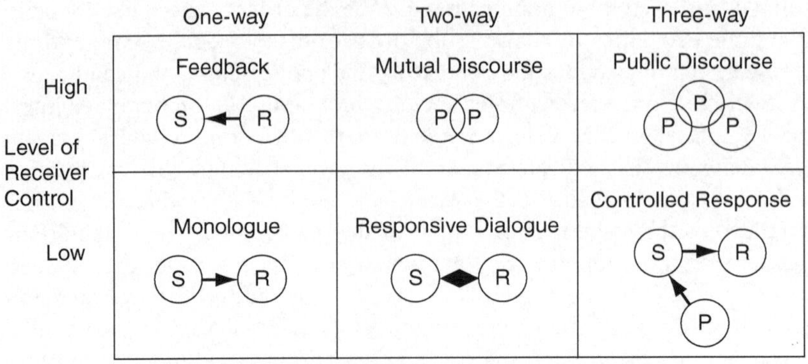

Figure 4.1 A six-part model of cyber-interactivity.

sample of categorisations of actual usage that deviated from expected practice, allowed us to map our classifications to intended uses of features with some confidence.

A count for each feature was made, usually present or absent, but where appropriate, the number of items (press releases, videos, weblog posts for example) was also recorded. The categories are operationalised for the purposes of analysing website content (Figure 4.2) and the 1–10 scale on the x-axis is derived from McMillan's classifications of interactivity (Table 3.1) but in a simplified form to enable mapping across the six directional dimensions; the classifications are detailed in Table 4.2.

All site features were analysed and classified according to evidence of levels of sender/receiver control, and direction of communication in terms of user-to-user interactivity. Within this process we sought to identify the nature of the audience (passive or active), and direction of communication when looking at user-to-document interactivity and the intended nature of the audience (Figures 4.2 and 4.3). The latter dimension, also based on McMillan's schematic, identi-

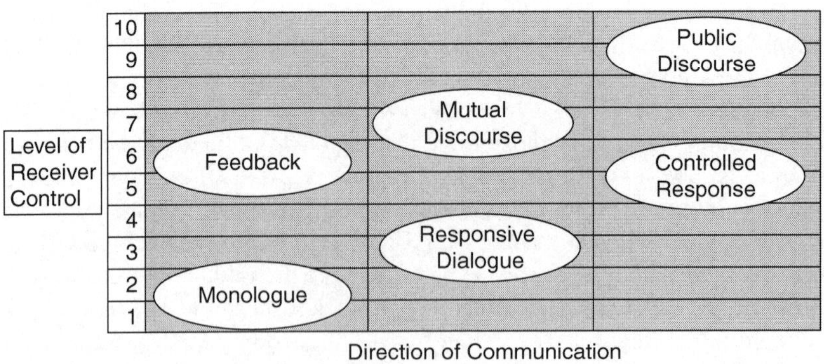

Figure 4.2 Revised user-to-user interactivity model.

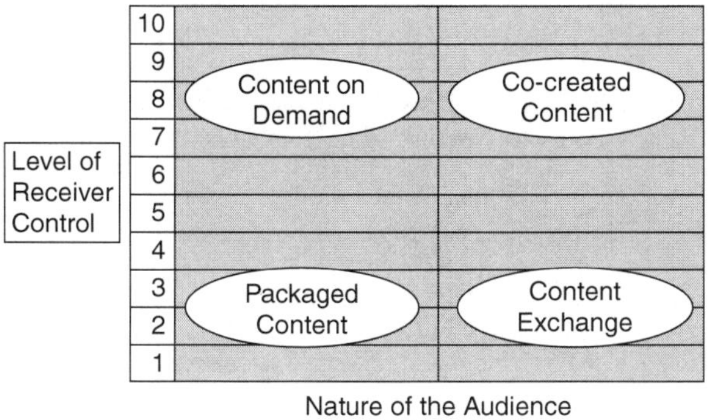

Figure 4.3 User-to-document interactivity.

fies how website features encourage a range of behavioural responses from passivity, with read-only documents designed to be informational and persuasive, through material that can be accessed by choice, and the exchanging of information to the highest level of activity: the co-creation of content within a website. While the latter only measures the number of opportunities and not the extent to which these are taken up by site visitors, we add commentary on this to provide detail of the success or failure of the design, or indeed the party or candidate, to elicit responses and work with their network of supporters and visitors.

The level of user control was quantified (from 0 to 10), the direction of communication classified (one-way, two-way or three-way) and whether the communication would be synchronic or asynchronous for the user-to-user interactivity model. In the case of the user-to-document model, the process was repeated using the nature of audience category (active or passive audience), as detailed above. To measure the level of interactivity, the websites were taken as a whole and assessed using the original McMillan categories (Table 3.1). These were operationalised, defining each point on the scale, and linking potential and actual user behaviour to numerical values (these are presented in Table 4.2). In addition, to ensure that interpretations and explanations were intelligible (Titscher *et al.* 2000: 164; Bondarouk and Ruel 2004), medium and situational variables were taken into account (Herring 2004); these included the context of any single part of the site and the stage in the campaign. These measures were intended to improve the trustworthiness of the study (Lincoln and Guba 1985; Bondarouk and Ruel 2008; Herring 2004).

The data that we present, therefore, is collected through a series of analytical descriptions and measures based upon an operationalisation of models, each derived from a range of studies that permit a full and rich analysis of the interactivity potentiated across candidate and party websites or linked auxiliary online presences that will be applied to each of the websites of the key candidates or parties in each contest. Using these, we can evaluate sites for the presence of interactive tools, how the tools are used and could be used, and also how usage

Table 4.2 Scale for measuring levels of receiver control

Category	*Scale*	*Definition*
Low receiver control	1	One-way hyperlink with unclear destination
	2	One-way hyperlink with defined destination
	3	Hyperlinks created with user input, language is dynamic using second person
	4	User has control over read and link options, video play is optional, content can be downloaded
	5	Users have control over interfacing with content (above) and can send information
	6	Users can send and receive information, i.e. debate forums
	7	Users have multiple options to send and receive information, their input has transformational power – can be seen, i.e. text-only chat.
High receiver control	8	Users can upload content, questions, including videos, and can receive answers from receivers
	9	User can choose time, type and amount of information sent and received, the information sent is transformed by the receiver and the transformation is transparent. Communication is asymmetrical
	10	Sender and receiver have equal levels of control, communication is conversational

is encouraged through the language of the host. Furthermore, each party or presidential candidate will be awarded an overall interactivity score based on a mean average of assessments which, alongside counts of the use of Web 2.0 tools and the extent to which the website as a totality offered opportunities for interaction, can permit a greater sense of comparability and testing for lesson learning between nations over this four-year period.

5 France 2007

Tentative interactivity

French politics in 2007: cautious interest

The French Presidential Election of 2007 gained considerable media attention throughout both rounds of voting. The 2002 election had seen the far right Front National leader Jean-Marie le Pen get to the second round, so perhaps voters were more aware of the importance of voting; however, there also seemed to be greater interest in who would replace Jacques Chirac and what that would mean for the future of France (Le Monde, 23 April 2007). Whilst it was clear that it would most likely be a race between left and right, the winner of the first round of voting was by no means predictable from the early stages. Turnout on 22 April was high, 83.77 per cent, producing two clear candidates to move forward to round two: Nicolas Sarkozy, representing the *Union pour un mouvement populaire*; and Segolene Royal of the *Parti socialiste*. Whilst the left gained slightly more votes, across all candidates, within round one, it was Sarkozy that emerged as victor on the evening of 6 May. The contest, and its outcome, was close and difficult to predict (53 per cent versus 47 per cent), turnout in round two was again just below 84 per cent and it seemed it was issues that determined the outcome, with personality not emerging as an important theme even if it did gain voter interest (BBC News, 4 May 2007).

French electoral politics have not recently seen such high turnouts or engagement (Fauvelle-Aymar *et al.* 2000), though turnout is often higher for presidential elections than in the US or for UK general elections. The reason for le Pen getting through to the second round in 2002 was turnout, which was just over 70 per cent, and the left wing vote collapsed seeing Lionel Jospin, then prime minister, squeezed out by le Pen. The negative tone of the campaign, with Jospin and Chirac both claiming the successes and apportioning blame for problems on their opponent, is argued to have depressed support for both candidates (Bell and Criddle 2002). However, others suggest that it was Jospin that lost the contest by ignoring his core vote (Gaffney 2004; Kuhn 2002; Laver *et al.* 2006), though there may also have been a rejection of the traditional political class due to a range of cultural and social changes (Miguet 2002; Laver *et al.* 2006). Whatever the underlying reasons, a range of candidates gained a small amount of votes rather than there being clear favourites; hence le Pen's 16.8 per cent vaulted him into the second round. While there was a mood for change, Chirac won due to an anti le Pen reaction, where turnout reached 79 per cent. However, despite the turnout being high, suggesting high engagement and interest in electoral politics, French politics witnessed similarly high levels of disengagement, disillusionment and apathy, as is common for many democracies (see Table 5.1).

While this appears to indicate that France would benefit from the potential of a more interactive political communication discourse, this historically has been hindered by the shallow penetration of Internet usage. UNSD data showed France having 31.38 per cent of the population having access, compared to 42.31 per cent in the UK, 48.9 per cent in Germany and 55.14 per cent in the US (UNSD 2006[1]). This is due to the French Minitel national intranet, which lacks compatibility with the English language oriented World Wide Web (Global Reach). This factor has fundamentally limited the Internet's potential as a communication channel in France. It is also worth noting that it is suggested that the Chirac government hesitated over adoption due to the Anglo-Saxon and Anglophile predominance of the Internet, and thus social and political usage was restricted. In 1997 only le Pen's Front National created a website with the expressed intention of circumnavigating the media; therefore, there was a clear political divergence on Internet use (Bratten 2005). However, with concerns over the Internet on the wane, and in response to some public and corporate demand, over the last four years France has moved into the top fifteen online populations and is now number seven, and its unique home users spend around thirty-seven hours per month online (Comscore 2006). This seems to have reduced the digital divide noted by Chadwick (2006), with France seeing 51.8 per cent online at the time of the 2007 Presidential Election (InternetWorldStats 2008), though this is still lower than the 67 per cent, 71.8 per cent and 72.5 per cent in Germany, the UK and the US respectively at a contiguous point of time. However, there is

Table 5.1 Socio-political factors in France

Factor	*Mean (scale) in France*	*Mean average ESS nations*
Interest in politics	2.61 (1–4, 1 = very interested)	2.61
Politics is too complicated to understand	2.86 (1–5, 1 = always understand)	3.10
Trust in parliament	4.31 (0–10, 0 = no trust)	4.46
Trust in politicians	3.29 (0–10, 0 = no trust)	3.57
Trust in parties	3.21 (0–10, 0 = no trust)	3.60
Taken part in lawful demonstration	1.85 (1–2, 2 = no)	1.94
Close to one party	1.46 (1–2, 2 = no)	1.48
Party member	1.98 (1–2, 2 = no)	1.95
Satisfied with government	3.84 (0–10, 0 = extremely dissatisfied)	4.42
Satisfied with democracy	4.57 (0–10, 0 = extremely dissatisfied)	5.23

Note
Data from European Social Survey 2006/7.

certainly evidence that significant numbers of French citizens were participating in online debates on the election (Desquinabo 2008); therefore, while to some extent still lagging behind the UK and the US, the French population are quickly catching up in their move to Internet communication.

The lag in terms of penetration of the Internet in France, mainly due to cultural exceptionalism, has resulted in French parties and candidates being an election cycle behind their Anglo-Saxon counterparts. French politics has not previously seen new media strategists become an integral part of campaign planning and execution, as was the case in the US in 2004 (Howard 2006), but French parties were quick to build websites in time for the 1997 General Election and it became a *de rigueur* electoral tool. The French tradition for being politically active, coupled with a demand for greater input into the political process (Villalba 2003: 121), suggests that if the Internet is used to facilitate participation and interaction then French citizens will not be reticent in accessing those sites. However, this would mark a departure from tradition in French political communication. The monopoly control of Minitel by the state-owned France Telecom has limited citizens' access, and participation has been the preserve of social elites (Vedel 2000). Villalba's (2003) study of the use of the Internet before and during the 2002 Presidential Election reinforces the pessimistic predictions for interactivity. He found that the majority of parties offered a range of information to visitors to websites, and simple ways to interact such as email, discussion fora, online polls and joining the party were facilitated. However, any sense of true interaction was limited, and the majority of communication was unidirectional. This approach was mirrored during the 2004 European Parliament Elections, leading Van Os (2005) to conclude that party websites were basic, content driven and had very little impact. Similarly, Bratten (2005) assessed le Pen's website during the 2002 Presidential Election and found that its role was essentially one-way to promote the Front National's policies. This is fairly common of Internet use by political parties, and a trend mirrored across most of northern Europe (Jankowski *et al.* 2005).

Interest in the Internet increased during 2005 with the referendum on the European Constitution, and innovation crept into political communication. While the French Government used content-driven websites to provide basic facts and details to support the Yes campaign, the No campaign made use of weblogs to encourage public debate on the issues (Soufron 2007). The No campaign also exploited the networking feature of Web 2.0 to identify possible activists, and circulated favourable stories and newspaper commentaries, so adding to the reach and depth of the debate (Soufron 2007). Indeed, Jean Phillippe Clement, suggesting that the Internet had an impact on the result, opined that 'the media said yes, and the web said no' (cited in Perrier 2007). Thus, in the run-up to the 2007 Presidential Elections a number of commentators believed that the Internet would play an enhanced role. For example, Wood (2007) suggested that political debate was moving from the Left Bank cafés to cyberspace. Uther (2007) went further and predicted that the Internet, particularly weblogs, would help candidates gain an advantage with an ever-growing Web-savvy electorate.

Facilitated by the use of video-sharing sites such as YouTube and social networking tools to communicate with voters, it is suggested that 2006/7 marked a turning point for political communication (Castells 2007). The French Presidential Campaign of 2007 seemed to be the first campaign to offer evidence to support Castells' claim. While public interest and participation remained high throughout the contest, the aspect that seemed to set this campaign apart was the use of ICT (XiTi Monitor 2007a, 2007b). During her French presidential campaign, Ségolène Royal established her presence in Second Life (Kyricau 2007) and put interaction via new media in the spotlight. The candidate was reaching out to the voters in a way previously unseen (for example, see Scott 2006 and Benhold 2007). Interest came from both journalists and the online community. Weblog authors began asking if this was an effort to enhance democratic life, or just another campaign gimmick (Uther 2007). As Sarkozy developed a parallel online presence, journalists and weblog authors frequently asked whether both candidates were striving to interact with their voters, and if interaction was possible, was it appropriate and actually desirable?

Domestic French media, as well as commentators in the wider global media, commented on the use of blogs, embedded videos and Second Life, suggesting a different style of campaigning was emerging. Though both candidates found themselves the victims of user-generated content posted to YouTube, their own sites did not suffer from visitors posting critical remarks. This was argued to be due to the level of control the site hosts and gatekeepers had over content, which led one blogger to comment that Sarkozy and Royal 'still see the world from the old top-down, command-and-control perspective' (King 2007). But, their use of ICT was still vaunted as encouraging participation of a previously unseen level and extent (XiTi Monitor 2007b). Therefore, we pose the question whether this was true interactivity, a 2.0 Election, or a chimera of interactivity that was more about impression management than conversation.

Mapping the sites

In order to examine to what extent the French Presidential Election of 2007 included an interactive dimension, the sample studied was the official campaign websites of the two main candidates, Ségolène Royal (www.desirsdavenir.org) and Nicolas Sarkozy (www.sarkozy.fr). The websites, in this case, represented the heart of the candidates' online presence and, apart from the use of Second Life which was impossible to capture, were identified as the totality of Internet usage by the candidate. Other sites dedicated to the candidate and a Facebook fan page supporting Nicolas Sarkozy appear to have been created independently, and there was no link to them from the candidate's site proper; hence their sense of being official was highly questionable and these were not included in the sample.

Web mapping allowed an overview of the complete site and its purpose; desirsdavenir.org, the official web page for the Ségolène Royal campaign, consisted of 1,754 individual pages separated into 28 distinct categories. The Web interface was divided by user activity into three main categories: 'S'informer' (Get informed), 'Participer' (Participate) and Blogs. The most prominent element invited visitors to get informed, however 'Participer', the largest section of the site, featured a range of opportunities to actively support the campaign in the form of donating, downloading banners or going to the debate forums. The Segosphere, the third element, featured links to her online support network and, while a key part of the ethos of the campaign, remained a peripheral part of the experience for visitors to the home page.

The structure of sarkozy.fr was organised around a central node. The content was more visual and presented in a monochrome design. The navigation was outlined through a linear menu. The 610 unique pages were separated into three domains: www.sarkozy.fr, www.supportersdesarkozy.fr and www.boutique-sarkozy.com/. The coherence of presentation throughout gave more of a feel of a single site than that of Royal, though Sarkozy's television (NS-TV) was within a separate section. The site was very much about Sarkozy in every aspect, thus the small supporters section enabled active support rather than encouraging participation in the way offered by Royal.

The sampling units for content analysis were those contained in the websites www.desirsdavenir.org and www.sarkozy.fr. Any information outside the original path was discarded to limit the boundaries of the research, with the exception of six microsites: http://video.desirsdavenir.org, www.boutique-sarkozy.com, www.supportersdesarkozy.com/home, http://videos.desirsdavenir.org, http://emilitants.desirsdavenir.org and http://blogs.desirsdavenir.org. The specific pages identified for use within the discourse analysis stage were both sites' home page; Royal's debate forum *E-debaters* and her biography, and Sarkozy's 'Ask a Question' area and his biography entitled My Life.

Defining identity online

Two of the first elements that came to light after the first two phases of the research were completed were differences in the constructed architecture, and purpose of the websites. The differences in those elements permeate throughout, and are important to understanding both the perceived and actual interactivity of the sites. Royal's website was built around a dynamic platform that changed its content by showcasing user-generated content, posts and alternative voices; Sarkozy's website, on the other hand, was designed to allow the voice of the candidate to predominate and reach supporters and undecided voters through targeted messages inserted into made-for-Web videos. NS-TV, with its eighteen channels, was the backbone and main feature of a website with a high level of message control. However, amidst these contrasts there was a key similarity: the majority of information followed a downward communication flow across both websites.

The characteristics and extension of the documents provided created two separate effects. Ségolène Royal's website scored highly in the downward information and communication flows, and included, among many other documents, a 600-page *Cahiers d'esperances* (Notebooks of Hope) that report the results of participative live and online forums that were held to develop the candidate's manifesto. The intent of placing this document on the website could not have been for users to read, as users rarely read politicians' manifestos (Castells 2007) and large amounts of text reduce a website's usability and readability (Nielsen 2004; George 2005). The 'Notebooks' are in reality a metaphor of the participative democratic proposal that is behind the inclusive discourse in Ségolène Royal's campaign, consistent with her socialist and communitarian ideology (Pène 2007). The same can be said of the Republique des blogs (Republic of blogs), the myriad of voices found in the home page (17 distinct voices), and the amount of user-generated content posted on parts of her website. The abundance of statements as questions (interrogative grammatical mood, Fairclough 1995), in addition to the site's graphic design, created a multi-coloured, polyphonic platform that was much closer to the ideal of the public sphere than the targeted messages of the campaign-oriented Sarkozy website.

Sarkozy's website reflected his more authoritarian and nationalistic ideological position on the right. The design reinforced the idea of a unified France with a clear direction, and an integrationist view on the French culture through a monochromatic style with one font face and uniform positioning of the text across each page. Everything in the design was a metaphor for consistency and unity, with the colours of the French flag in the background. Even in the biography section, Sarkozy's position on unity, clear direction and traditional values is highlighted by reflexive forms. While the manifesto title 'Together everything becomes possible' gives the impression of inclusivity, the tone is one of offering leadership, with Sarkozy setting the parameters for what should be achieved 'together' and the means for doing so. While, within a marketised era of politics (Lilleker *et al.* 2006), we would expect clear linkages between manifestos and issues, there is little sense of collaboration. Equally, within the 'Posez une question' section, nineteen individuals' videos are included with detailed answers and there is a clear process of selection by the site gatekeepers. Furthermore, within the section 'Ils me soutiennent' (They support me), there is a series of endorsements from both elite figures and ordinary people, suggesting some form of collaboration, but again within clearly defined parameters. In contrast, the values of democratic participation, diversity and collective construction were housed under the umbrella of 'France for president: Ségolène Royal for president' in desirsdavenir.org. The campaign slogan stresses the femininity of the candidate and the nation; and the Royal website gave the spotlight to the voters. The value of the candidate herself is underplayed to highlight the collectivist style of campaign image she wanted to project.

While it is frequent that political parties' websites outside the US and the UK 'lack a clear rationale for their online activities, other than maintaining an image of professionalism and being seen as up-to-date' (Gibson and Ward 2000b: 302), this was not the case for the French presidential websites. On the contrary, the results of both the content and discourse analysis provide enough evidence to suggest that the design and function of the websites is consistent with Howard's (2006) description of a hypermedia campaign. Within such a campaign, all multimedia tools are integrated into the general campaign strategy. This is evidenced by the consistency in interface design, message and language use of each website with their candidate's platform and brand differentiators.

Furthermore, the functionality of the French presidential candidates' official websites was evaluated, and found to be consistent with Gibson and Ward's original 2000 findings. The websites were indeed used for the five main functions of information provision; campaigning; resource generation; networking and organisation strengthening; and promoting participation. With this in mind, after briefly highlighting what features were present, we offer an overview of the results that pertain to each function, followed by an analysis and discussion to access the levels of interactivity, the fit with the big ideas of Web 2.0 and the mode of discourse found within the two French presidential candidates' websites.

The features present across the sites

Both sites had a high degree of sophistication and appeared as multimedia platforms with a range of both Web 1.0 and Web 2.0, as would be expected. The focus within both sites was presenting information rather than allowing visitor input; while presenting information is not seen as normatively bad practice, as one key function of any party or candidate website is to inform visitors, the fact that a significant amount of the site was purely information does not suggest a move towards embracing the technologies or philosophies of Web 2.0. While we return to this point later in this chapter, this should not be taken as a suggestion that the site was completely non-interactive. Visitors were able to interact with the site in a range of ways. An overview of the features present is shown in Table 5.2.

Table 5.2 demonstrates that essentially, the sites concentrated mainly on Web 1.0 features. Where Web 2.0 did feature, these were features which largely allowed visitors to interact with the site rather than the host or other visitors. A striking feature is the lack of any social networking activity; while both Sarkozy and Royal are now highly active on Facebook, this was not always the case due to the low take-up of the site in France prior to 2008. Equally, tools such as Twitter had not gained a critical mass of users. Hence, the campaign centred solely on the websites, as opposed to using a hypermedia granular campaign with multiple points of access. In this context of a largely user-to-site interactivity approach, Sarkozy's site offered a greater degree of sophistication, particularly the NS-TV, which allowed videos to be embedded within other sites and downloaded to players. However, Royal did explore some innovative features, in particular allowing citizens to join Segoland, her supportive blog community, and to participate in a forum. The latter, however, was not a real-time discussion and so, in the same way as Sarkozy's 'Ask a Question' and 'They Support Me'

Table 5.2 Features of both candidates' websites: France 2007

Categories	*Royal website*	*Sarkozy website*
Downward information flows		
Documents (e.g. manifesto)	Yes	Yes
Policies summed	Yes	No
Issues examined	Yes	Yes
Number of issues discussed	16	21
Statement of values/ideology	Yes	Yes
Newsletters	Yes	Yes
Number of newsletters archived	77	0
Media releases	Yes	Yes
Number of releases	170	119
Candidate profile	Yes	Yes
Election information	No	No
Event calendar	Yes	Yes
Frequently asked questions	No	No
Number of FAQs	0	0
Negative campaigning	Yes	Yes
Overall per cent of negativity	0.4%	60%
Videos	Yes	Yes
Number of videos	469	819
Targeted pages	Yes	No
Number of groups targeted	3	0
Targeted download form	No	No
Targeted online enquiry form	No	No
Targeted online transaction	No	No
Upward information flows		
Volunteering possible	Yes	No
Donations possible	No	No
Merchandise for sale	No	Yes
Cookies	No	No
Lateral/horizontal information flows		
Number of partisan links	3	1
Number of reference links	0	0
Number of internal links	0	0
Interactive information flows: Asynchronous		
Download logos/posters (number)	33	29
Site search	No	No
Enmeshing	No	Yes
Navigation aids	Yes	Yes
Online games/gimmicks	No	No
Email contact	Yes	Yes
Email feedback	Yes	Yes
Online feedback form	Yes	Yes
Join email list	Yes	Yes
Questionnaires	No	No
Visitor-initiated questionnaires	No	No
Polls	No	No
Visitor-initiated polls	No	No

Table 5.2 Continued

Categories	*Royal website*	*Sarkozy website*
Petitions	No	No
Visitor-initiated petitions	No	No
Join online campaign	Yes	Yes
Subscribe to e-newsletter	Yes	Yes
Membership form to download	No	No
Online membership enquiry form	No	No
Online membership transaction	Yes	Yes
Bulletin board	No	No
Blog tools	Yes	Yes
Ability to share videos/pics (embed code)	No	Yes
Podcasts	No	Yes
Social networking links	No	No
Twitter	No	No
RSS	Yes	Yes
Interactive information flows: Synchronous		
Ability of visitors to upload content/comments	No	Yes
Number of opportunities to upload content/comments	0	2
Ability of visitors to share information	Yes	Yes
Number of opportunities to share information	2	8
Ability of visitors to update information	Yes	No
Number of opportunities to update information	2	0
Public conversations allowed via comments or wall posting	No	No
Number of opportunities for public conversations	0	0
Forum	Yes	No
Chat room	No	No
Online debate	No	No
Number of opportunities to debate with candidates/leaders	0	0

sections, showed where visitors had participated rather than showing participation as it happened and which could be directly interacted with. Hence, as the discussion of the functions and Web 2.0 features below demonstrates, the overriding purpose of the websites appeared to be informing visitors about the candidates and presenting them with a brand image; a typical use of communication during an election campaign.

The functions of the French candidates' websites

Information provision

The function of information provision was well served on both websites. The majority of content had a downward communication flow, a total of 63 per cent of Royal's site and 97 per cent for that of Sarkozy. Users were offered a range of opportunities to access information about the candidates' stance on issues, as well as their speeches and media appearances. However, discourse analysis also demonstrated clear differences between the candidates' approaches. For instance, the level of personalisation through language was higher in the Sarkozy web page, where the voice of the candidate was consistently used as the narrator as well as showing a predominantly reflexive formula (i.e. what I think, what I believe) (Marnette 2005). Even Sarkozy's biography, distinctively the most linear section in both websites, was written in autobiographical style. The assumed intention was to increase user engagement by personalising the discourse and mixing the personal identity with the public persona of the candidate (Wood and Kroger 2000). This strategy can create a type of user-to-user interaction called para-social interaction (McMillan 2002b). In it, 'the most remote and illustrious men are met as if they were in the circle of one's peers' (Horton and Wohl 1956: 215), a strategy which is argued to have the potential to establish a bond and rapport between the user and the candidate (McMillan 2002b).

On the other hand, the Ségolène Royal website used her supporters' voices to engage the user. It was 'their' voice inviting users to participate in events or discuss issues, evidenced by the continuous use of the pronoun 'we' (nous). This pronoun helps create a sense of community and participation, and so would have an impact on the levels of perceived interactivity (Fairclough 2003) and could raise the level of user satisfaction and overall experience. Where the main voice is that of Ségolène Royal herself, she uses the language of inclusion (i.e. 'What you have said, I have heard'), speaking directly to the user and inviting him or her to participate: 'Together we will implement it [the presidential pact]'. While still rich in information, it gives a sense of a collectivist message, so reinforcing the message of 'France for president': an inclusive, collectively decided and collectively executed style of campaigning and governing. This core principle of her campaign continues through the debate section and the 'Presidential Pact', a collection of a hundred proposals developed out of participative debates. However, the interactivity presented is again closer to the definition of para-social interactivity than that of interactivity as defined by Kiousis (2002). Therefore, across both websites, information is presented as if the candidate is talking directly to the user. In Royal's case talking of a co-created and shared political platform; for Sarkozy more a sense of him synthesising public needs, wants and desires; each approach reflecting the ideology of the candidate. However, this is perceptual interactivity only and there is no sense of a real-time symmetrical conversation interrupting the brand-communicating monologue.

Campaigning

The campaigning function is implicitly served throughout both websites. Discourse analysis highlighted the absence of the traditional campaign discourse, which places direct references to asking visitors to vote at the forefront. This consistent absence may be explained by the knowledge that visitors to specific candidates' or parties' websites during a campaign cycle have already decided their vote and visit the site either to gather information for or against their candidate, to network with other supporters or make a donation (Norris 2001b; Boogers and Voerman 2002). However, we suggest that it is not just those already persuaded who go online and visit candidate and party websites; an alternative explanation for the lack of explicit campaigning is that it is implicit in the promotional messages presented in narrative or predictive genres. For instance, while most of the Sarkozy website consisted of narratives describing how Sarkozy would run the French nation, through declarative and imperative sentences, the text (including video) explicitly offered a predictive narrative of French politics and society following a Sarkozy victory. The traditional genres were mixed and the persuasive promotional intent was veiled in a descriptive construction, which is consistent with Fairclough's description of the promotional culture that permeates contemporary media.

The use of video by the Sarkozy campaign must also be noted. While desirsdavenir.org revolved around a cooperative platform of information exchange, with 36 per cent of the total site offering some form of public discourse, www.sarkozy.fr used bespoke video as the backbone for the website. NS-TV provided the user with 18 targeted channels and 819 videos. Most videos presented short, targeted messages similar to those traditionally broadcast on television (Delaney 2006). The importance of video spots as communication tools in political campaigns has been well established in political literature, as well as the relationship between the short direct style of the videos and elevated voter response stemming from the advertising tradition (Benoit 1999). The use of videos also allows the simple communication of messages directly to potential voters (Benoit and Benoit 2000); consequentially, the Sarkozy campaign profited from the characteristics of media convergence that the Internet provides. However, NS-TV did not evidence a new style of campaigning. Indeed, the videos, coupled with both his narrative and experiment in Second Life that permitted test-driving his leadership skills as a resident of Isle de France, all offered a packaged image of how a Sarkozy Presidency would impact on the politics and society of France.

Negative campaigning

Criticising the opponent can be a key part of any marketised political campaign (Lilleker and Scullion 2009). While in Ségolène Royal's case a visitor would have to manually search for references to Nicolas Sarkozy and would find very few, in contrast www.sarkozy.fr contained a section entitled 'The obligation to answer'. Here, members of Sarkozy's team or recruited experts responded to the claims and comments of their opponents. The answers were in the form of videos, accompanied by a transcription of the commentary. However, in contrast with traditions of advertising use in American political campaigning, the format was less of an attack style but is in informational mode, consistent with the current promotional nature of contemporary culture of presenting information with the intention of persuading (Fairclough 2003). Furthermore, the campaign never uses the voice of the candidate (Sarkozy) to answer claims made by the opponent or to attack their strategy. It is always a third party, a 'field expert'.

However, in the voice of the third party, Sarkozy is mostly present, creating a sense of polyphony in the discourse (Marnette 2005) while distancing the candidate from negative commentary. For example, the most frequent interviewee is Sarkozy's own spokesperson Xavier Bertrand, whose role it is to reiterate campaign discourse and official messages; however, Sarkozy's presence is not empirically verifiable, and it is left to the audience to read these video responses, form an attitude towards or impression of the messenger and decide on the connotations.

Resource generation

Ségolène Royal and Nicolas Sarkozy present the user with all possible options for making donations (download form, online enquiry form and online transaction) to their campaign. In addition, Nicolas Sarkozy created his own 'boutique' where users could purchase campaign merchandise, something Ségolène Royal did not exploit. Resource generation was one of the website functions first mastered by political candidates in the US as well as in the UK, and seems to be of paramount importance in candidate and party website design (Kamarck 1999; Gibson 2003; Wolf 2004). Though we note that for a range of political, legal and cultural reasons there is more of an emphasis on fundraising in the US (Anstead and Chadwick 2008), and membership in the UK (Jackson 2006b). France seems to sit somewhere in the middle, as donations could be made but the demands for money were less prominent than would be expected in the US. Sarkozy's boutique was an innovative way of gaining revenue from visitors, but represents a fairly small development in the use of the online environment for generating resources. Royal, in contrast, used her site to develop a network of supporters, and this was perhaps viewed as the most important resource within a French political context.

Networking

The networking function is of particular interest, especially considering Ségolène Royal's 'Segosphere' initiative and the 'Segoland' map. Her campaign not only exploited the use of official weblogs, but also harnessed supporters' weblogs to reinforce her messages throughout the net. The site provided supporters with graphics, text and arguments that could be re-posted across the blogosphere. The Independent Presidential Observatory (www.presidentielle2007.fr) showed 285 networked weblogs that not only linked back to the official site but also used the materials from www.desirsdavenir.org. In addition, the website provided users with a space to showcase their weblogs and upload their own supportive comments and materials. In some senses this gave a greater impression of allowing open participation, particularly as many of the weblogs gained further links and so built up an interactive network talking about Royal and using her branding. However, this approach was not without problems and on occasions threatened to undermine Royal's campaign as a whole.

Nicolas Sarkozy took a more traditional approach, supplying supporters with images and materials to place on their own weblogs, but not linking to sites beyond the control of the campaign or opening up his site for visitor uploads. This route proved the safest one since, in the two-way linking approach, message control becomes impossible. The Ségolène Royal campaign encountered a problem when one of the supporter's blogs made anti-Semitic claims interpreted to be a direct attack on Sarkozy's ethnic background (Fouetillou 2006). The Royal response was to erase links with the specific site, but the damage was already done. This example demonstrates the risk of using the Web's interactive capabilities to increase participation. As Stromer-Galley reported in 2000, the risk of losing control of the message is one that few politicians are willing to take on official websites, though perhaps on social networking profiles less control is maintained (Jackson and Lilleker 2009a and b).

Promoting participation

Despite the risks of allowing users to generate content, participation was encouraged by the inclusion of interactive features within the websites. There were two kinds of participation sought. Democratic participation promoted through the text and the language of the websites; and particularly on the home page of the candidate, and directly related to the campaigning function. The second type of participation is within the campaign as supporters, group leaders or bloggers. The former approach was pursued exclusively by Sarkozy, the clear aim of his site being to reach as many voters as possible and persuade them to support his bid for the presidency. Royal, on the other hand, was more inclusive and gave opportunities for contributions from others to the site; therefore she scored higher for public discourse features and her site featured more co-created content. The differences are emphasised through the results of the discourse analysis. Sarkozy's personalisation of the discourse invites the user to follow the events and efforts organised by the candidate and his staff. Royal, in contrast, in employing 'us' and 'you' in the plural form, gave a collective meaning to the campaign, which is reflected in the use of the website to organise and disseminate local as well as national support events, cultural demonstrations and online debates. This type of participation is also directly linked to the levels of interactivity found across both websites.

A 2.0 election

Turning to Anderson's (2007) six big ideas, which we use to frame evidence of campaigning adapting to Web 2.0 as a social phenomenon, could we detect the presence of these features, and to what extent were they used to foster engagement?

The capacity for individual production and user-generated content

As with the above discussion of discourse, largely we found a variance in the capacity for visitors to produce and upload content to the sites. Nicolas Sarkozy allowed no content to be contributed by anyone apart from his campaign team and his range of carefully selected endorsers; in contrast, Royal's *Notebooks of Hope* represented a body of ideas that had been co-created with her support network. However, while demonstrating interactivity had taken place, there were few real-time opportunities to contribute to the Royal website during the campaign itself, apart from when a supportive weblog was linked from the site. There were opportunities to submit items, such as events, or comment on a small number of posted items within external sites that were linked to from her main website; however, this limited open participation. Therefore, largely the websites were essentially Web 1.0 and the produser was excluded from shaping visitor experiences.

Harnessing the power of the crowd

Consistent with the approach to co-production, visitors were allowed to promote the candidate and the site in a number of ways; not only through forming links but also through the provision of buttons and widgets which could be embedded on visitors' sites and weblogs. Equally, and more in keeping with the Web 2.0 philosophy, one could argue that the *Notebooks of Hope* was the power of the crowd writ large. Not only did participants inform Royal's manifesto, but they also provided a useful marketing tool that was consistent with her overall ideological position. Furthermore, Royal's creation of the Segosphere and willingness – despite this having to be more tightly controlled after some embarrassment was caused by one weblog author – to link to supportive sites and weblogs suggests she was more in tune with the notion of being in touch with a broader online audience. This inclusivity again reflects the tradition of French socialism she was representing and perhaps was influenced less by the availability of the tools, but this represented an extension of her political persona which was enabled by Web 2.0 technologies. Sarkozy, in contrast, and also consistent with his ideological positioning, allowed the crowds to promote him but not to have any direct influence on the content of his website or broader campaign.

Access to data on an epic scale

Both candidates provided a lot of information for site visitors, Royal linking to external sites more than Sarkozy, suggesting less of a desire to control. Sarkozy's videos clearly represented a mass of data provided by him that was over and above anything achievable using mass media alone. The narrative of the Sarkozy Presidency was largely enabled by Internet technologies, and was able to provide a more nuanced and in-depth understanding of the candidate than would have previously been possible. Equally, Royal's website presented a mass of information on her policies, ideology and personality that would provide the visitor with a richer understanding of her political platform. The use of videos, pictures and other more sophisticated tools were heavily reliant on technologies that provide a rich user experience, but visitors to the sites were largely viewing highly packaged content on demand. They could choose to watch or not, but they had limited opportunities to add to or adapt the data and hence were largely passive members of an online audience. This is consistent with studies of why parties tend to eschew interactivity (Stromer-Galley 2000), and observations of party use of Web 2.0 in the UK in 2008 and during the European Parliamentary election of 2009 (Jackson and Lilleker 2009a; Jackson and Lilleker 2010).

An architecture of participation

Neither candidate offered anything that resembled a participatory forum in a meaningful way within their website. One could suggest, tentatively, that the Segosphere allowed a degree of participation, however this was geared more towards linking to those already using the Internet and Web 2.0 tools, and encouraging and widening greater participation. Hence, the sites were largely based around a Web 1.0 philosophy, even if Royal used Web 2.0 language when talking of inclusivity and linked to external Web 2.0 sites where co-creation and co-production were possible.

The network effect

If Sarkozy sought a network effect, it was solely with the aim of creating a promotional network across the French Internet. Royal clearly sought to include others, and the Segosphere represented a network in itself. However, despite her ideological inclusivity, the network was not open to all, and those linked to were selected and screened by the candidate and her campaign team prior to being allowed into the sphere. While this approach was vindicated by the problems of linking to independent bloggers, it still did not prevent Royal facing threats from her network; yet one could also argue there was a benefit to her in that her supporters may have been stronger advocates due to the two-way endorsement mechanism that tied supporters closely to the campaign.

Openness

As discussed above, openness was evidenced to some extent within the Segosphere; however, largely both websites were open only to audience members and not participants. Overall, we argue that there was tentative usage of Web 2.0 tools, but largely the philosophical notions which underpin the social aspects of interactivity were not embraced by either candidate. To some, if limited, extent Royal displayed interest in aspects of the big ideas of Web 2.0, though largely the actual participation took place either prior to the campaign proper commencing, or was kept at a distance within the Segosphere of related weblogs. Hence, essentially, the websites had the look and feel of Web 2.0 in terms of sophistication, but the style of communication was locked into the traditions of Web 1.0, where content is controlled and communicated to a mass audience who remain passive receivers expected to be susceptible to persuasion.

Evaluating interactivity

The above analysis offers little indication that interactivity was deemed worthwhile to the campaign, as it featured so little within the websites to any significant extent. However, to determine that, evaluation of the levels of interactivity found across the pages of the candidates' websites was conducted over two stages. First, the presence or absence of technical features that allowed interactivity was assessed through applying the amended Gibson and Ward schematic; this was followed by an analysis of the type of interactivity present through discourse analysis and the application of the revised Ferber *et al.* interactivity model regarding user-to-user and user-to-document interaction.

The first step of the research showed that both websites presented the user with all possible options of asynchronous interactive features (i.e. email links, downloadable material, user registration), while limiting the opportunities for synchronic communication. The lack of synchronic communication suggests allowing uncontrolled communication to appear on an official website and was deemed too great a risk, so restricting interactivity (Stromer-Galley 2000; Tedesco 2007; Jackson and Lilleker 2009a).

Due to the uniform presence of technological features, both sites were identical in terms of the level of interactive information flows. However, by taking interactivity as a process, with conversation and public discourse being seen as the ultimate form of interactivity, the results are slightly different. This is clearer when measuring the level of interactivity through the operationalised version of the Ferber *et al.* model (see Table 5.3).

Applying the revised user-to-user categories, we find that asymmetric communication was most common; symmetrical elements were mostly limited to the use of hyperlinks. Hyperlinks allow user-to-document interaction, but are not in themselves user-to-user; though arguably, the links from the Royal website to the Segosphere did allow participatory dialogue with other supporters and voters if not the candidate herself. Even in the elements with the highest perceived interactivity (i.e. the message board in Ségolène Royal's home page or the debate sections on both websites), there was a time delay between users posting and the message appearing and a sense that posts submitted were selected to suit the campaign independent of their popularity among Web users. The fact that issues raised followed broad national concerns, and ones which were established policy items for the candidate, reinforces this as linking into offering a sense of a market orientation (Lees-Marshment 2001; Lilleker and Negrine 2006) as opposed to desiring open dialogue with the site users. Thus, the role of the moderator became that of a gatekeeper and the extent of this role was discretional. This suggests that even with the most up-to-date technical features available, little conversation was taking place and most communication was monologic.

Table 5.3 User-to-user interactivity: France 2007

Level of receiver control	*Direction of communication*		
	One Way	*Two Way*	*Three Way*
10			SR – 7 NS – 10
9			SR – 1 NS – 2
8			
7		SR – 1 NS – 1	
6			
5	SR – 5 NS – 3	SR – 6 NS – 7	
4	SR – 676 NS – 1328	SR – 1 NS – 1	
3	SR – 2 NS – 2		
2	SR – 103 NS – 26		
1			

The section with the highest interactivity level was the debate section in www.desirsdavenir.org, where the sender could control the text posted and the post affected the presentation of the web page, the debate index and the home page, which showed extracts from the debate section (even if there was a time delay). The direction of communication was qualified as three-way, for users could post comments answering questions posted by the organisation, the candidate or other users, thus continuing a conversation started by the latter. However, discourse analysis revealed that the discussions were fragmented and disjointed interventions.

Even though animated graphics and video elements may give the illusion of higher interactivity, when applying the measures designed by Gibson and Ward they did not score higher than simple textual hyperlinks. While flashy, visually attractive elements can act as a pull factor, drawing users to visit the website, such features do not translate into higher interactivity. It does, however, affect perceived interactivity, which impacts upon levels of engagement, trust (Welch and Hinnant 2003), user satisfaction and general attitude towards websites (McMillan 2002a). The French presidential candidates were found to have a higher level of perceived interactivity than in the 'brochure-like websites' studied by Gibson and Ward (1998), and Kamarck (1999); however, the majority of elements still belong to the monologic style of one-to-many user-to-user communication.

As shown in Table 5.4, the majority of elements in both websites belong to the packaged content on demand category, an assessment based upon the

Table 5.4 User-to-document interactivity: France 2007 (number of items per category)

	Royal	*Sarkozy*
Downward flows (Packaged)	746	969
Upward flows (Content on Demand)	1	1
Lateral flows (Content on Demand)	3	1
Asynchronous (Content Exchange)	43	42
Synchronous (Co-created Content)	5	10
Number of features	798	1,023

assumption that it takes more than just the ability to click to make an active audience, they must also contribute content (McMillan 2002b). While this can be seen as fairly typical of any aspect of the communication emanating from a professional campaign, greater use of content exchange and co-created content was witnessed. Rather than locking visitors within the single branded site, visitors could take away logos and symbols to demonstrate their support; equally, they could offer content, though it is not always transparent how such material was used. Navigation aids are the fundamental way in which users of the Sarkozy site can shape their own experience, if only in an isolated way. It is argued that through the provision of links, candidates allowed visitors to create their own experience within the website and follow links to related sites. However, this is the limit of users' ability to shape the nature of their experiences as visitors.

As explained before, the Ségolène Royal website took more advantage of interactive and content-sharing features than that of Nicolas Sarkozy, and was rated overall higher in user-to-document evaluation as well. The co-created content is largely related to navigation, apart from the *Notebooks of Hope* and debate area which increased the extent to which Royal's site both reflected and permitted user participation. However, apart from within these areas, which were large in size but accessible only from one link within the site, participation is not promoted and so not prioritised. Therefore, although the technological features of websites have improved, the websites were still primarily used for the traditional functions of providing information, requesting donations and attempting to mobilise supporters. In fact, in terms of offering users choice over access, Sarkozy's site offered more links which specified interest areas while Royal packaged the content within her home page in an attempt, perhaps, to ensure greater reach than if content was made only on demand.

However, the differences between these two websites may symbolise two different approaches to the campaign process. Royal to some extent embraced the interactive features of the Internet; Sarkozy used the features while maintaining control over all messages. Equally interesting is that the approach seems to be perfectly consistent with the ideological stance projected by each candidate; therefore, the various characteristics that have been argued to influence adoption of the Internet and now Web 2.0 may well be secondary factors in comparison to ideology.

Tentative interactivity

Essentially, both candidates' websites were pieces of marketing communication that were used to build positive voter perceptions and promote their unique selling points. The strategy underpinning the sites' creation can be inferred as vote maximisation among both core and non-aligned voters, with each candidate positioning themselves ideologically so as to have a gravitational pull effect on centrist voters who are either left or right leaning. The sites thus offered a significant amount of symbolism, not only in the language but in the style and features. Interactivity was largely spectral; it was a shadow that could be seen in the language. This suggests a vote maximisation strategy that seeks to persuade voters. With both candidates attempting to position themselves as ideological magnetic polls, Royal drawing around her a leftist coalition and Sarkozy seeking to win over all sections of the French right (Sauger 2007; Vedel 2007), while also fighting over the centrist voters they sought to build strong brands focusing on the core issues that united broad swathes of French society. While Royal did employ a symbolic campaign theme which built upon traditions of socialism, encapsulated in her participatory style, this was argued to have lacked visibility on and offline. The uniformity, simplicity and clarity of Sarkozy's approach delivered message recall and perceived credibility; factors which delivered him victory by uniting the right while also capturing centrist voters uncertain of Royal's ability (Sauger 2007).

There are scatterings of evidence that optimistic predictions about the effect of the Internet and Web 2.0 are bearing fruit. Yet, on the whole, both sites essentially reinforce previous studies that witness politics as usual (Margolis and Resnick 2000; Vedel and Michalska 2007). Any change in campaigning strategy and tactics is minor and at best incremental (Lilleker and Negrine 2002). While the nature of online interactivity in the French presidential candidates' official websites is consistent with Stromer-Galley's (2000) assertion, they still offered greater use of interactive tools than previously had been seen. Rather than witnessing free-flowing conversations, we note that there appears to be an ever present involvement of political advisors and webmasters exercising a gatekeeping function.

When examining the language on the websites as an enabler of interactivity, the results were consistent with para-social interaction (McMillan 2002b). In addition, the discourse analysis showed that the elements of promotional culture described by Fairclough (2003) and the mixture of genres he predicted in websites were confirmed here. The combination of multiple genres present in the websites is characteristic of innovative texts (Fairclough 2003), as well as the shifting boundaries and unclear rules regarding the formation of the text. The similarities between the websites studied were scarcer when the websites were analysed through CDA to determine the voices present in the website. While Ségolène Royal's website was characterised by a multiplicity of voices and a collectivist outlook to the campaign process, the Nicolas Sarkozy website was centred on the sole voice of the candidate, and the unity of the campaign was reinforced through both visual and textual mechanisms. Yet in the end, both sites shared similar functions and goals; these seem to lead to a rejection of symmetrical interaction and the accompanying loss of control over communication. In other words, from the discourse perspective, they were very typical 'politics as usual' campaign sites.

Perhaps the fact that the least interactive candidate, who presented the most uniform and controlled image, was victorious may indicate Royal's interactivity had little real impact or, perhaps, her inclusive style and 'weaker' presence made her appear too non-presidential; or at least outside the norms of what is expected of a French president. Pierce (2005) argued that both culturally and constitutionally, the French president is positioned as a strong leader, and voters seek the characteristics of experience and ability. It is possible that the very act of consultation made Royal appear weak to traditionalists among swing voters and so not an ideal leader. Clearly, she positioned herself as an interactive candidate in touch with the voters, and this contrasted with the branding of Sarkozy as highly traditional and linked to symbols of the nation. Perhaps, the glimpses of interactivity and conversation may not have been suitable marketing tools for the context of a French electoral contest. Equally, however, one could also note that the approach to the Internet was consistent with what may be expected of each candidate. Sarkozy's right-wing authoritarian style hardly suggests he would welcome co-production; Royal, however, emerges from a tradition of the left which hinges around collectivism. While she faced the dangers of the approach, and withdrew from some elements of openness, Royal has the greatest room for manoeuvre without being criticised for cynical electioneering, while interactive moves from Sarkozy could have been viewed as nothing more than attempts at vote winning.

Returning to the notion of a Web 2.0 election, there is little evidence of a radical or revolutionary style of campaigning emerging here. There was little encouragement to join a current, live conversation with the candidate or among users. Interaction is limited and pushed to the fringes of the campaign, and campaigning retained its top-down, repeat-remind nature designed to gain recall of messages and candidate attributes only. Philosophically, both candidates were largely tied to the top-down model of communication, though Royal's withdrawal from some aspect of Web 2.0 may have been more as a result of bad experiences than inherent unwillingness to engage with a wider audience and allow them to participate in her campaign. The result, however, suggests that neither in the end was able to comfortably embrace the big ideas of Web 2.0. The use, or rather the limited use, of the Internet was shaped in France by cultural and political factors, which will be different in other countries, a factor important when considering comparative work on online campaigning (Anstead and Chadwick 2008). Therefore, based on this election we suggest, as campaign teams learn lessons from one another, that interactivity may be used very tentatively and the lessons that political strategists can take from the French example may not be positive. After all, the dangers of user-generated content from YouTube, and the fact that linked bloggers can embarrass the candidate by association, show there are significant dangers out there. While these may be unavoidable, the key lesson relates to the purpose of the campaign. Sarkozy, the more uniformly branded and controlled candidate, was successful; the candidate who offered a co-created manifesto lost. The margins were reasonably narrow, but it is possible that the interactive style had a negative impact on Royal's quest for the presidency. However, we should not assume there to be a direct effect based on online behaviour and other factors played out in the contest; this will equally be true of our other studies. Will they see interactivity also as too risky, or will there emerge stronger evidence of a move to Elections 2.0?

Strategists looking for lessons from the French election may gain mixed impressions. While the adventures in Second Life were quickly replicated in the US by failed democratic candidate John Edwards, the key lesson is perhaps the link between the candidates' branding, the context of French politics and how these informed campaign strategy. Perhaps France was not ready for greater interaction, however the use of the Internet and social networks, still in infancy in France, is widespread and has been normalised into the US, German and UK cultures. Hence, perhaps the key comparative lesson here is the political context, and that interactivity may be interpreted in a number of ways by voters. Given the more engrained use of the Internet, and the familiarity to candidates using the Internet for a range of functions, the US candidates may well integrate interactivity within their campaign strategies to a much greater extent.

6 The US 2008

A giant step for interactivity

US politics in 2008: time for change?

The 2008 US Presidential Election captured global interest, in particular interest focused on Barack Obama; the first black candidate to stand a serious chance of winning. Interest began during the race for the party nominations, a series of state-based primaries to win delegates at the party conventions; the Democrats' was held 25–28 August and the Republicans' 1–4 September. While the Republican nomination battle proved fairly straightforward, with John McCain emerging in March as having sufficient delegates to ensure his victory, for the Democrats it proved to be a close battle that was not resolved until 7 June when Hillary Clinton conceded. The final race between Obama and McCain saw Obama victorious, with 365 Electoral College votes to McCain's 173; there were 12 minor party and independent candidates on some or all of the state ballot papers, but none received over a single percentage of the overall votes. While in terms of states won it may appear to have been a landslide victory, this disguises the fact that out of 131.2 million voters, a turnout of 63 per cent – which is the highest in terms of percentage since 1960 – Obama only received ten million more votes than his opponent. However, with the weighting attached to states within the Electoral College, Obama's victory proved to be crushing; due particularly to his targeting of states crucial to success (Arterton and Greener 2009), suggesting that he followed Brams and Davis's 3/2 rule.

The US has long been seen to be the home of innovation for political communication and election campaigning. If for no reason beyond resources alone, US election campaigners are able to construct the most sophisticated and persuasive campaigns. Beyond the standard tools, which for at least ten years have included the Internet, Howard (2006) identifies the US as developing a hypermedia campaign. Voters are ruthlessly targeted by political organisations and their data stored and analysed, so communication can be carefully constructed to mobilise key publics to donate or to take further active roles on behalf of the organisation. It is within this broad communications context that the 2008 Election of the US President should be judged, in terms of the extent to which the targeting not only sought to identify voters' interests and the buttons to push to mobilise them, but also to gain their donations, as was largely the case in past elections (Bimber and

Davis 2003). A key question is to what extent candidates' websites facilitated voter entry into the campaign as active participants as opposed to passive receivers of, and respondents to, persuasive communication devices (Trippi 2004; Kline and Burnstein 2005).

In 2008 there was perhaps a sense that voters took a stronger interest in the contest and so were easier to communicate with, despite media fragmentation. Dissatisfaction with the administration of George W. Bush meant there was a widespread desire for change (Walsh 2008). Perhaps also there was a desire for a new direction in US politics. Bush is perhaps to be recorded in history as a failed first-term president, who was handed a second-term due to the unprecedented events of the terrorist attacks of 9/11 and his launch of a War on Terror (Wroe and Herbert 2008). His emotional, gut-reaction, style of politics, juxtaposed with the intellectual yet impersonal style of Democrat Al Gore, delivered Bush a narrow victory in 2004. Yet his performance was tarnished by questions regarding personal probity, the toll of war deaths and the economic crisis, which culminated during the 2008 election campaign. Furthermore, Bush has to be the most mocked president in history. While satirists have poked fun at every leader at some point, the communication gaffes of Bush have become the material of legend, and are widely circulated and shared by users of Facebook and YouTube. There is even an application for *i*-Google, the personalised Google home page, called the Chimp-o-matic, which delivers 'Bushisms' such as 'Make no mistake about it, I understand how tough it is, sir. I talk to families who die' daily to the desktops of users. This is not to say that Bush had no characteristics that were appealing to the American voter. It is argued that, like Clinton before him, his down to earth authenticity was his selling point (Devine 2009). At the very least, this suggests that a presidential candidate has to demonstrate they have more than a simple range of skills or knowledge, and must also engage voters emotionally, while also being aware that anyone can act as a political commentator if they wish.

Engagement has long been a serious issue in American politics. The 1996 election saw a serious dip in turnout, the only time it dropped below 50 per cent, and the increase to 51.31 per cent in 2000 was not remarkable (Federal Election Commission figures www.presidency.ucsb.edu/data/turnout.php). It is claimed that inequalities in participation are most serious with young people and ethnic minorities, though the young have actually been participating more in 2000 and 2004, and the trend continued in 2008 (Levine and Lopez 2002; US Census Bureau 2006; Barr 2009). More importantly, engagement in politics is found to be on the whole low, linked to widespread cynicism and dissatisfaction with the system. A Pew Research Center report (2006) found a majority lack feelings of political efficacy (58 per cent), and believe government is inefficient and wasteful (80 per cent), suggesting disengagement is comparatively high in the US. This research also found that 42 per cent of Republicans and 76 per cent of Democrats agreed that 'Washington politicians should step aside and make room for new leaders'; thus it is suggested that any incumbent would be well advised to demonstrate they represent a clear break from the traditions of Washington-based politics (Arterton and Greener 2009: 176).

Such lessons were perhaps not lost on those that sought to be the 44th President of the USA. While the Republican race seemed the least predictable, it was John McCain, a somewhat maverick figure, who emerged as the nominee very early. This gave him a clear head start in his bid for the White House. The Democrat contest was initially seen as a two-horse race between Senators John Edwards and Hillary Clinton, the latter being seen as the most likely winner of the nomination (Flanders *et al.* 2007). Thus, interest quickly grew, as for the first time it was envisaged how a female president might approach the role. However, this was not counting on Barack Obama. As he emerged as the main challenger to Clinton, and then eventual winner of the nomination, Obama's chances were re-evaluated. Now focus was on whether a black man of mixed race, with a convoluted genealogy that included Muslim forebears, would be the right man to lead the world's most powerful nation. The question of voter uncertainty was openly discussed in the media, with commentators speculating on the Bradley effect and what may go through voters' minds as their pencils hovered over the voting sheet (Johnson 2009). Equally, a range of commentators, official newscasters and political bloggers debated whether America would accept Obama as Commander-in-Chief; thus attention on him remained strong, though this was not necessarily a positive focus (Groeling 2008). Even McCain's selection of outspoken right-winger Sarah Palin as his running mate did not seriously divert attention from Obama for long (Arterton and Greener 2009). His campaigning style not only made media and academic headlines, Obama's creation of a movement offline and online indicated a new direction in campaigning and politics. It is this aspect which suggests that the US moved towards a Web 2.0 election phase, which may have the potential to shape all future contests.

Perhaps we should not be surprised that it is the US that is closest to a Web 2.0 election. The US has witnessed most of the innovations in electioneering and political communication, and hence has led the way in Internet use for elections. Ex-wrestler turned politician Jesse Ventura usurped candidates from the major parties through mobilising the non-aligned and disaffected, by building a grassroots network of supporters through the use of the Internet in his successful campaign in the Minnesota gubernatorial contest of 1998 (Greer and LaPointe 2004; Klotz 2004; Kluver *et al.* 2007). Howard Dean built upon this and was almost within reach of the Democratic nomination in 2004 by offering further online innovations. Drawing on the lessons of MeetUp.org, Dean was able to gain significant funding through the Internet, linking communication of his stance on issues to a strategy of talking directly with issue publics. This highlighted the birth of the hypermedia campaign where 'people with Internet access can express their opinions, learn about issues that concern them, and contribute to the political groups with whom they find affinity' (Howard 2006: 180). Second, he harnessed supporters across the blogosphere and got them to amplify his message (Kline and Burnstein 2005). Underpinning these innovations is the fertile environment offered by the Internet in the US. While suggesting that diffusion of the Internet is a driving factor for a greater impact from online campaigning or that political actors using the Internet would be erroneous (Anstead and Chadwick

2008), it clearly is a contingent factor. In 2005, 76 per cent of Americans were recorded as being online (International Communication Union 2005), though this had reduced slightly to 74.7 per cent in 2009 with no available figures for the exact period of the campaign. More importantly, 77 per cent have gone online to search for information on Government Agencies or to contact them, though they remain more likely to turn to the telephone or face-to-face contact (Horrigan 2004). It is argued, however, that more will use the Internet for information seeking, while also wishing to offer their own opinions and gain feedback (Fox *et al.* 2005), and indeed this trend was evidenced in use of the Internet during the early stages of the Iraq War. Americans increasingly accessed a range of government and independent sites to get news, as well as using email to offer views of support and opposition; furthermore, opponents increasingly turned to the Web to propagate their points of view and to start campaigns (Rainie *et al.* 2005). The prime motive for citizens interested in the election to go online was to gain political information, but a secondary purpose was to have their views heard.

Such trends were not ignored as the candidates prepared for the contest for the party nomination. The Democrats were certainly the most innovative, consistent with past usage (Anstead and Chadwick 2008); perhaps like Royal due to their more grassroots-style of campaigning and inclusive leftist ideology. There also may have been some nervousness in the Republican camp about public participation. In 2006 a YouTube video of Republican Senator George Allen calling a black employee of his opponent a macaca destroyed his chances of retaining his seat (Anstead and Chadwick 2008). This was a clear demonstration that the online community represented an uncontrollable, and potentially dangerous, force that could destroy a candidate's image as well as enhancing their electoral chances. With lessons learned from the Dean campaign informing their approach (Chadwick 2007), the three most prominent candidates, John Edwards, Hillary Clinton and Barack Obama, began amassing fans on SNS. This early start may have paid dividends, as by Election Day Obama had 6,471,027 supporters on Facebook, ten times that of John McCain, who managed no more than 620,359; while not crucial to his victory, it is a demonstration of reach if nothing else. Other innovations included the use of Second Life by John Edwards, and all candidates began to use Twitter to advertise their daily activities. Edwards led the way with this microblogging tool, opening his account and tweeting first as early as March 2007 (Jones 2007; Johnson 2007): Obama soon followed, and by May they were joined by Clinton and John McCain. Cumulatively, this suggests a greater and more strategic use of the Internet than has previously been seen, and for Web 2.0 technologies to feature to a greater extent than in any previous contest.

Politics generally, and political communication online in particular, is not just driven by the elite actors in the strategy teams and media corporations. Political candidates in the US do not just compete against their opponents, but also the range of other actors who produce content and post it to the Internet. There are 116 million Americans that regularly consume some form of user-generated content (Wood 2009); furthermore, 42.8 per cent of US Internet users (88.8 million individuals) contribute online content (Verna 2009), with the US said to be responsible for 90 per cent of the content on YouTube. There is a trend for the creation and sharing of user-generated content within the US (E-marketer 2006). The impact of this level of public participation can be seen with the creation of mock campaign videos, or videos featuring the Democratic candidates. The video of Hillary Clinton, depicting her as the Orwellian Big Brother from the classic political novel *1984*, received 5,849,914 views, far more than the most popular of her campaign videos. The media amplified the highly negative message in the video, with questions about who created it and their motives being discussed throughout the early months of the campaign (National Journal 2007). The creator, Philip de Vellis, was an active supporter of Obama and worked for Blue State Digital, the organisation that managed Obama's website; Vellis going on record to say he acted independently prevented Obama also suffering from the fallout. In contrast, it was the somewhat jokey contribution by Obama Girl that placed user-generated content at the heart of the Obama campaign. The video of Amber Lee Ettinger (Obama Girl) received 14,880,295 views (www.barelypolitical.com/) and was amplified by the media, and Ettinger became something of a media star for a short time. Juxtaposing these images, we see the user denigrating Clinton while expressing love for Obama. Obama also captured the imagination of rap artist Will-i-am, singer with the Black Eyed Peas, who mixed Obama's Yes We Can speech, overlaid images of Martin Luther King and created a global hit on YouTube. Again, this sort of endorsement, viewed by millions online but also broadcast by major television news corporations, did Obama little harm even if it won him no votes. Of course, election-related user-generated content does not only cover these highly sophisticated contributions, but the thousands who blogged for both contenders, the semi or fully independent actors creating satirical sites, and those who commented on news and blog posts all contributed to public discussions of the election in their own small and immeasurable way. All this indicates that, in the US, there may be a trend towards a more participatory politics. True it represents participation in myriad forms, from wishing to support a candidate to expressing general or specific political views. Moreover, given that there was a general preparedness to participate among a section of the online audience, it suggests that US candidates had to decide whether this participatory impetus was worth harnessing and working with, or shunning and keeping at a distance.

Mapping the sites

Obama's website's key function was to harness the online political activist. While there was a traditional home page with a links menu and news items, the front screen offered visitors the opportunity to sign into their own personal space within www.mybarackobama.com (MyBO). MyBO was, in essence, a campaign-related SNS which allowed users to link up to others in their neighbourhood. This was not the tool that created the movement; this was based upon interest in

Obama as a candidate and support for his message and style. However, his background as a grassroots political campaigner taught him how to mobilise people, and MyBO was a key part of this strategy. It allowed his supporters to interact with one another, encouraged the creation of, and participation in, events and allowed the campaign to interact with the support base, offer training in telephone and door-to-door canvassing and mobilise them as offline activists. His strategy was thus not simply about persuading through informing, rather his campaign sought and succeeded in mobilising broad sections of US society to support his campaign. In terms of harnessing those who wished to participate in politics online, this was not a participatory discussion in order to shape policy or political direction; however, it allowed a range of participatory activities which furthered the objectives of the Obama campaign. The site was the hub of activity in this respect.

Following archiving, the site was mapped and it was possible to identify three distinct areas, defined by how users were permitted to engage. The functional and informational elements, which largely contained content on demand, are areas that would be expected on any campaign website: News, Events (though this had a feed from MyBO, so was co-created to an extent), Donate, Store and Fight the Smears; the latter being an area devoted to rebutting some of the more extreme attacks, as well as commenting on political issues and the way his opponents characterised his stance. By far the largest single area of the site, representing 59 per cent of total pages and totalling 6,170 entries up to the end of 4 November 2009, each soliciting an average of 184 comments, was the blog, as this was one part of an area that encouraged open participation. Alongside the blog was the MyBO section and an area for volunteers; here, not only was there a large amount of information but also an opportunity to share ideas and best practice tips. While one can question whether all the participatory elements were from real people or whether the team was astroturfing using 'sock-puppets', this huge area gave the sense of a site that was not simply that of the candidate, but a sense of belonging to the movement. This is a new type of interactivity which could be argued to be a by-product of many social networking sites; however, uniquely this formed the backbone of the site of a political candidate. The final parts, created immediately after securing the nomination, are areas designed for Hillary Clinton supporters, designed to be persuasive; there was also a large area consisting of targeted pages for a range of social groups including specific pages for each state. There was an additional Obama Everywhere section linking to a total of sixteen separate social networking pages, which also allowed interaction with the campaign.

John McCain's website offered something of a contrast to that of Obama's, mainly due to its traditional structure and functions. The home page was highly linear with links to his biography, issue pages, including comparative documents which were thinly veiled attacks on Obama's policies, 925 pages of news releases with no simple search tool, an events page including media appearances and the coalitions section. The latter included targeted pages, with some specifically for Hispanic voters, yet there was little attempt to encourage participation.

The volunteers' section had a large feature on donating, Action included links to his three social networking fan pages and the store. The blog was the one area that allowed participation, but tended to be politically charged, if informal, often negative, and was underdeveloped as a campaigning tool.

These maps provide a useful overview for understanding the sites, their overall design and the way in which users were able to navigate around the pages. As with those of the French presidential candidates, a selection of pages were sampled; these included the home page of each site, a randomly selected issue statement (both statements on health care) and the biography page. The language and discourse were analysed to gain an understanding of how the candidates positioned themselves in relation to their audiences.

Identifying online identities

While web mapping reveals highly contrasting approaches, the discourse used by the candidates demonstrated a strong synergy in strategy. Both sites are highly promotional and present information about the candidate, and compare them to their opponent when discussing points of principle and specific issue politics. McCain shows the greatest propensity to go on the all out offensive, while Obama is far more subtle and focuses his attacks on the elitism of the system as opposed to individuals; a strategy he also employed against Hillary Clinton in his advertising prior to winning the nomination (Lilleker and Scullion 2008). That minor strategy issue apart, however, the key point of difference is the sheer level of co-created content within Obama's site. Whole areas are created by a combination of campaign staffers and other site users, and without specific identification of individuals it is impossible to know who were 'official posters' and who were ordinary users, and in fact one insider account suggests a blurring of the distinction given the fluidity between the support network and those who were, or saw themselves, as officially part of the campaign (Harfoush 2009). It is within this area we find the greatest open negativity, as users with various non-de-plumes used the blog comments to launch attacks on McCain and Palin, as well as expressing an almost adulatory support for Obama. McCain's blog was also a focal point for anti-Obama messages; however, these tend to be more personal, bordering at times on the racist, as opposed to the often quite erudite critiques of McCain's politics. It is this clear difference that suggests a dichotomy in approaches. Obama's website as a totality is virtually all co-created and participatory; McCain's, in sharp contrast, offers less opportunities for participation than those of Royal or indeed Sarkozy; hence suggesting McCain did not draw on lessons from previous US contests or more global examples. Hence, it appears that if this was a Web 2.0 election, it was a highly one-sided contest in terms of offering interactivity.

However, when talking of the clear differences, it is also worth noting the strong similarities in terms of presentation. Obama's home page offered more internal and external links, and presented a video of Obama speaking directly to the visitor on the home page; however, on the whole this was largely packaged and monologic communication. McCain's was far more static and lacking in outward links, and of course lacked the equivalent of MyBO, but allowed some element of participation. Volunteering was encouraged, in particular recruiting supporters by telephone, and users could enter their state, coalition and issue to gain bespoke polling data on the candidate's standings. Obama matched most of these to some extent; donations were promoted more on his home page and throughout. He also offered a Obama–Biden Tax Calculator where users could work out the personal economic impact of his presidency and, in the final days, a link to information on the Violence Against Women Act, a personal campaign of Barack and Michelle Obama.

The position statements also reflected synergy between the campaigns. Obama's read very much as a press release which provided internal links, McCain's appeared to be built for the Web and ran over five screens. Videos and text on the Obama website quoted his own speeches heavily, while McCain presented policies as a fact checker with a large number of references to his opponent. However, he is not alone in presenting a comparative perspective on issues, as Obama also refers to McCain's political stance and provided links to www.JohnMcCainrecord.com, a site built around attacks against his opponent's record as a Senator. Across both candidate websites it is the voice of the candidate that predominates, and both areas are designed to be persuasive. There is one clear difference; while Obama positioned himself as reflecting the aspirations of the less well off voter in stating 'I believe that every American has the right to affordable health care', McCain focused more on attacking Obama and his running mate Joe Biden. The opening line argues that 'Barack Obama and Joe Biden have consistently lied to Americans about John McCain's plan', and he talks of a 'blatant mischaracterization' and presents detailed comparisons with statistics and tables. Obama presents a simple case and his mention of McCain is in an informative style, saying that policy under his opponent 'would represent the first time in our nation's history that health care benefits would be taxed'. While one could argue the merits of each approach, both clearly present the user with a sense of credibility, McCain's in terms of its level of detail, Obama's in its simplicity. However, there is one dialogic difference. McCain's is highly impersonal, written in the third person with no reference to 'I' but only of 'John McCain'. McCain is described as 'believing that no American should be denied access to quality and affordable [health] coverage', while Obama offers a more personal approach. While also largely in the third person, when Obama is quoted his language is inclusive, of 'our nation'; this suggests a strong consistency between the campaign message and the strategy that underpinned Obama's use of the Internet, and is encapsulated within one word that was emblematic of his campaign. Obama constantly spoke of 'We' meaning the people of the US; McCain very much spoke about 'I', and 'We' only referred to his political partnership with Vice Presidential Candidate Sarah Palin.

The use of the third person continues into the biographies of both candidates. The style is not of something personally written, an autobiography, but in the style of a portrait by a journalist. Interestingly, McCain's focuses mainly on his war record and seems to finish in 1967; Obama's is an overview of his life including recent activism in relation to help given to those displaced by Hurricane Katrina, and the humanitarian crisis in Darfur. However, both lack the personal touch that Royal was willing to express, and as this cannot be explained by the political stances of either candidate, it would suggest that both present these in a way consistent with tradition and use the third person to appear more credible than open self-promotion may appear.

There are other subtle differences in style between the candidates. Obama used his blog to present news. Equally, he shared a lot of information on endorsements from experts, celebrities and foreign national leaders, such as the support for his plans for the Middle East both from within the American Jewish community and Dennis Ross, a former diplomat to the region. Thus, similar to the approach adopted by Sarkozy, but to a far greater extent, Obama presented a polyphonic experience to site visitors that included high profile endorsers, ordinary people and his own words, often delivered through videos. McCain's weblog, on the other hand, offered a greater amount of gossip and less formal comment on the campaign; something that one commentator picked up to argue that McCain's was more interesting (Romano 2008). However, across the majority of the site, McCain tended to depersonalise every aspect of his argument, with much written in a third person style. McCain also concentrated on direct attacks to a far greater extent, with one section of his policy area called *Rhetoric v Record* devoted to comparative attacks. Thus, McCain's overall strategy appears to have been dedicated to mobilising his support base and the anti-Obama camp among American voters, as well as those who were perhaps unsure of Obama as a president but who also might have been concerned that McCain would be a continuation from the Bush years. He did not, however, appear to be reaching out to new voters or to position himself as anything but a traditional politician; this represents the antithesis of the strategy employed by Obama, which spoke of inclusivity and the mobilisation of the politically disengaged and excluded.

Features present across the sites

Having mapped the websites and made assumptions regarding their links to the strategies of the candidates, we now focus on the extent to which the websites offered users a range of features and the extent to which overall they were monologic and dialogic. Websites provide an opportunity for a candidate to present themselves directly to their potential voters, and therefore there must be a monologic element. Thus, both sites offered a significant level of downwardly flowing information, though McCain's was much heavier in supplying page after page of press releases, a total of twenty-six pages, twenty-five of which had the titles of and links to thirty-seven press releases per page. Obama, in contrast, offered his press releases in a blog format, so allowing visitors to comment, as well as utilising the more user-friendly medium of video to relay information, which combined speeches to camera addresses as well as behind-the-scenes footage from

Table 6.1 Features present on presidential candidates' websites: US 2008

Categories	*Obama website*	*McCain website*
Downward information flows		
Documents (e.g. manifesto)	Yes	Yes
Policies summed	Yes	Yes
Issues examined	Yes	Yes
Number of issues discussed	23	21
Statement of values/ideology	No	Yes
Newsletters	No	No
Number of newsletters archived	0	0
Media releases	Yes	Yes
Number of releases	166	925
Candidate profile	Yes	Yes
Election information	Yes	Yes
Event calendar	Yes	Yes
Frequently asked questions	Yes	No
Number of FAQs	20	0
Negative campaigning	Yes	Yes
Overall per cent of negativity	0.0003%	25%
Videos	Yes	Yes
Number of videos	1867	329
Targeted pages	Yes	Yes
Number of groups targeted	74	3
Targeted download form	No	No
Targeted online enquiry form	Yes	No
Targeted online transaction	Yes	No
Upward information flows		
Volunteering possible	Yes	Yes
Donations possible	Yes	Yes
Merchandise for sale	Yes	Yes
Cookies	Yes	No
Lateral/horizontal information flows		
Number of partisan links	114	4
Number of reference links	6	18
Number of internal links	3	6
Interactive information flows: Asynchronous		
Download logos/posters (number)	45	34
Site search	No	No
Enmeshing	Yes	No
Navigation aids	Yes	Yes
Online games/gimmicks	Yes	No
Email contact	Yes	Yes
Email feedback	Yes	No
Online feedback form	Yes	No
Join email list	Yes	Yes
Questionnaires	No	No
Visitor-initiated questionnaires	No	No
Polls	No	No

continued

Table 6.1 continued

Categories	*Obama website*	*McCain website*
Visitor-initiated polls	No	No
Petitions	No	No
Visitor-initiated petitions	No	No
Join online campaign	Yes	Yes
Subscribe to e-newsletter	Yes	Yes
Membership form to download	No	No
Online membership enquiry form	Yes	No
Online membership transaction	Yes	Yes
Bulletin board	Yes	No
Blog tools	Yes	Yes
Ability to share videos/pics (embed code)	Yes	Yes
Podcasts	No	No
Social networking links	Yes (16)	Yes (2)
Twitter	Yes	Yes
RSS	Yes	Yes
Interactive information flows: Synchronous		
Ability of visitors to upload content/comments	Yes	Yes
Number of opportunities to upload content/comments	11,452	3
Ability of visitors to share information	Yes	No
Number of opportunities to share information	11,452	2
Ability of visitors to update information	Yes	No
Number of opportunities to update information	11,452	2
Public conversations allowed via comments or wall posting	Yes	No
Number of opportunities for public conversations	11,452	1
Forum	Yes	No
Chat room	No	No
Online debate	Yes	No
Number of opportunities to debate with candidates/leaders	11,452	0

Campaign HQ, Obama on the road and one of the candidate with his wife and two daughters. Obama also gave a more interactive feel by offering Frequently Asked Questions, suggesting prior interaction, and his events calendar included those created by the activists within MyBO.

Both candidates offered opportunities to volunteer to participate as campaign activists, though the sheer number of opportunities within MyBO outstrips anything McCain offered. Obama promoted the donation feature more prominently, though both candidates were clearly using the Internet to fund their campaigns; the evidence is that Obama was far more successful, raising $643 million dollars compared to the $259 million raised by McCain; indeed, Obama received 40 per cent of all donations made to all candidates (Hook 2008; Corrado and Corbett 2009). Unlike France, social networking is used by both candidates, however McCain's fairly basic fan pages secured him few supporters. Obama gained ten times the number of followers than McCain on Facebook alone, and many posted supportive comments which could be read by visitors as endorsements.

However, the clear difference with any previous campaign is the opportunities visitors are offered by both candidates to contribute content; and for Obama the amount is staggering. Counting all blog entries, opportunities to create or edit campaign events across the states, contribute to forums and post to Walls on social networking profiles, the total number of discrete opportunities to shape content was 11,452. McCain asks visitors to share thoughts, though there is no evidence of these being made public as there is a simple form requesting a name, email and comment that is submitted. McCain also had profiles on MySpace and Facebook, so allowing some level of interaction between visitors, though his voice was largely absent. Obama in contrast not only supported twenty-one different profiles across eighteen different social networks, but MyBO (www.mybarrackobama.com) was a bespoke social network for activists. While both had an Action Center which offered opportunities for, and guidance on, participating in the campaign both online and offline, Obama allowed these activists to chat within his own site, so providing a platform for horizontal conversation within a purpose-built community of activists. It was this that enabled him to build a relationship with a cohesive movement, which worked at a highly interactive level, with him as one voice within the movement. Obama's voice may have been rare, and his contributions do suggest he is an elite figure, however he interacts with the movement within the site, via email and across the networks he joined and those he created around his campaign.

The functions of the US candidates' websites

Information provision

As stated above, information provision was a necessary priority for the websites of both candidates. Users were able to view speeches, read policy statements and download policy documents. While Barack Obama combined information with interactivity, by providing a news feed in blog format, John McCain had a news section as well as an area containing 925 discrete media releases. The latter really only offered the impression of a lack of sophistication from the McCain web developers, as it made the site fairly text heavy. Apart from journalists and committed followers, few visitors would likely be interested in press releases: having such a large archive seems to offer little value to host or user. While Obama's site offered a similar level of information, the fact that users could comment on these added a new dimension to information provision. While it could be suggested that there was a left–right dichotomy evident in the style of the candidates, with the more right-wing McCain being highly traditional and choosing to adopt an informative monologue, this may not be wholly accurate. Obama's inclusivity certainly reflects an ideological stance that gave credence to accusations that he was a socialist or even a Marxist (Kristol 2008), though perhaps this is due to the unusually left-of-centre character of Obama's stance within the tradition of American politics. However, there is less of a sense in some areas of this clear dichotomy. The language adopted on the Obama site is as traditional as that of McCain, and some parts could have almost been written by the same Public Relations officer. The reality is, though, that Obama's site is almost schizophrenic. The information is delivered in a highly traditional manner, while elsewhere it is his movement that speaks. McCain eschewed any sense of polyphony; rather it is the voice of an impersonal campaign that could be heard throughout.

Campaigning

As was the case with the French presidential candidates' websites, McCain's site does not specifically ask for the votes of visitors to his website. The requests are indirect and couched in language such as 'It's Time to Make History', which is more about mobilising supporters behind the campaign and converting them into activists; this demonstrates clearly how McCain was targeting the committed Republican voters as opposed to those who need persuading. McCain's strategy is consistent with established views of a website as being a focal point for the committed (Norris 2001b; Boogers and Voerman 2002), but this may be outdated in the modern American context, where there is an increase in those seeking political information online and of those willing to seek this directly from the candidate (Rainie and Horrigan 2007).

Clearly, it seems Obama felt this was outdated, and his campaigning function followed two distinct strategies. While building interest in him as a candidate, and so forging a support base, in the course of his contest for the nomination, Obama encouraged use of his website for all those interested in his candidature. Visitors to www.barackobama.com then had the choice of finding specific information, browsing the site or joining the MyBO network. Those who joined the network were encouraged to be active, both by returning to search updates and local information, but also through regular email contact sent out in the name of Obama himself, Joe Biden or his campaign manager, David Plouffe. Those who chose not to join would be encouraged to do so, but also find a fairly traditional and persuasive front end reinforced by a co-created back end built around the weblog. To contribute to the weblog you had to create a profile within MyBO, just one of the many MyBO recruitment tools employed. Campaigning was also served through the multifarious requests for donation that were embedded across the site, as well as all Obama's social networking presences and those of his network of supporters.

The network of supporters was as vital to the campaign, and central to the campaigning function of his website, as perhaps any other aspect. Not only were activists contributing to the campaign at the street level, they were mobilising other supporters online, encouraging greater participation. They were also at the forefront of demanding the votes of others across the Internet. Supporters donated their Facebook status to ask their friends to vote Obama, badges and posters were embedded across social networking profiles and weblogs, and those with the technological ability and software created mash-ups and multimedia productions to reinforce Obama's messages. This effort was encouraged and orchestrated through the Obama website, and the calls from the central campaign HQ, together with those contributing to the weblog, built up to a crescendo on election day. As the day progressed it was almost impossible for any social network user not to find some pro-Obama message, and be pressed to going out to vote and to take a friend. This network was not simply young Democrats in America, but a global network stretching across Australasia, Europe, the Middle East and wider Americas. Thus, the campaigning messages matched the site's polyphony, and added weight and credibility to Obama's campaign.

Negative campaigning

Barack Obama made a conscious effort to avoid the overt negativity that is a recurrent feature of American election campaigns (Blumler and Kavanagh 1999; Lau and Pomper 2004). This did not mean that the Obama campaign made no reference to that of McCain, however on the whole, his message was comparative. This means that he presented his argument as one that evaluated his position against that of his opponent, and often he compared his vision against the current systemic problems of corporate lobbying and 'broken' politics. Within the Fight the Smears section of his site there was the clear objective of rebutting McCain's arguments, much of which can be classified as having a negative tone. There are also references to McCain supporting Bush, suggesting a vote for McCain would be for continuity; thus preying on the prevailing desire for change (Greener and Arterton 2009). However, on the whole, the majority of the website was positive and personal, and in contrast, it was often Obama's support network that provided the negative content when responding to blog posts; in fact, many simply offered a rant about John McCain, despite this being irrelevant to the original post. One example is the comment 'looney tune McCain..he mentally unstable' (*sic*) offered by 'dmgforchange' in response to a post of 21 October by staffer Molly Claflin 'Do something to help make it happen', a narrative about canvassing. Yet, a number of sites existed that claimed independence, such as www.johnmaccainsrecord.com, which are frequently linked to from blog posts and are wholly negative. While these cannot be coded as part of Obama's website due to their claim to be independent, he draws them into his Websphere and both gives them credibility while also reinforcing his arguments by referencing their data; hence, on the fringes of Obama's Web presence was a wealth of anti-McCain material he was happy to promote or have links to across the site.

McCain was more direct and traditional in his recourse to negativity, and was happy to brand Obama and Biden liars when referring to claims made about the impact of his policies. He also mocked Obama's style, with one video depicting him as Charlton Heston's Moses, capable of miracles on an epic scale. Despite this, his campaign was not without innovation, and he used the online Republican network to amplify a range of negative messages. The satirical Moses video was posted by McCain to YouTube and then reposted 80 times by other YouTube users, as well as being flagged as a favourite by 142 users. He also mocked Obama's celebrification, comparing him to Britney Spears and Paris

Hilton; however, this rebounded on him following the Barely Political website publishing a video featuring Hilton herself calling him 'wrinkly, white-haired guy' and 'old dude' (Fenn 2009: 219). This demonstrates the dangers of using satire; online, anyone with the technology can present a rebuttal and, if newsworthy, can gain greater reach than the original. Hilton's reply gained over a million views across seven different postings to YouTube, with McCain's gaining just less than a third of that number. McCain used negativity online, but perhaps not very effectively.

Resource generation

Both candidates' websites sought donations, but what was remarkable were the differences in success rates. The *New York Times* monitored spend on television advertising alone and reported that Obama spent $207,410,911 compared to McCain's $119,906,703; this is unremarkable until you factor in that Obama's money came entirely from donations from supporters, not corporate sponsorship. Drawing on the lessons of Howard Dean, Obama ruthlessly fought for donations across his online presences as well as through street level activities. Both candidates also had online stores, selling a range of campaign material including T-shirts, baseball caps and bumper stickers. McCain also tried to create an 'I am Spartacus' type movement following the intervention of a member of the public who claimed to be supporting McCain as he was worried about Obama's tax reforms. Joe the Plumber became a minor celebrity during the final part of the campaign, and was frequently mentioned during their final televised debate. McCain launched the 'I'm Joe the Plumber' gear range straight after in a bid to have some form of antidote to the success of the Obama range, which, whether staged or not, could be seen worn at all Obama's public events.

However, the most important innovation in resource generation was potentiated by MyBO. The Obama community was able to mobilise activists that would campaign for Obama within their neighbourhoods. His campaign team, when encouraging activism, placed particular focus on encouraging those within the swing states such as Ohio, worth the most votes within the Electoral College. However, MyBO evidences that activism was taking place across all US states, even Republican heartlands such as Alaska. Thus, alongside the huge amount of donations received, it was the foot soldiers who canvassed door to door and by telephone, who delivered leaflets, organised events and maintained a campaigning presence at a street level that seemed the key aspect of Obama's resource generation strategy. This was a tool that was exploited to a minor extent by McCain, who did try to recruit volunteers within his online campaign Action Center, but in terms of scale his efforts were massively outstripped, as his potential volunteers could only email or fill out a form as opposed to the community-based MyBO that linked the online community to one that was offline. It is argued that the human resource generation element was a pivotal tool of mobilisation (Harfoush 2009).

Networking

One of the key differences between the candidates was their use of networks. McCain sought to build links between his campaign and the various Republican-supporting coalitions across the country; a strategy characteristic of this was to focus on his loyal voter base. Beyond this, McCain also offered a version of his website in Spanish in order to be accessible to the Hispanic community, though this is now de rigueur for any serious national candidate; here ended the serious networking activities of the John McCain campaign. Obama reached out to every voter group using a range of available means. The sixteen social networks included ones that were popular among Democrat Party members, Hispanics and African-Americans. He also promoted himself within poor neighbourhoods, as well as more affluent middle-class areas. He forged links with community politicians from all racial and ethnic groups, and built up a strong following within colleges and universities. All of this was not purely via the Internet, however MyBO and his sites tailored to each state, to thirty-eight distinct voter groups and a further eighteen voter segments (including Republicans and Hillary Clinton loyalists) facilitated ongoing relationship building between him and the members of these groups that engaged with his campaign. Obama also employed the online network to co-create his campaign at the local level.

Promoting participation

A feature at the heart of what could be defined as a Web 2.0 election, participation was clearly encouraged of visitors to www.barackobama.com. McCain invited visitors to ask questions and they could comment within his small blog area; however, these additions to US campaigning were overshadowed by the innovations introduced by his opponent. Barack Obama's site was overwhelmingly about participation, and in a myriad of ways ranging from volunteering to commenting on blogs and contributing to future user experiences. In fact, when assessing the extent of participation, due to the relative size of areas where participation was permitted, 83 per cent of the overall site falls into the category of public discourse, which contrasts with 14 per cent for that of McCain. Equally, while McCain had only 10 per cent of co-created content present, Obama presented the visitors with 78 per cent of content that may not have been solely created by site visitors and users, but had been shaped by user input. Thus, two very different approaches to campaigning emerged from the US Presidential Election of 2008, one that appears highly consistent with Web 2.0, and one that cherry-picked very small parts of the Web 2.0 suite of tools while retaining a strong sense of command and control.

A 2.0 election

Turning to the framework offered by Anderson (2007), we now ask whether there is evidence of the presence of the features that indicate adherence to the big ideas of Web 2.0, and to what extent were they used to foster engagement?

The capacity for individual production and user-generated content

The key area for participation shared by both candidates was their weblog area, though the sheer size and scale of Obama's rather put his opponent into the shade. Equally, the level of participation gained was at times phenomenal, with some posts gaining over a thousand comments. The level of participation is quite surprising in many ways. Romano (2008) is correct in suggesting McCain's blog was the most entertaining, as it was essentially about campaign gossip and commentary on political events; as such it was very readable. Essentially, Obama's was his news area, so presenting a mixture of press releases, videos, calls for mobilisation and some gossip-esque or comment-based journal entries. McCain's separation of news and the blog means users are only encouraged to comment on the blog itself; it appears that on Obama's site users were encouraged to offer fairly wide-ranging contributions on any subject they wished. Within the comments area it can be difficult to track comments to posts, as it appears these are pulled in to the most recent post from other posts rather than always being directly beneath that to which they respond. Equally, users have a tendency to say what they want as opposed to making relevant comments. However, the participatory nature of the blogs is irrefutable.

In the case of Obama, however, participation did not stop with comments on his blog, or indeed the many ways that users could post items to the public open access areas of his SNS. Going beyond harnessing independent bloggers to campaign on his behalf, as was the case with Howard Dean in 2004, Obama created in MyBO an area where supporters could be courted and placed at the heart of the campaign. The success of this form of participatory campaigning connected fully the online activity to the offline, grassroots and street-level campaign to win the Democrat nomination, to secure donations and support throughout the contest and finally to get out the vote.

Harnessing the power of the crowd

Continuing this theme, MyBO represented one key aspect of harnessing the power of the crowd. In presenting himself as the complete outsider, the new kind of leader that significant numbers of Americans from across the political spectrum had claimed to want in 2008, Obama was able to build a supportive movement that would campaign for him. However, such a strategy is not without risk, and this was evidenced with Obama's decision to back an Immunity Bill, to allow companies engaged in surveillance activities to be free from prosecution. His shift from opposition to support of the Spying Bill in June 2008 led to severe protests within MyBO, and across his social networking presences. Such was the force of opposition that Obama released an 852-word explanation of his new position (Melber 2008). While this can easily be interpreted as evidence of the danger of allowing public participation, what Obama seemed to be able to achieve was to answer critics with a strong rebuttal and maintain their trust. Therefore, this crowd's opposition may be dissipated, but even if not, if they retained trust in Obama due to his quick and detailed response (they seemed to, as membership was not reduced), they could become stronger advocates for him and use this affair as a metaphor for his style of leadership.

Access to data on an epic scale

As noted earlier, both candidates scored highly for downward information flows, and provided a wide range of information for visitors to their sites. Obama had a combination of issue positions and portable document files (PDFs) that could be read or downloaded, and most were also available to be shared by readers with their friends. The same was largely true of the McCain site, however areas were extremely text heavy and much could only be read online. Features such as the large amount of press releases could be described as unfriendly to any user except possibly journalists; though of course one could make similar comments about the Obama blog, apart from the fact this symbolised participation as opposed to monologic communication.

An architecture of participation

While this was partially present in areas of the McCain website, in particular his blog and the 'ask a question' feature, and his site stands up reasonably well when compared to those of Sarkozy and Royal, what this lacked was any sense that participation had been (as was the case with Royal), or was, at the heart of his campaign. McCain's problem was that his online strategy compared very badly with that of Obama, whose entire website was within a participatory framework. For those who joined MyBO, everything was seen from within a participatory social network. Those who preferred to remain outside of the network would still see participation happening, and be encouraged to take part. What is clear from the sites is that in the case of Obama's, it is hard not to view participation taking place; with McCain's there is a more traditional style of allowing participation, but not advertising it to any significant extent. Hence, one could suggest that a participatory architecture was placed within an annex of the McCain website; for Obama it was in the entrance hall.

The network effect

It is probably for this reason that Obama rode the wave of a supportive network, while McCain was limited to relying upon those who we would describe as long-term converts to the GOP. McCain was able to draw to the campaign individuals that would publicly express their support for him on weblogs and on the SNS, but in terms of reach, Obama was far ahead in every aspect. While McCain limited himself to Facebook and MySpace, Obama targeted a wide range of groups, amassing over ten million supporters worldwide. This included 12 individual groups within MySpace, where he had a total of 1,801,305 friends on his own profile, but alongside these were Students for Obama with 8,906 members, the 10,464 strong Women for Obama and Latinos for Obama with 3,557 members. His profiles on Black Planet gained 481,427 friends, there were 51,127 on MiGente, the network for English-speaking Latin Americans, as well as 1,994 on GLEE (Gays, Lesbians and everyone else). This level of overt support, the act of befriending, coupled with the level of sharing of videos across social networks, asking friends and supporters to post badges and donate their status updates to the call of 'Vote Obama' are all demonstrations of Obama making the network work in his favour. While the sites where Obama gained the majority of his friends and supporters are global, this perhaps does not matter. As one commentator argued, Obama's support abroad could not only signal a recasting of the US's relationship with the world, but also be read by US voters as a signal that they should vote Obama for more reasons than the purely personal or indeed national factors headlined in his campaign (Brownstein 2009).

Openness

What all this signals is that the Obama campaign was open to all. While the MyBO network necessitated signing up with a US zipcode, this was not impossible for an outsider to the US. The content was clearly designed for US residents, however there were multiple points of access that allowed anyone to join and publicly support his campaign; it could be argued that any element that was not restricted to US voters only was a waste of effort, but the number of supporters from across the globe acted as a wider endorsement that added a degree of credibility to his bid to be president that few previous candidates have had. Inclusivity is perhaps the key element. Not only did he reach out beyond the traditional voter segments to the gay and lesbian community for example, he offered them a place within his network as equal participants. While McCain's campaign was not exactly closed, it may have appeared to have been designed predominantly for the mainstays of the Republican movement. The language was set within a very political discourse and was quite impersonal. While Obama spoke of we, and claimed he spoke for the nation or a clearly defined segment, McCain offers a more personally driven agenda. The use of 'I believe', for example, does not denote inclusion; this contrasted sharply with the keynote sound bites that are encapsulated in Obama's 'Yes We Can' campaign motif and slogan.

Evaluating interactivity

Focusing on the overall interactivity offered by the candidates' websites, we find a fairly stark disparity that is perhaps obvious from the preceding discussion. Obama's site predominantly, in terms of physical number of pages, offered a range of ways for users of the site to enter into public discourse that could be viewed by any visitor. While the precise extent of censorship is vague, it is claimed that this task was delegated to the community in a similar way to the Facebook policy of allowing users to report slanderous or inappropriate content (Harfoush 2009), though we should recognise some form of moderation as a

Table 6.2 User-to-User Interactivity: US 2008

Level of receiver control	*Direction of communication*		
	One Way	*Two Way*	*Three Way*
10			BO – 57465 JM – 284
9			BO – 2 JM – 2
8			BO – 2
7		BO – 1	
6		JM – 1	
5	BO – 127 JM – 30	BO – 8 JM – 6	
4	BO – 2172 JM – 1294	BO – 2 JM – 1	
3	BO – 4 JM – 1	BO – 1	
2	BO – 120 JM – 29		
1			

necessary task as opposed to underhand behaviour. What is clear from analysing a sample of the contributions is that these were largely from ordinary users. From comments on detail of policy such as health insurance to a request from one female contributor for a pair of Obama's 'pants … (washed or not)', there is the clear sense that participation was encouraged and it was taking place. Furthermore, participants were not simply adding graffiti in the way found on UK party SNS profiles in 2007 (Jackson and Lilleker 2009a). Debate took place between contributors and, on occasions, this discussion was picked up by the campaign team in later posts. Thus, arguably, the Obama site presented evidence that a three-way conversation can take place which involves the candidate both as the starting point for debate, but also as a contributor, if not within the comments area then in subsequent posts as well as in public appearances.

There is very little comparison to this on the McCain website. McCain's communication is predominantly one way, with a few areas that invite feedback. Given the size of the website overall, which is fairly small, and the comparative size of the blog, the site offered a largely Web 1.0 experience to visitors. While his approach is consistent with that of Sarkozy, if perhaps slightly less sophisticated, this seems out of step with current trends within the US in relation to innovation in online campaigning (Anstead and Chadwick 2008; Chadwick 2007; Howard 2006).

The disparity is replicated when looking at the passivity of the user. Of Obama's total webspace, 83 per cent was co-created compared to less than 10

Table 6.3 User-to-document interactivity: US 2008 (number of items per category)

	Obama	*McCain*
Downward flows (Packaged)	2,163	1,302
Upward flows (Content on Demand)	5	3
Lateral flows (Content on Demand)	123	28
Asynchronous (Content Exchange)	77	46
Synchronous (Co-created Content)	57,266	284
Number of features	59,634	1,663

per cent for McCain; this is not including the level of co-production that was occurring across the social networks. Thus, Obama clearly set about harnessing the produser, and setting them to work on his campaign within his own website.

A further disparity is the extent to which Obama offered content on demand through links and invitations; McCain's content was packaged and little information was offered to hint whether content was of interest or relevant to the visitor prior to following links to view documents.

Overall, Obama embraced Web 2.0 and interactivity to an unprecedented and perhaps quite radical extent; in contrast, McCain offered the most packaged communication of all candidates up to this point in this study. Perhaps this was a sign of insecurity in using such innovative technologies, a belief that those he was targeting wanted to be informed but not to participate online, an indication that he was ideologically against interacting with voters, or that he felt that he did not have the resources to avoid the pitfalls of open participation. Insider accounts do suggest McCain had a low resourced and at times dysfunctional campaign team, which also offers a stark contrast to the highly motivated and coherent Obama campaign team (Heilemann and Halperin 2010). Whatever the reason, McCain presented a highly packaged campaign designed for a passive audience of loyalists, while Obama fought for the support of every visitor to his website and tried to convert each one into a participant.

Extreme interactivity in a controlled environment

Based on the above evidence, one could suggest that there is a dichotomy between the approaches; that McCain offered a wholly controlled environment, whereas Obama gave up control in order to lead a movement of political participants. However, this dichotomy is not wholly accurate. While McCain was the more controlling and offered a majority of packaged, monologic content, Obama equally retained strong message control and allowed the greatest participation within specific, although physically large and easily accessible, areas. This was perhaps a deliberate attempt to reduce the risks that hostile elements might use inappropriate or controversial contributions against him. Whilst it is difficult to assess the level of control that was maintained over comments on the blog, there was a clear lag between comment and appearance and one cannot imagine that visitors were free to add what they liked; this would have made MyBO a playground for Obama's political opponents. Therefore, what Obama managed to do was build a campaign that meets the definition of a Web 2.0 campaign. While he did not use every Web 2.0 feature available, in building a social network around the campaign and giving its members complete access to his website it could be argued that his social network were produsers of the entire campaign (Germany 2009). McCain, on the other hand, remained consistent with pre-Web 2.0 patterns of Internet use within election campaigns. Resources clearly had a role to play, as monitoring visitor usage is highly time consuming and requires paid professionals to monitor a site 24/7. Yet, the approaches were equally contiguous to the ideological styles of the candidates. McCain's maverick approach allowed some elements of interactivity to feature, but not to the extent that this weakened the style of leadership he offered; Obama offered rhetorically and practically a new style of leadership. This was reflected in his use of Web 2.0, the fact he drew on a grassroots movement and mobilised from the bottom up as well as in his messages and image.

Analysts have been quick to seize upon Obama's strategy, and point to his online innovation, to explain his victory. However, we should look at this campaign within a wider context. Obama's strategy was one borne out of his experiences as a community organiser (Obama 2008); he worked with people to create a campaign in that role and did the same as a candidate for the Presidency. His support was not simply the product of his campaign, it was a combination of the right candidate and communicating the right message using every media available. The Web 2.0 environment suited his grassroots style, and he avoided the gaffes that had thwarted previously successful online campaigners such as Howard Dean. Kerstin Plehwe (2009) identifies ten key strategies that contributed to Obama's victory, and these include: being in touch with the zeitgeist of the US in 2008; his authenticity and branding; his realistic requests for donations and the new ways employed to encourage fundraising; his individualised mode of communication, from him to other individuals; his harnessing of a network of ambassadors rather than winning over voters; and his consistent communication about what he was doing, in Plehwe's words 'do good and talk about it ... and get others to discuss it also' (Plehwe 2009: 156). All these strategies were not enabled specifically by the Internet or Web 2.0, however these new technologies made them easier, and extended the reach of the candidate and his style of communication beyond the meeting halls and rallies. What appears to have been the case is that the Obama strategy was facilitated and enhanced by the Internet, and the potential was recognised and exploited; McCain saw little potential for the Internet so perhaps adopted certain tools within the tradition of the bandwagon approach, but with little sense of how they fitted strategically to the campaign.

The question that has been asked more widely and in particular within events for political strategists in Germany and the UK is: can we, in a parliamentary as opposed to presidential system, 'do an Obama'? Responses from the academic community and independent political analysts are at best cautionary. The reason is that it is not simply about the tools, but also about the individual.

While Obama put both the Internet and Web 2.0 on the map for political communicators, it is less clear what lessons can be learned beyond finding a candidate that has both the charisma and the communicative ability of Obama. However, it may be that Obama marks a watershed in campaigning, and that subsequent elections may not have the resources or the levels of engagement, but there may be attempts to replicate what Plehwe (2009: 175) describes as 'the Internet magic' used by Obama.

7 Controlled interactivity

Parties' online campaigns in the 2009 German National Elections

Eva Johanna Schweitzer

German e-campaigning has never sparked so much interest in the public as in the 2009 national elections. Even one year before Election Day on 27 September, journalists started to produce an avalanche of op-eds, features and reports to speculate about the new 'political generation 2.0' (Thies 2009) and parties' online strategies. Consultants announced that the Internet would be – for the first time – the 'heart' of their campaigns (cf. Bialek 2009; Pfannenmüller 2009). Pollsters, pundits and PR practitioners initiated several studies, dossiers and project platforms to observe the political web (e.g. www.wahl.de; www.wahlgetwitter.de; www.wahlradar.de; www.parteigefluester.de; date: September 2009). This 'media-hype' (Vasterman 2005) around parties' online activities was triggered mainly by four factors that shaped the 2009 election:

First, Internet usage in Germany had grown to 67.1 per cent including the 50–70 demographic (cf. van Eimeren and Frees 2009). In that way, the World Wide Web had truly become another channel for political communication that parties and candidates were eager to employ for voter information and mobilisation.

Second, new Web 2.0 applications, like YouTube, Twitter, and social networking sites (e.g. StudiVZ, Facebook, MySpace), had made their political debut in the 2009 European parliamentary elections and were now to be utilised for the first time in a national race. Their growing usage in the population, specifically among young voters (cf. Busemann and Gscheidle 2009), initiated questions about their potential and effects. This also intensified public and academic debate.

Third, Internet politics had generally become a matter of national concern in 2009 due to investigations of child pornography on the Web. This led to a fierce controversy about online censorship which motivated the so-called Pirate Party, an Internet-savvy civic movement founded in 2006, to campaign in the 2009 elections. In their fight against state interventions, they not only relied on flashmobs to disturb the offline canvassing tours of Germany's parliamentary parties (cf. Bingener *et al.* 2009; Osel 2009), but the Pirates made use of all cyber weapons in modern e-campaigning to raise interest and to win supporters. In this way, they drew additional attention to the political Web. In fact, in the mass media they were cited as the genuine technological front runners that had put established parties under considerable pressure (Fischer and Voß 2009; Roggenkamp 2009).

Fourth, the proximity of the American presidential election further intensified the public focus on e-campaigning and parties' online innovativeness. This race had taken place just one year before the 2009 German national elections and was closely followed by both journalists and politicians. All major parties had sent observers into the United States to learn from the candidates' experiences. Obama's successful online campaign truly became a role model for German politicians. They not only sought to improve their campaign logistics, to gain publicity and to address new target groups; rather, they were striving to meet the growing public expectations on e-campaigning. In particular, parties had hoped to establish an aura of modernity and responsiveness that could overcome tendencies of partisan dealignment, growing public cynicism and shrinking voter turnouts (for an overview see Scarrow 2004). In the past, these developments had led several commentators to decry the end of Germany's mass membership parties and the traditional parliamentary system (cf. e.g. Müller 1999; Sarcinelli 1998; Starke 1993; Wiesendahl 2001). With the electoral success of Obama, some early expectations about the democratic potential of the Internet were revisited. Journalists referred frequently in their media reports to his promising example so as to compare and evaluate the online performances of national parties (cf. e.g. Gillmann *et al.* 2009; Volkery 2008; Von Marschall 2009). In this way, they fuelled the public attention for the 2009 e-campaign.

Most observers agreed that the World Wide Web would play a larger role in 2009 than in previous national elections. As regards the quality of parties' online activities, however, journalists were less unanimous. Whereas some spoke of the 'power of the Internet' (Reichart 2009) and the end of television as the prime campaigning medium (Laufer 2009: 24; Pfannenmüller 2009: 28), others bemoaned a total 'Internet deception' (Tillmann 2009: 10) and 'digital straw fires' (Bay 2008: 54). Parties were said to be amidst an overall 'blogisation' (Vitzthum 2008: 4) and 'web 2.0-isation' (Brauckmann 2009) of politics, while at the same time they were criticised for being 'laggards' (Hanke 2009) in cyberspace that were not only devoid of basic ICT skills (Rybarczyk 2009) but literally 'light years' away from modern e-campaigning (Patalong 2009) – 'Winning like Obama? No we can't...' (Gillmann 2009). These inconsistent judgments are not surprising given the standards and work principles that influence the practice of today's news reporting: journalists base their arguments usually on standalone examples rather than on statistical data (Zillmann and Brosius 2000). They prefer superlatives and fancy headlines to raise attention (Brosius *et al.* 1991), and adapt their reports to typical news values like conflict, negativity or surprise (O'Neill and Harcup 2009; for Germany see Reinemann and Eichholz 2006). In addition, reporters organise their articles as impressionistic narratives rather than as scientific in-depth reports and thus provoke technically determinist, decontextualised and ahistorical claims (Roberts Frith 2005; Rössler 2001). Heterogeneous comments are often a consequence, with a lack of both explicit criteria of evaluation and missing reflections on the epistemological limits that are at the very heart of these observations. From a scientific point of view, these news reports thus do not provide a reliable basis to assess parties' online activities.

To give a valid account of the status quo in German e-campaigning in the 2009 national elections, the following chapter seeks to overcome these restrictions through a systematic empirical approach. As part of the comparative Elections 2.0 project, the Internet presences of all six parliamentary parties (CDU: Christlich Demokratische Union Deutschlands; CSU: Christlich-Soziale Union; SPD: Sozialdemokratische Partei Deutschlands; FDP: Freie Demokratische Partei; Greens: Bündnis 90/Die Grünen; Left: Die Linke) were examined in the last four weeks before Election Day. These parties represent the main political forces in Germany and thus define the electoral landscape. The study combines a structural, hyperlink and content analysis to examine the overall style and substance of parties' online communications. In this way, the enquiry also sheds light on the way in which German political actors succeeded in engaging voters in Web 1.0 and Web 2.0.

The campaign context

Political context

The 2009 campaign was carried out under the condition of a grand coalition of Conservatives (CDU/CSU) and Social Democrats (SPD). This unusual constellation had come into being after the 2005 early elections in which Angela Merkel (CDU) became Germany's first female chancellor. In 2009 she sought re-election and a change in government in favour of a pure bourgeois coalition of CDU, its Bavarian sister association CSU and the liberal minor party FDP. This goal was achieved with a landslide defeat of the Social Democrats and their candidate Frank-Walter Steinmeier. The campaign, however, was not marked by special incidents. Rather, pundits and journalists criticised the 'dullness' of the race, with CDU/CSU and FDP leading the polls even months before the election. The shared government responsibility of Conservatives and Social Democrats had contributed to the lack of excitement: the grand coalition reduced the number of mutual attacks on the opponents' past records that are otherwise common in national races (see also the results section on negative campaigning). In fact, even in the televised debate between Merkel and Steinmeier that took place on 13 September 2009, i.e. two weeks before Election Day, assaults and polarisations were hard to find. In addition, no single issue dominated the news agenda during the final phase of the campaign. As a consequence, citizens turned off from the race, particularly in the Eastern part of the country: with 70.2 per cent, turnout was not only 6.9 per cent lower than in 2005, it was also the lowest ever in national elections since 1949; though this is high compared to the US, France and the UK.

Electoral context

Parties tried to counter the anticipated voter fatigue through their electoral campaigns. In the last four weeks before Election Day, the so-called 'hot phase', they put up posters in the streets, published ads in newspapers and magazines, and produced spots for both public and private television or radio stations. In Germany, political advertising is subject to the rule of 'graded allocation', i.e. major parties receive more opportunities for self-promotion than minor or fringe parties (for an overview on the legal framework, see Holtz-Bacha 2006). Major parties are also more prone to buying additional advertising space, for example on commercial television channels, due to their privileged financial status: they receive larger sums of state subsidies based on their vote shares in past elections. On all stations, however, parties' spots need to be announced and highlighted as 'political advertising', which is seen as detrimental to their persuasive effects. In recent years, parties have therefore lost interest in this traditional mode of electioneering. Rather, they are turning more and more to e-campaigning since its usage is currently not restricted by electoral laws. This offers a strong incentive for all political actors to go online.

Web context

The first Internet presences were established in the mid-1990s, and the 1998 national election is usually cited as the political race in which German e-campaigning made its debut. Since then, the parties' online activities have been marked by a clear trend towards *professionalisation* (cf. Schweitzer 2008a): all parliamentary parties rely on external consultants and specialist Web agencies to organise their cyber campaigns. To this end, they spend between 1 and 5 per cent of their budget, i.e. between 100,000 and 250,000 Euro, on online political communication (cf. Schweitzer 2008a: 242). Prior to major national elections, the main websites are usually subject to complete relaunches that are staged as pseudo-events to gain additional publicity. In 2009 this happened at the beginning of the year so as to use the European parliamentary election in June as a test field for the national elections that were to follow in September. In the long run, these technical makeovers have turned the initial 'electronic brochures' from 1998 into dynamic multimedia platforms (see below). Moreover, parliamentary parties have started to extend their Internet presences with satellite home pages for fundraising, volunteer recruitment, rapid rebuttal and social networking. This *functional differentiation* has been accompanied by a *digital diversification*, i.e. the inclusion of various types of online formats in parties' e-electioneering (e.g. websites, blogs, Twitter, YouTube channels) by a *presentational sophistication*, i.e. the gradual improvement of informational, interactive and navigational features on the websites (cf. Schweitzer 2008b, 2010b), and by a growing *strategic convergence* of online and offline campaigns. Parties not only refer in spots and on posters to their Internet presences but also use cyberspace to plan and design their offline paraphernalia (see the results section on resource generation). This kind of professionalisation, though, is clearly limited to the e-campaigns of Germany's two major (CDU, SPD) and four minor (CSU, FDP, Greens, Left) parties in parliament. Fringe parties that fail to pass the 5 per cent threshold to enter the *Bundestag* have been found to lag dramatically behind the main political forces in terms of their website quality in both European parliamentary and national elections (cf. Schweitzer 2008b, 2009). This gap in website professionalism (a) is visible in all functions of e-campaigning (e.g. information, mobilisation, interactivity, design), (b) continues over time (2002–9) and (c) is even stronger in the Web 2.0 than in the Web 1.0 arena (Schweitzer 2010b). In this way, the Internet has not levelled the playing field for insiders and outsiders in the political competition. Rather, the World Wide Web has reinforced the inequalities and power differences that exist in the offline world between parliamentary and non-parliamentary parties. The main reason for this 'normalisation' in German e-campaigning (cf. Schweitzer 2008b) lies in the privileged position of major and minor fractions in the *Bundestag*: as outlined above, they have far more financial and human resources at their disposal and better infrastructures so as to continue their superiority in campaigning, even in cyberspace. In the following, this has to be kept in mind since the present study concentrates on these parties only. The findings thus do not reflect the whole range of political actors on the Web but rather the leading edge of Germany's party-based e-campaigning.

Method in the German case study

To examine the style of parties' online communications, the analysis included all Internet presences of the parliamentary groups in the 2009 national elections. This encompasses their main websites as well as the satellite home pages (e.g. for fundraising or volunteer recruitment) and all additional online platforms or profiles (e.g. on YouTube, Twitter, or social networking sites) that were established for the race and linked to the main websites. In this way, the enquiry provides a complete set of all authorised and organisation-centred campaign activities of Germany's parliamentary parties in cyberspace. To save the respective online content, the author relied on different programmes for downloading, crawling and annotating the home pages, including packages like Teleport Pro, Xenue's Link Sleuth, Zotero and PDF dumping software. As with the other analyses, this was conducted during the week prior to Election Day on 27 September 2009.

The whole website was manually coded to assess the presence and absence of features and, where specified, their magnitude (see Table 7.1). Additionally, this study employed a computer-assisted hyperlink analysis that counted and classified all outgoing hyperlinks from the main sites to other online offerings. In order to shed light on the discursive patterns of parties' e-campaigns, a content analysis was conducted of all news releases that were published on the front pages of the websites in the last four weeks before Election Day (N = 370). The quantitative findings of this analysis are reported in detail in another article (cf. Schweitzer 2010b). For the present study, the text-based messages are used to describe parties' online approaches in a more general manner. The focus on the text-based messages is motivated by three reasons. First, the online news releases are the most prominent feature on parties' websites. They are the first content that is seen by journalists, voters and members when visiting the party home pages. Moreover, these messages are reproduced on other campaign platforms as well, e.g. in newsletters and on social networking sites, which increases their circulation. A content analysis of these messages thus allows conclusions about parties' strategies for self-presentation, as they represent the Web content that has the widest public reach and the largest potential exposure effect among Internet users. Second, parties' online news releases are published instantly during the campaign. In contrast to other parts of the website that are pre-produced long before the actual race starts (e.g. sections on values, issue standpoints, or programmes, etc.), these messages provide insights into parties' real-time communication practices in the hot phase of the election. This includes argumentative tactics and spontaneous reactions in the light of certain campaign events or developments. In content analysis, this kind of context-sensitivity is a crucial premise to secure valid conclusions. Third, while German parties' websites differ in their overall structure and style, they all place online news releases on their front pages. To rely on this type of communication thus ensures that the discursive patterns of different political actors are deduced from identical units of analysis across all websites. Through this, the study achieves internal methodological equivalence when making comparisons.

Mapping the websites

In the 2009 national elections, German parties tried to establish distinct digital images on the Internet. The choice of colours and fonts as well as the spatial alignment of their websites contributed to brand-like corporate identities. In this way, the parliamentary groups sought to unite their various online platforms under a common stylistic umbrella that was easy to recognise and to remember for voters. The CDU, for example, relied on orange–grey as the main colours that resonated with the party's offline campaign materials. The CSU continued to use blue–white in the background as a reminder of the regional affiliation to the state Bavaria. The FDP preferred a classical liberal layout with frames of blue and yellow on an otherwise white page. The most colourful and flashy websites were the home pages of SPD and Greens, which were almost completely branded with the traditional party colours of red and green. The Left Party appeared to be an exception, as it used deep red (its signal colour) only as shading for the start menu and for navigational items on the front page. All other parts of the website remained white with black letters, as in earlier elections. The Left was also the only parliamentary party that kept up a primarily text-laden Internet presence with strong vertical orientation. All other parties sought to break up this organisational structure in 2009: they either offered animated media boxes with video streams, short text teasers and photos on the front pages

Table 7.1 Elements on German party websites in the 2009 National Elections

Categories	*Party Status*					
	CDU Major	*CSU Minor*	*SPD Major*	*FDP Minor*	*Greens Minor*	*Left Minor*
Downward information flows						
Documents (e.g. manifesto)	Yes	Yes	Yes	Yes	Yes	Yes
Policies summed	Yes	Yes	Yes	Yes	Yes	Yes
Issues examined	Yes	Yes	Yes	Yes	Yes	Yes
Number of issues discussed	38	10	8	212	48	190
Statement of values/ideology	Yes	Yes	Yes	Yes	Yes	Yes
Newsletters	Yes	Yes	Yes	Yes	Yes	Yes
Number of newsletters archived	0	0	0	0	0	6
Media releases	Yes	Yes	Yes	Yes	Yes	Yes
Number of releases	22	14	109	186	35	46
Candidate profile	Yes	Yes	Yes	Yes	Yes	Yes
Election information	Yes	Yes	Yes	Yes	Yes	Yes
Event calendar	Yes	Yes	Yes	Yes	Yes	Yes
Frequently asked questions	Yes	No	Yes	Yes	Yes	Yes
Negative campaigning	Yes	Yes	Yes	Yes	Yes	Yes
Overall percentage of negativity	10.5	10.2	40	93	74	16.9
Negative campaigning (% of statements in online news releases)	40.0	28.2	52.7	61.8	56.9	63.2
Videos	Yes	Yes	Yes	Yes	Yes	Yes
Number of videos	56	11	17	44	62	22
Number of groups targeted	5	11	4	0	0	1
Targeted download form	No	No	Yes	No	No	No
Targeted online enquiry form	No	No	No	No	No	No
Targeted online transaction	No	No	No	No	No	No

continued

Table 7.1 continued

Categories	*Party Status*					
	CDU Major	*CSU Minor*	*SPD Major*	*FDP Minor*	*Greens Minor*	*Left Minor*
Upward information flows						
Volunteering possible	Yes	No	Yes	Yes	Yes	Yes
Donations possible	Yes	Yes	Yes	Yes	Yes	Yes
Merchandise for sale	Yes	Yes	Yes	Yes	Yes	Yes
Cookies	Yes	Yes	Yes	Yes	Yes	Yes
Lateral/horizontal information flows						
Number of partisan links	3	11	32	11	15	4
Number of reference links	225	129	51	15	16	2
Number of internal links	2,207	1,100	769	136	108	32
Total number of links	*2,435*	*1,240*	*852*	*162*	*139*	*38*
Interactive information flows: Asynchronous						
Download logos/posters (number)	Yes	Yes	Yes	Yes	Yes	Yes
Site search	Yes	Yes	Yes	Yes	Yes	Yes
Enmeshing	Yes	Yes	Yes	Yes	Yes	Yes
Navigation aids	Yes	Yes	Yes	Yes	Yes	Yes
Online games/gimmicks	No	No	No	Yes	Yes	No
Email contact	Yes	Yes	Yes	Yes	Yes	Yes
Email feedback	No	No	No	No	No	No
Online feedback form	Yes	Yes	Yes	Yes	Yes	Yes
Join email list	No	No	No	No	No	No
Questionnaires	No	No	No	No	No	No
Visitor-initiated questionnaires	No	No	No	No	No	No
Polls	No	Yes	No	No	No	No
Visitor-initiated polls	No	No	No	No	No	No

Petitions	No	No	No	No	No	No
Visitor-initiated petitions	No	No	No	No	No	No
Join online campaign	Yes	No	Yes	Yes	Yes	Yes
Subscribe to e-newsletter	Yes	Yes	Yes	Yes	Yes	Yes
Membership form to download	Yes	Yes	Yes	Yes	Yes	Yes
Online membership enquiry form	Yes	No	Yes	Yes	Yes	Yes
Online membership transaction	Yes	No	Yes	Yes	No	Yes
Bulletin board	No	No	No	No	No	No
Blog	Yes	No	Yes	Yes	No	Yes
Ability to share videos/pics (embed code)	Yes	Yes	Yes	Yes	Yes	Yes
Podcasts	No	No	Yes	No	No	Yes
Social networking links	Yes	Yes	Yes	Yes	Yes	Yes
Number of links to social networks	6	3	2	3	2	2
Twitter	Yes	Yes	Yes	Yes	Yes	Yes
RSS	Yes	Yes	Yes	Yes	Yes	Yes
Interactive information flows: Synchronous						
Ability of visitors to upload content/comments	Yes	Yes	Yes	Yes	Yes	Yes
Number of opportunities to upload content/comments	275	17	233	108	15	112
Ability of visitors to share information	Yes	No	Yes	Yes	Yes	No
Number of opportunities to share information	274	12	234	111	13	103
Ability of visitors to update information	No	No	No	No	No	No
Number of opportunities to update information	0	0	0	0	0	0
Public conversations allowed via comments or wall posting	Yes	Yes	Yes	Yes	Yes	Yes
Number of opportunities for public conversations	270	14	231	106	14	110
Forum	Yes	Yes	No	Yes	Yes	No
Chat room	No	No	No	No	No	No
Online debate	Yes	Yes	No	Yes	Yes	No
Number of opportunities to debate with candidates/leaders	4	1	0	13	1	0

(CSU, FDP, Greens), or initiated portal sites that were placed ahead of the main website (CDU, SPD). The latter encompassed dynamic news sections in the upper half of the screen as well as basic mobilisation features for voters (i.e. options for donations, volunteering, membership) and promotional hyperlinks to all other Internet platforms of the party, including Twitter, YouTube, or profiles on social networking sites like MySpace, Facebook or StudiVZ, a widely used German social networking service for students.

In this way, the websites not only became tools for direct resource generation, they also worked as digital collections of parties' official activities on the Internet that could be used as starting points for users to delve deeper into the site. Other navigational elements, like start menus, sitemaps or search engines, that had prominent positions on parties' former Internet presences were instead partly removed to the bottom (CSU, FDP, Greens), or became visible only if users wanted them to (SPD). These changes reflect the growing ICT skills of average citizens that parties had anticipated in the design of their new websites.

Functions of the party websites

The Elections 2.0 project sheet included more than 60 website elements that were checked for presence and absence or magnitude on parties' home pages. These options were categorised into two basic groups (information and interactivity) and further differentiated according to the flow of communication (downward/upward/lateral; asynchronous/synchronous) that is realised through these structural features (see Table 7.1). In the following, the results of this coding will be summarised for the main functions of e-campaigning, i.e. information provision, campaigning, negative campaigning, resource generation, networking and the promotion of participation in Web 1.0 and Web 2.0. In total, the findings will show that German e-campaigns diverge only on the surface (see above). As regards the degree of innovativeness in 2009, the technical facilities and the options to engage voters, all parliamentary parties – i.e. major and minor ones – are marked by a *digital standardisation process*. This results from mutual co-orientation among competitors as well as from collective learning processes in the observation of successful e-campaigns that are conducted in other countries, specifically in the United States.

Information provision

In the longitudinal comparison of parties' Internet presences between 2002 and 2009, the top-down provision of information has always been the major function in German e-campaigning (cf. Schweitzer 2008b, 2010b). Political actors seek to bypass journalists and news organisations in cyberspace so as to provide interested voters, members and supporters with unlimited, unfiltered material. All parliamentary parties offer basic informational features on their home pages, such as manifestos, issue positions and ideology sections as well as newsletters, candidate profiles and event calendars. General information about the political system or the German institutions (apart from the basic electoral procedures), however, is missing. Parties thus do not seek to contribute with their websites to voters' civic education. Rather, they focus throughout on self-promotion and leave out other aspects of the democratic process.

Campaigning

The information offered to visitors met a number of campaigning-related objectives. In 2009 CDU/CSU, SPD and the Left provided specific materials about the party and the election programme for target groups such as the over 50s, migrants (specifically from Turkey, the largest immigrant group domiciled in Germany) and first-time voters. In this way, they customised their Web content for those segments of the population that were said to have a strong but unpredictable influence on parties' final results. In fact, this customisation of parties' websites reflects a turn towards lifestyle politics that has come about with the modernisation and individualisation of society (cf. e.g. Bennett 1998; Blumler and Kavanagh 1999; Shah *et al.* 2007).

In addition, the websites were built to address journalists, through media releases, photo and 'sound bite' archives as well as through hotlines and options to become accredited for special campaign events. This service is based on the fact that German journalists rely in their work more and more on the Internet and use parties' Web presences as information subsidies (cf. Machill and Beiler 2009). With extensive material for the mass media, political actors have a chance not only to leave a favourable impression among reporters but to influence their offline news coverage through agenda-building and digital spin-doctoring (see also Ku *et al.* 2003; Meraz 2004; Tedesco 2005). In this way, journalists become amplifiers of parties' online messages that reach even those parts of the population that normally would not turn to the Internet to search for political information. E-campaigning thus revives the two-step-flow model of communication (cf. also Norris and Curtice 2007): the media report about parties' e-campaigns (see introduction) and through this create additional publicity that helps to overcome the original pull-medium character of the World Wide Web.

German political actors sought to enhance this effect by adopting a journalistic news style on their home pages. As the content analysis shows, parties did not address voters directly in their text-based messages. Instead, they used a detached third-person voice with citations of the top candidates and with information that is presented in a chronologically reversed order, similar to the inverted pyramid structure in traditional offline coverage. Moreover, they focused primarily on the horse race aspect of the election and their campaign activities ('metacoverage') while substantial policy discussions moved into the background (see also Schweitzer 2005, 2008b, 2010b). In this way, they mimicked the characteristics of today's political journalism to raise attention and to create an impression of impartiality, authoritativeness and credibility (cf. also Schweitzer 2010b).

Negative campaigning

Another way to gain publicity and to define the news agenda on the Web and beyond is the use of verbal attacks on a political opponent. This tactic is not uncontroversial given the normative democratic ideal that citizens should base their votes on an ethical, rational and issue-based public discourse (cf. e.g. Kaid 1991). PR consultants and campaign managers, however, see negative campaigning as an effective strategy to bolster candidates' name recognition and to cast doubt on the opponents' viability for office (cf. Perloff and Kinsey 1992). In fact, empirical research has shown that political attacks not only trigger more media coverage (e.g. Ridout and Smith 2008), they also overcome voters' selective perception (e.g. Lau 1982), are easily remembered (e.g. Newhagen and Reeves 1991), lower competitors' public esteem (e.g. Garramone *et al.* 1990) and mobilise supporters of their own camp (e.g. Freedman and Goldstein 1999). In the United States, negativity has thus become a pervasive strategy that marks both offline and online campaign channels to almost the same degree (for television advertising see Geer 2006; for e-campaigning see Druckman *et al.* 2010; Wicks and Souley 2003).

In Germany, negative campaigning has long been said to be an ineffective and unethical strategy that conflicts with the country's overall coalition-based and democratic–corporatist political culture (cf. e.g. Kaltenthaler 2000; Holtz-Bacha 2001). Past analyses on the use of negativity on German party websites in state, national and European parliamentary elections show, however, that assaults on the opponent have become as prominent in the Federal Republic as in the United States and with very similar patterns (cf. Schweitzer 2010a): on average, there are more attacks than acclaims in the online news releases that parties publish on their home pages in the last four weeks before Election Day. The amount of negative campaigning is generally higher in national (first-order races) than in European or state elections (second-order races). In addition, challengers are more likely to go negative than incumbents. The attacks are usually formulated by third- or second-rank politicians and not by the top candidates themselves, and concentrate on opponents' competence or leadership abilities. In contrast to the US, attacks on individual candidates are scarce. This reflects the party-centredness of the German political system. Moreover, the assaults are most often placed within the election context itself and hardly ever lead to substantial follow-up discussions (cf. also Schweitzer 2010b).

In 2009 these trends in German e-campaigning continued. Even though negativity is restricted to small parts of the whole website (between 4 and 16.9 per cent of all subpages; see Table 7.1), parties' attacks in these sections are quite intense: in the online news releases that were coded on parties' home pages in the last four weeks before Election Day, 51 per cent of all statements (N = 1,067) were attacks. In comparison to earlier national elections, in which negativity had a share of 56.9 per cent respectively, this means a slight decrease. This finding is due to the special situation of a grand coalition of CDU/CSU and SPD that forced both parties into cooperation and into joint government decisions that were difficult to criticise afterwards. Negative campaigning was thus more prominent among the minor oppositional parties in parliament, i.e. FDP, Greens and Left, who showed the highest shares of assaults as challengers. CDU and CSU, on the other hand, relied more on positive self-promotion (see also Table 7.1). The Social Democrats proved to be an exception here since they launched more attacks than acclaims while being in an incumbent position. In fact, their average number of assaults in the online news releases continuously increased throughout the campaign season from about 1.9 in the first to 3.6 in the last week before Election Day (cf. also Schweitzer 2010b). This development can be explained by their role as junior partner in the grand coalition preceding the election. In 2009 they not only sought to end the cooperation with the Conservatives, they also tried to regain the chancellorship from Angela Merkel. This turned them into strategic challengers who were more prone to go negative than the Conservatives. The personal competition between Frank-Walter Steinmeier (SPD) and Angela Merkel (CDU), however, did not affect the overall patterns of negativity in e-campaigning. The attacks still remained targeted at the parties as collective entities rather than at individual candidates. Moreover, they focused primarily on competitors' political records and their leadership abilities, i.e. on qualities that are directly related to office-holding. In contrast, politicians' personalities and their private lives were hardly touched.

In fact, German e-campaigns are marked by a continuous trend towards *depersonalisation*: as past content analyses show, the top candidates are hardly mentioned in parties' online news releases (less than 4 per cent in national elections). Compared to their dominance in news reports or televised ads, they are seldom addressed as statement objects (about 25 per cent) and are cited as main sources on the websites only in about one fifth of all statements (cf. Schweitzer 2005, 2008, 2010a). Between 2002 and 2009, the share of sound bites by the major candidates further decreased in e-campaigning from 26.7 to 16 per cent. This trend can be explained by the functional differentiation and digital diversification of parties' online activities. As described above, German political organisations rely on several Internet platforms for various tasks in electioneering, such as fundraising, volunteer recruitment, or campaign coordination. The portrayal of German candidates is thus outsourced to other, more effective instruments of personalisation in cyberspace, such as individual home pages or profiles on social networking sites. This unburdens parties' main Web portals and leads to a stronger focus on the pluralistic interests and goals of the organisation.

Resource generation

Next to informing, the generation of human and financial resources has always been the second most important function in German e-campaigning (cf. Schweitzer 2005, 2008b, 2010b). Parties seek to enhance their competitiveness and their electoral viability by persuading voters to donate, volunteer, or become members. All parliamentary groups provide these options on their websites. There was only one exception: since the CSU campaigned together with the

CDU, they maintained a common platform for volunteer recruitment and campaigning called www.team2009.de (the letters A and M were supposed to represent the initials of Angela Merkel, the joint chancellor candidate of the Conservatives). The CSU home page was linked to this website so that users interested in supporting the party could register there. A separate volunteer option on the CSU website was not given. Aside from this, political organisations offered their TV spots, posters, or other paraphernalia for download and maintained an online shop for merchandising. The Internet presences thus become cornerstones for parties' corporate identities: they accelerate the distribution of campaign material, reduce the costs for transmission and allow citizens to identify with a party. In addition, all parliamentary groups established intranets for volunteers and members to exchange exclusive information, to coordinate the offline campaign and to build task forces. On the websites of CDU and FDP, volunteers could also upload a personal profile and photos to become publicly visible as supporters. These networks enhance the overall efficiency of parties' electoral communication: they strengthen people's emotional connection to both the party and to each other, which in turn contributes to their overall team spirit and motivation. For this reason, parties' Internet presences have even been dubbed the digital 'backrooms of the campaign' (Bieber 2000), the modern 'test fields' (Hebecker 2002: 48) and 'seismographs' (Schemel 2004: 35), and the new 'think tanks' in electioneering (Gellner and Strohmeier 2002: 171). In 2009 German parties also used the Web to design their offline campaign material: both the personal logo of SPD chancellor candidate Frank-Walter Steinmeier and the Liberals' campaign slogan ('Leistung muss sich lohnen' = 'Work needs to pay off') were chosen by Internet votes and the CDU allowed users to upload personal remixes of the official campaign song on the Internet. By including amateurs and Internet-savvy supporters into the planning process, parties are able to energise their campaign using an element of crowd-sourcing: they make free use of the creative potential of the population, demonstrate responsiveness to people's ideas and moods, and increase the parties' overall competitiveness and strength.

Networking

Apart from social networking with supporters, members and friends, parties have the ability to build a technical network via hyperlinks. This tool allows political organisations: (a) to enhance their overall web presence (*extension*), (b) to direct interested voters to other online platforms of the party (*guidance*), (c) to enhance their visibility in search engines that are based on hyperlink algorithms (*visibility*), (d) to compensate for information deficits on their home pages through the reference to complementary online contents (*accommodation*), (e) to provide evidence for certain claims on the website by citing independent Internet sources (*justification*), and (f) to symbolically demonstrate solidarity as well as ideological proximity to certain groups, individuals and institutions (*positioning*). All parliamentary parties in Germany make use of these options, even though to varying degrees and with different foci (see Table 7.1). The results of the computer-assisted hyperlink analysis show that the status and size of a political organisation are reflected in its technical network structure: the major people's parties, CDU/CSU and SPD, provide more than ten times as many hyperlinks as the minor fractions in parliament. Most often they link to internal subgroups of the organisation, such as the party associations in the sixteen federal states, special working groups and committees (e.g. for women, senior, or young members), or to national and international political institutions like ministries, the federal council (*Bundesrat*), or the EU. References to partisan groups, NGOs, or partners from economy, education, culture, or science, however, are scarce. This pattern has also been observed in earlier national and European parliamentary elections (cf. Schweitzer 2005, 2009). German parties thus do not rely on technical networks to externally validate their claims or to symbolically exhibit their affiliation to non-political organisations. Rather, they utilise hyperlinks primarily for the purposes of digital image-building, i.e. for the tasks of extension, audience guidance and visibility.

Promoting participation

The last function of Web campaigning that has been considered in this analysis is the field of participation. This aspect encompasses all features that allow members, voters and supporters to initiate, maintain, or foster an online exchange with the party in a synchronous or asynchronous way. In the Elections 2.0 project, this means not only email contacts, chat rooms, opinion polls, digital petitions, or Web 2.0 applications (blogs, social networking sites, Twitter, video and photo sharing), but also navigational, transactional, entertainment, or update elements if they provide a basis for further user engagement on the website (e.g. through enmeshing, search options, online games, or customised subscription and feedback options). In past studies on German e-campaigning, voter participation has always been the least important function on parties' websites. For the main part, they concentrate on traditional, top-down information provision and resource generation while genuine interactive features are largely neglected (cf. Schweitzer 2005, 2008b, 2010b). Through this, parties seek to maintain their message control in cyberspace and to preserve the overall centralisation in campaign management. In the 2009 national elections, this pattern has hardly changed. Even though all parliamentary groups embraced new Web 2.0 features like Twitter accounts, blogs, profiles on social networking sites, or channels on YouTube, substantial policy debates with voters were scarce (see also Table 7.1). This restricted use of interactivity will be illustrated in the following short notes according to the key criteria of the Elections 2.0 project.

A 2.0 election?

Individual production and user-generated content

Some elements of user-generated content were found on the German party sites, mainly within the weblogs of CDU, SPD, FDP and Left Party, and the social networking profiles they had all created. However, cumulatively across the parties there were only twenty-nine individual points at which visitors could upload material and twenty-one opportunities to share information.

Harnessing the power of the crowd

There were limited ways in which the parties attempted to gain public endorsements on the Internet. Mostly, they relied on social networks to demonstrate popularity. Here, candidate profiles were generally more successful than member groups of individual political organisations. In comparison to the United States, though, the support gained in these networks was rather meagre. At the end of August 2009, i.e. four weeks before Election Day, Angela Merkel (CDU) had won about 14,000 fans on Facebook while her competitor Frank-Walter Steinmeier (SPD) was backed by only 5,000 followers. The main websites, on the other hand, were aimed at harnessing the power of the media. Rather than using the online audience to promote their ideas, German parties continued to target journalists for the amplification of their campaign messages. In this way, they sought to increase their publicity in both print and television news, and to preserve their message control.

Access to data on an epic scale

The party sites contained large amounts of information, with FDP and Left Party breaking policy down into fine detail. This suggested a certain kind of transparency. However, the purpose of the data was to persuade rather than to educate; the extent to which it was delivered with negative slants demonstrates this clearly. Party sites also provided several hyperlinks to internal networks. This created a web of data that would reinforce their messages.

Architecture of participation

The participatory architecture was not in place within Germany. There were some minor elements on the websites that allowed genuine participation (e.g. through weblogs or feedback forms), however German parties remained highly cautious of allowing public, open debate. Thus, the real participatory architectures were constructed and locked behind passwords to gain intra-party discussion as opposed to talking with the wider online audience.

The network effect

Apart from basic sharing options (such as social bookmarking or subscriptions to RSS feeds), German parties made use of the network effect only in terms of preparing and conducting their offline campaign. Crowd-sourcing was used, for example, to design their paraphernalia (see above), and intranets were established to inform and coordinate volunteers, members and supporters in the canvassing tours. This happened under the strict guidance and observance of the campaign headquarters. A free, independent and self-reinforcing network was not intended.

Openness

Levels of openness and transparency were generally limited. All websites provided basic information about user privacy, data protection and the deployment of cookies. However, the political content of parties' Internet presences was driven by the constraints of campaigning. In this way, the websites were locked into the logic of branding, informing and persuading. Bottom-up discussions, for example in party-based wikis, about policies and programmes were not encouraged.

Evaluating interactivity

Although limited in terms of offering participatory features, there were uses of elements that adhered to the big ideas of Web 2.0. Site visitors could subscribe to newsletters or RSS feeds, share content with other users through social bookmarking or forwarding options, or respond to parties' news releases via online feedback forms. Petitions, visitor-initiated polls, chats, or personal updates, however, were not provided. Moreover, parties' forums required separate registration procedures and the conversations exchanged were often not visible to other users. In this way, parties preserved more critical and programmatic debates to an exclusive and easily controllable audience.

In fact, when taking the Elections 2.0 matrix for user-to-user interactivity as a basis (see Table 7.2), it becomes clear that 88.5 per cent of all 7,112 items coded on German party websites (including their individual quantities) concentrated on one-way communication with low to medium degrees of receiver control (levels 2 to 5). In contrast, genuine two or three-way interaction was present in less than 12 per cent of all elements. This imbalance was observable for all parliamentary parties irrespective of their size, ideology, or campaign status (i.e. incumbent or challenger). German e-campaigns thus still adhered to the one-way feedback type of interactivity that has been theoretically proposed in the research literature (cf. e.g. Ferber *et al.* 2007; Jackson and Lilleker 2009).

The use of Web 2.0 features in the 2008 US Presidential Election has not altered this controlled style of online political communication. Rather, as with earlier digital innovations, German parties adopted the new applications primarily at a surface level so as to jump on the international bandwagon, improve

Table 7.2 User-to-user-interactivity on German party websites

Level of receiver control	*Direction of communication*		
	One-way	*Two-way*	*Three-way*
10			CDU – 266 CSU – 11 SPD – 228 FDP – 106 Greens – 11 Left – 107
9			CDU – 2 CSU – 1 SPD – 2 FDP – 2 Greens – 1 Left – 2
8			CDU – 2 CSU – 1 SPD – 2 FDP – 2 Greens – 2 Left – 2
7		CDU – 1 SPD – 1 FDP – 1 Greens – 1 Left – 1	
6		CSU – 1	
5	CDU – 2440 CSU – 1245 SPD – 857 FDP – 167 Greens – 236 Left – 43	CDU – 9 CSU – 6 SPD – 9 FDP – 8 Greens – 8 Left – 9	
4	CDU – 91 CSU – 36 SPD – 135 FDP – 240 Greens – 156 Left – 77	CDU – 1 SPD – 1 FDP – 1 Left – 1	
3	CDU – 3 CSU – 2 SPD – 3 FDP – 3 Greens – 3 Left – 3	CDU – 1 CSU – 1 SPD – 1 FDP – 1 Greens – 1 Left – 1	
2	CDU – 43 CSU – 26 SPD – 16 FDP – 217 Greens – 53 Left – 202		
1			
Σ	6,297	65	750
%	88.5	0.9	10.5

Source: The figures were provided by Darren Lilleker.

their image, demonstrate campaign professionalism and modernity, and to symbolically connect with voters (cf. Schweitzer 2005, 2008b). Web 2.0 was an aesthetic tool to influence perceptions as opposed to connecting with voters at a more cognitive level. A genuine 'architecture of participation' (O'Reilly 2005) was not established. Parties' Web strategies thus resembled digital window dressing.

This is further evidenced when looking at the user-to-document interactivity figures displayed in Table 7.3. The majority of information flows were lateral, driven by the heavy use of internal hyperlinks. Most of the content was monologic and packaged to be persuasive. There were the usual opportunities to donate and volunteer, and all the parties offered merchandise for sale. Asynchronous flows tended to conform to the interactivity-as-product paradigm, with the smallest amount of features being on the margins of interactivity-as-process (Stromer-Galley 2004).

Summary and conclusions

The 2009 German national elections saw an unusual public interest in e-campaigning. National controversies about Internet politics, the proximity of the 2008 American Presidential Election, and the debut and growing usage of Web 2.0 features had led citizens, journalists and consultants to expect a rise in online political communication and a digital empowerment of voters (see introduction). These far-reaching democratic hopes, however, were not fulfilled. Instead, parties deployed new Web instruments in the very same manner as they had previously made use of older formats in cyber campaigning. The major observations in the 2009 elections can thus be summarised in four conclusions:

1 German e-campaigning is marked by a *national standardisation process* as regards the six political organisations that are represented in the federal parliament. As the country's most influential political organisations, these parties are the early adopters of online political communication. They implement digital innovations first and integrate them readily into the overall campaign strategy. With the exception of the hyperlink structure, the functional and formal differences between these parties are rather narrow or nonexistent. This standardisation process can be explained by four factors: parties' mutual co-orientation on the national level; the close public scrutiny and the weight of expectations that puts them all under considerable pressure to perform equally well on the Internet; their privileged position, with enormous financial and human resources and established infrastructures that enable similar degrees of campaign professionalism; and the comparably large number of supporters that actually make use of these Web offerings.
2 The standardisation in German e-campaigning has led to a *democratisation of the parliamentary competition.* That is, minor parties in the Bundestag (CSU, FDP, Greens and the Left) compete with the major people's parties (CDU and SPD) on equal grounds in cyberspace. Their websites are as

Table 7.3 User-to-document interactivity: Germany 2009

	CDU	*CSU*	*SPD*	*FDP*	*Greens*	*Left*	$\sum$	*%*
Downward flows (Packaged)	132	57	150	454	156	278	*1,227*	*17.4*
Upward flows (Content on Demand)	7	5	6	6	6	6	*36*	*0.5*
Lateral flows (Content on Demand)	2,435	1,240	852	162	232	38	*4,959*	*70.2*
Asynchronous (Content Exchange)	21	15	18	19	16	18	*107*	*1.5*
Synchronous (Co-Created Content)	267	12	229	103	12	108	*731*	*10.4*
Number of features	2,862	1,329	1,255	744	422	448	*7,060*	
%	40.5	18.8	17.8	10.5	6.0	6.3		

Source: the figures were provided by Darren Lilleker

sophisticated and comprehensive as the home pages of the leading political forces. In this way, they are able to compensate for their smaller size and for the lower media attention that they usually receive in offline campaign coverage (cf. Jandura 2008). Consequently, the true digital divide in German e-campaigning does not run between major and minor organisations in general, but rather between parliamentary and non-parliamentary parties. Only the Pirate Party proved to be an exception in the 2009 national elections, since they were the only fringe group that closed the gap in Web professionalism and even surpassed the leading parliamentary organisations in the use of interactive campaign features, specifically in Web 2.0 (cf. Schweitzer 2010b).

3 German e-campaigning is *inspired by international role-models* and successful examples in online political communication. Web 2.0 features were available long before the 2009 national elections, yet German parties started to incorporate these elements on the national level only after the Obama campaign had shown how to effectively deploy them. German parties thus play safe in cyberspace: new developments in online political communication are adopted in major elections when their practical use and their electoral gratifications have been tested and proven in other countries. Largely, the United States is the primary benchmark here. The sheer multitude and frequency of gubernatorial, congressional and presidential elections, as well as the personalised voting system, the advanced industry of political consultants and high Internet penetration rates, are known to foster digital campaign innovations (cf. Filzmaier and Plasser 2001: 157–8; Gibson 2004: 103). These spread from the US to other countries with similar social and cultural backgrounds (cf. Howard 2006: 203; Schneider and Foot 2006: 23; Ward 2008: 4). This diffusion process is enhanced by both the few legal regulations that surround the use of e-campaigning in different states and the global compatibility of ICT basics. The 'Americanisation' of political communication, a concept which has long been refuted by European scholars in terms of offline campaigning (cf. e.g. Baines *et al.* 2001; Negrine and Papathanassopoulos 1996; Pfetsch 2001), might thus still be valid on the Internet.

4 Even though Web 2.0 platforms (like YouTube, Twitter, or social networking sites) were largely embraced by all parliamentary parties in the 2009 elections, *past trends in German e-campaigning were not abandoned.* Rather, typical patterns continued and affected even the way in which new digital features were applied in the election. Specifically, top-down information delivery and resource generation remained the most important functions on parties' websites, while interactive elements were scarcely used or offered with restrictions (i.e. prior registration or secure login) so as to maintain control. The mere presence of these features is therefore no guarantee for a change in the basic style of communication with which parties address voters. Their primary goals, i.e. cost-effective electioneering, publicity, voter persuasion and the maintenance of political power, still affect

their overall approach in e-campaigning. This defies technological determinist assumptions that postulated a revolution in public discourse due to the specific quality of digital inventions (cf. e.g. Rash 1997; Rheingold 1995; Morris 1999; Trippi 2004; Weinberger 2007). Instead, the 'tried-and-true real world campaign techniques' (Resnick 1998: 64) are transferred to the Internet and lead there to a normalisation of cyberspace that is rooted in the social shaping of technology (cf. Williams 1997). In Germany, the channel of campaigning has thus changed, but not the nature of parties' electoral communication.

8 The UK 2010

Interacting within echo chambers

The parliamentary systems in Germany and the UK have many similarities, yet one difference is highly significant as it impacts upon campaign strategy and conduct: the electoral system. The UK uses a simple first-past-the-post single member system, where members of the national parliament are elected to represent constituencies, and the party with the largest number of members is allowed to form the government. This system is designed to deliver a majority for one party or another to encourage the likelihood of strong government, but this results in greater inequality between parties contesting UK elections, as fewer enjoy representation in the House of Commons, the UK lower chamber. Two parties, Labour and the Conservatives, are seen as the main contenders for government (gaining 356 and 198 seats respectively at the 2005 General Election). A third party, the Liberal Democrats, (with sixty-two seats at the previous election) plays a minor role. The other parties represented are either all regionally based parties representing constituencies in Scotland, Wales and Northern Ireland, or, as with Respect[1], contested only a limited number of seats in 2005. No other parties which stand across the nation have seats in parliament. This means in practice that there is a two-and-a-half party system, though the media and public focus tends to be on Labour and the Conservatives, and their leaders Gordon Brown and David Cameron. This orthodoxy was shattered in 2010.

While the UK is essentially a two-and-a-half party system, there is a range of other parties that can have an impact on election outcomes. In Northern Ireland, Scotland and Wales, there are parties who stand only in these countries that consistently win parliamentary seats.[2] Equally, alongside a range of single issue or regional parties there are three emergent contenders who have representation at the local council level as well as within the European Parliament who are vying for parliamentary representation. Although the voting system tends to prohibit advances from parties with lower resources, the Green Party, UK Independence Party (UKIP), which campaigns for independence from the European Union, and British National Party (BNP), a party with a neo-fascist history which campaigns for greater rights for indigenous peoples, were all in a position to have an impact. Indeed, for the first time in a UK parliamentary election there was the possibility of any or all of these three parties gaining representation. Even if they did not, their impact would certainly be in capturing votes that could swing the result in some constituencies. Given the increased talk of a hung parliament in the final weeks of the campaign, with no party having overall control, many of these parties, along with the Liberal Democrats, saw this as empowering.

In addition to the expectations of these three minor parties, the election context was also beset by the economy and a long-running MPs' expenses scandal. The immediate run-up to and contest proper were overshadowed by worldwide jitters caused by serious concerns about the Greek economy. As well as losses to share prices worldwide, the crisis focused attention on what the next UK government would have to do to address the growing budget deficit of £163 billion in 2009. Indeed, concern that the UK's economic situation could become worse than that in Greece turned the spotlight during the campaign onto the parties' policies for cutting the deficit. The slower-burn issue was that of MPs' expenses. In May 2009 The *Daily Telegraph* published the first of a series of stories about MPs' expenses. The more ridiculous and faintly pantomime expense claims included cleaning a moat and buying a floating duck island. The more insidious claims suggested avoiding paying capital gains tax on properties, in part funded by the taxpayer, and potentially fraudulent claims for mortgages already paid off. Whilst not all of the 146 MPs stepping down were doing so because of their expenses, many were. This, combined with the fact that Labour lost just under 100 seats, meant that the 'churn' of MPs in 2010 was significantly greater than in recent elections.

The run-up to the 2010 General Election was very different, with some commentators speculating that this could be the first Internet election (Bernstein 2009; Pullin 2010). Such projections were consistent with a belief in the rise of postmodern campaigning (Norris 2000), whereby traditional mass communication channels were being replaced by direct communication channels. In fact, on the face of it, television would appear to have dominated the campaign. After some fifty years of discussion, the UK finally got its first live televised leaders' debate. Three ninety-minute debates between the leaders of the three main parties, Gordon Brown (Labour), David Cameron (Conservative) and Nick Clegg (Liberal Democrat), gained good ratings and much interest. The impact of the first debate was fairly immediate. Nick Clegg, possibly through the novelty factor of not being that well known, was widely considered to have 'won'. As a result, his party's poll ratings increased by 10 per cent. From then on, the 2010 UK election was truly treated as a three-party race. This then meant that one of the big issues of the campaign was what each party leader would do in the event of a hung parliament. Then, just as the effect of the television debates was waning, the headlines were again dominated by this medium. A microphone attached to the then Prime Minister Gordon Brown picked up a private conversation with aides during which he called a voter he had just met 'some bigoted woman'. Television, thus, appeared to be the primary communication channel.

Labour won a landslide in 1997 and has dominated parliament ever since, however it was widely predicted that Labour would lose in 2010 despite the fact that the Conservatives needed a swing of 6.9 per cent or greater in order to win a majority. In the end, predictions were correct. The Conservatives won the most seats with 307 seats, which was 19 short of the magic number of 326 required to govern alone; Labour did not lose as many seats as was predicted, finishing with 258. The gains that the Conservatives made, and Labour suffered, were primarily in England, and there were few changes in Scotland and Wales. Despite the surge in support linked to the first televised debate, and increasing their overall vote by a percentage point to 23 per cent, the Liberal Democrats only won 57 seats, a loss of 5. The Green Party won their first ever seat, and nationally gained 1 per cent of the vote; UKIP enjoyed a higher share of vote with 3.1 per cent, but this was spread nationally and won them no representation; the same was the case with the BNP, with 1.9 per cent of the overall share. The only other parties and independents, amounting to twenty-eight seats, were elected within Northern Ireland, Scotland and Wales. The result meant that a five-day period of negotiation took place prior to the Conservatives and Liberal Democrats forming the first formal coalition government in the UK for over 70 years. Three-party politics now exists, but within a two-party system.

The 2010 UK general election campaign had the potential to be a game changer in a number of ways. It was seen to be likely to be the closest contest since 1992, with polls showing very different results and public support appearing unpredictable and event driven. For the first time in decades there was a real likelihood of the election delivering a hung parliament, so a coalition government was highly possible. The contest was also one that had been on the media and parties' agenda for two years. Since the change of leadership of Labour, the governing party, from Tony Blair to Gordon Brown, there had been speculation about an election. Brown's poor standing in the opinion polls was an ongoing narrative as the election drew nearer. Turnout has been a concern in recent years, with a sharp drop to 71.4 per cent in 1997, down from 77.7 per cent in 1992, and this fell even more sharply to 59.4 per cent in 2001. A slightly less foregone conclusion may account for the increase to 61.4 per cent in 2005, but despite the unpredictability, 2010 did not see turnout rise to 1992 or 1997 levels; instead, the increase was a modest 4 per cent, to 65.1 per cent. Yet despite these fairly modest levels there were reports that in some cities, polling stations could not cope, with some angry electors unable to vote when the polling booths shut down at 10 p.m. These figures, however, mask the reality of constituency-based contests, that in the constituencies where the margin between parties has been narrowing, there is a greater intensity of campaigning and so higher turnout; the reverse is the case in safe seats. Turnout ranged from 53 per cent to 73 per cent in 2010 across constituencies, mirroring patterns in previous contests.

It was against this context that we need to view the role the Internet might play. Interest in the role of the Internet during elections emerged at the 1997 contest (Gibson and Ward 1998), which even saw a voting advice application used. Yet, through that and the subsequent two elections there has been limited progress in the party use of the Internet (Coleman 2001; Jackson 2007). However, there was a sense, probably because of the Obama effect, that the 2010 campaign could be different. The role of the Internet during by-elections, often involving non-elite actors, the uptake of social networking sites by UK society and tools such as Twitter, all suggested in 2010 that the Internet might come of age as a discrete campaigning tool. Parties themselves have shown less enthusiasm; while a variety of tools have been used for some time, there has been less innovation in terms of political communication (Jackson and Lilleker 2009a; Lilleker *et al.* 2010). Consultation exercises such as Labour's *Big Conversation* and the Conservatives' *Stand Up, Speak Out* were used to gather perspectives and amalgamate them into policy documents. These were similar to Royal's *Notebooks of Hope*, though in the former cases there was less clear link to party manifestos or policy proposals. The initial hype surrounding the use of social networking subsided, and in the weeks prior to the election it was argued that this would not be a game changer. Participants from the parties and media at a symposium in London in March (City University 2010) played down the importance of all forms of Internet campaigning, and this was reinforced following the first televised leader debates when it was television that was viewed as having the major impact. Conservative blogger Iain Dale, writing in *The Daily Telegraph* (Dale 2010), summed up opinion: email may have a function in mobilising supporters and the Internet provided information for those who wished to search for it, and there were the occasional rashes of online rebuttal and user-generated posters and videos that found an audience; but on the whole the Internet was deemed useless as a campaigning tool. Yet still all the parties had websites and they fulfilled a key role in the campaign; unsurprisingly, given that 76.4 per cent of the population of the UK are online and 25.6 per cent had broadband access. In fact, our data suggests that there was an online strategy, and the Internet was more embedded within campaigns than was previously the case. Though innovations were sporadic and focused explicitly on meeting campaigning objectives, the Internet played more of a role in the parties' strategies than in 2005 (Stanyer 2005; Jackson 2006b) and was closer to the heart of the campaigns of the major parties than previously had been the case.

Mapping the sites

The UK party websites all follow a general pattern of design. The home page acts as a central hub which presents the latest campaign video as the central object, surrounded by links as drop-down menus or sidebar click-thrus to various parts of the site. Apart from UKIP, which clearly put fewer resources into design elements, all the sites were colour branded, with logos across all the pages. The key function for the sites, as derived from the design, was to inform visitors within a partisan, non-mediated environment. Manifestos were the prominent feature, with all parties having online versions and offering the full document for download. Conservatives and Liberal Democrats also had policy-specific sections, with the former also making these available in podcasts. News was also an important feature, with rolling party news sections on most front pages and all sites offering a large archive of news items and press releases. Typically, there were also areas where campaign material could be downloaded, and the facility to join the party, donate to the campaign and sign up by email. These aspects of the sites' topography bear little difference in terms of functionality to those of the previous three elections; information is delivered in more sophisticated ways in 2010 with embedded videos common across the sites, but it does not represent a departure from traditions of online political communication.

The above summation is true of the entirety of the sites of UKIP and the Green Party. The latter offered some Web 2.0 aspects with links to their social networking sites, and the party Twitter feed scrolled on the lower right-hand side of the home page; UKIP remained firmly in a Web 1.0 paradigm. Labour's site offered many more opportunities to contribute, including the 'change we see' initiative, which invited followers on Twitter to upload comments and photographs showing local achievements resulting from Labour's time in office; this fed onto the site's front page. The campaign area of the site shared a variety of local stories, many appearing to be user-generated so giving an impression of co-creation. The large Membersnet area acted as a community for supporters and was dominated by Constituency Labour Party (CLP) groups, many of whom offered links to weblogs or campaign event pages. This was not easily searchable, however, and did not really encourage access via the main site, rather giving the impression that this was for members only who accessed via their CLP. There were pages which targeted socialist societies and Trade Unions, and pages devoted to Women and Faith Groups, the latter with a discrete newsletter and archive. However, on the whole, the site lacked innovation and seemed to be solely about pushing the party message as opposed to building a community online.

The Liberal Democrat site diverges slightly; entry is via a splash screen promoting leader Nick Clegg and prioritises opportunities to donate and sign up for the e-newsletter. Information on party and policy, including the constitution dominates, however their site also contained a live participatory LibDem Act Network. This section focused on building communities; there were 259 campaign-related events organised by 308 campaign groups, and any network member could create a new group or event, or contribute within a collaborate workspace. This Web 2.0 campaigning approach was also mirrored in the Conservative site, but with greater emphasis placed on providing a Web 2.0 dynamic. The highly modern appearance of the home page included the party Twitter feed, a Tag Cloud, feed from the party Blue Blog to which anyone could comment, and promoted their Facebook page and number of supporters (70,563). The site also encouraged supportive visitors to join their bespoke social network MyConservatives (MyCons), which was a direct copy of the Obama MyBO feature. The site also had a Wall of citizen endorsers, the WebCameron videolog, videos from the Cameron Direct national tour where he answered questions from local people and a live campaign stream featuring speeches. While the Conservative site was highly innovative, the philosophy of Web 2.0 was most prevalent on the site of the BNP. While highly complex, with navigation made difficult by the number of layers, it also offered the greatest opportunities for participation. Every page was in a weblog format, offered commenting and sharing facilities, and on each page a sidebar promoted the party network, which is a central element to the site, holding avatars of active members. While extremely heavy on propaganda and ideologically loaded information, the site offered more of a communal voice, with 38,851 items (97 per cent of the total site) being co-created.

Identifying online identities

Overall, information was prioritised, but this is to be expected within an election. It was the presentational differences and abilities to participate that offered significantly divergent perceptions of strategy. Identity, however, was far more similar but reflective of the design elements. In order to gain a sound overview of the language used across the sites, consistent with the data collected for previous chapters, we selected the home page, the policy statement on the economy and the page that offered an overview of the party's history, in the case of the Liberal Democrats, or in the other cases the page that offered a positioning statement. UKIP presented a unified, single voice, which referred to 'us' as a nation as a way of positioning the party as in touch with the concerns of voters. Key to presenting policy was the construction of an 'other': it was 'THEM' who give away UK sovereignty to the European Union. Thus, they presented themselves as an in-touch defender of the nation through a top-down, often negative, persuasive message. This style was mirrored by the Green Party despite their left of centre ideology. Discourse was highly personalised around key party figures, and they equally constructed a pseudo-environmentalist other when talking of their competitors; this linked to their campaign slogan of 'the real alternative'. Though the us versus them discourse did not prevail on the Liberal Democrat site, top-down dialogue dominated and the use of we related to the party as opposed to a more inclusive construct. Largely, this is consistent with the Liberal Democrat approach to the use of Web 2.0 (Lilleker *et al.* 2010). Again, persuasive messages linked to the campaign theme of 'new politics', which presented the party as representing 'real change' or 'change that works for you'. It was only within the bracketed-off networks that more diversity of opinion could be found, but such voices were eschewed from the main site areas.

Labour and the Conservatives offered a more parasocial style of discourse, aided by the inclusion on the party home pages of feeds from Twitter, weblogs and Facebook. Labour tended towards a persuasive tone, consistent with them having to defend their record of eighteen years in government. The Conservatives experimented with presenting a more community-based campaign experience. The Wall, a mirror of the endorsements found within Nicolas Sarkozy TV, had a wide cross-section of UK society stating why they were voting Conservative. This adhered to the model of polyphonic communication, yet was clearly persuasive, and constructed and packaged with consumption in mind. Other areas which allowed participation went beyond the parasocial to give a feel of inclusivity and accessibility. However, the majority of the site, in particular the videos on WebCameron and the Cameron Direct mini-sites, as well as the live stream, showed dialogue that had taken place and had been packaged for visitors' consumption as opposed to real-time conversation. Thus, the site gave a mixed experience of communication packaged for persuasive purposes, and free conversation with light touch moderation.

The most complex series of impressions were presented on the BNP site where the discourse was somewhat schizophrenic: while to an extent much of the party created text spoke as the organisation, 'we believe', 'we know', the majority of the site offered multiple voices speaking in chorus, open yet highly orchestrated. The party's nationalistic discourse is presented as one single narrative with no divergent views offered, however the narrative has multiple authors. The site contained 332,231 individual contributions, though this should not be read as the number of individual contributors, and evidence suggests that there were no more than 1,500 active members of the site; as estimated from the number of avatars appearing within posts across the community. Thus, the site, despite its overt inclusivity and adherence to Web 2.0, appears to be co-produced by a tight, ideologically coherent group of activists who have little divergence of opinion on the core premises of BNP policy. Thus, while there is real-time conversation presented, it is no more a hub of debate than any of the other party sites; as is consistent with party websites, it is a place to reinforce beliefs in the party dogma. Equally interesting is that, unlike candidate websites in France and the US, but as was the case with German parties, there is little difference that can be traced to the ideological stance of the parties. The three major parties who straddle the spectrum of centrism offer similar styles of discourse, with the most right wing, the Conservatives, being the most polyphonic. The two most monologic sites are the left libertarian Greens and the right wing UKIP; the most polyphonic, the far right BNP. This suggests that in these parliamentary democracies, discourse online does not reflect ideology to the same extent as is the case where it is an individual, with a personalised ethos, presenting themselves to their audience.

Reiterating observations relating to the site maps and the discourse present, Table 8.1 shows that informational elements relating to policy are common features across all the sites, as are the ability to donate, join and sign up using email. There is more divergence across a range of features, but becoming *de rigueur* for parties is the inclusion of some elements that permit users to upload comments and content, share and update information (updating including responding to information and adding anecdotal detail), and allowing posting directly to the site. These elements are common across all sites except that of UKIP. In contrast, however, opportunities to debate with the leaders are lacking on the whole and while they appear to be allowed by five out of six parties, only BNP Leader Nick Griffin, and Caroline Lucas, leader of the Green Party, actually can be seen responding to material posted. Thus, while this is potentiated, it is not a feature used that frequently; even when users do post comments that ask for a response. The leaders are more likely to spend their time offline campaigning rather than online. Thus, the websites tend to focus on meeting key campaigning functions, and it is to these our analysis now turns.

Table 8.1 Features present across the sites: UK 2010

Categories	*Lab*	*Cons*	*LDems*	*Green*	*UKIP*	*BNP*
Downward flows						
Documents	1	7	114	5	23	2
Policies summed	7	5	6	6	20	11
Issues examined	yes	yes	yes	yes	yes	yes
Number of issues discussed	14	28	10	16	38	16
Statement of values/ideology	yes	yes	yes	yes	yes	yes
Newsletters	yes	yes	yes	yes	yes	yes
Number of newsletters archived	0	0	9	0	0	13
Media releases	yes	yes	yes	yes	yes	no
Number of releases	480	1,1330	2,665	2,636	711	0
Candidate profile	yes	yes	yes	yes	yes	yes
Election information	yes	yes	yes	yes	no	no
Event calendar	yes	no	no	no	no	no
Frequently asked questions	no	no	no	no	no	no
Number of FAQs	0	0	0	0	0	0
Negative campaigning	yes	yes	yes	yes	yes	yes
Overall per cent of negativity	5	20	15	30	45	50
Videos	yes	yes	yes	yes	yes	yes
Number of videos	16	676	126	129	77	286
Targeted pages	4	3	5	2	0	13
Number of groups targeted	2	3	5	2	0	4
Targeted download form	no	no	no	no	no	no
Targeted online enquiry form	no	no	no	no	no	no
Targeted online transaction	no	no	no	no	no	no
Upward flows						
Volunteering possible	yes	yes	yes	yes	yes	yes
	yes	yes	no	no	yes	yes

Donations possible	no	yes	yes	yes	yes	yes
	yes	yes	yes	yes	yes	yes
Merchandise for sale	yes	yes	no	no	yes	no
Cookies	yes	yes	no	no	no	no
Lateral/horizontal information flows						
Number of partisan links	572	6	966	181	7	9
Number of reference links	0	25	0	1	2	1
Number of internal links	50	69	54	8	28	92
Interactive information flows: Asynchronous						
Download logos/posters (Number)	5	50	12	1	4	10
Site search	yes	yes	yes	yes	yes	yes
Enmeshing	yes	yes	yes	yes	yes	yes
Navigation aids	yes	yes	yes	yes	yes	yes
Online games/gimmicks	no	no	no	no	no	no
Email contact	yes	yes	yes	yes	yes	yes
Email feedback	no	no	yes	no	no	no
Online feedback form	yes	no	yes	no	no	no
Join email list	yes	yes	yes	yes	yes	yes
Questionnaires	no	no	no	no	no	no
Visitor-initiated questionnaires	no	no	no	no	no	no
Polls	no	no	no	no	no	yes
Visitor-initiated polls	no	no	no	no	no	yes
Petitions	yes	no	no	no	no	no
Visitor-initiated petitions	no	no	no	no	no	no
Join online campaign	yes	yes	yes	yes	yes	yes
Subscribe to e-newsletter	yes	yes	yes	yes	yes	yes
Membership form to download	yes	yes	yes	no	no	yes
Online membership enquiry form	yes	yes	yes	yes	yes	no
Online membership transaction	yes	yes	yes	yes	yes	no

continued

Table 8.1 continued

Categories	*Lab*	*Cons*	*LDems*	*Green*	*UKIP*	*BNP*
Bulletin board	no	no	yes	no	no	no
Blog tools	no	yes	no	no	no	yes
Ability to share vids/pics (embed code)	5	50	126	129	0	295
Podcasts	yes	yes	yes	no	no	no
Social networking links	yes	yes	yes	yes	no	yes
Twitter	yes	yes	yes	yes	no	no
RSS	yes	yes	yes	yes	yes	yes
Interactive information flows: Synchronous						
Ability to upload content/comments	yes	yes	yes	yes	no	yes
Number of opportunities to upload content/comments	7	1,372	2,658	132	0	5,342
Ability of visitors to share information	yes	yes	yes	yes	no	yes
Number of opportunities to share information	8	2,785	308	158	0	18,345
Ability of visitors to update information	yes	yes	yes	yes	no	yes
Number of opportunities to update information	1	347	308	2	0	4,480
Public conversations allowed via comments or wall posting	yes	yes	yes	yes	no	yes
Number of opportunities for public conversations	551	1,372	2,664	132	0	5,342
Forum	yes	yes	yes	no	no	yes
Chat room	yes	no	yes	no	no	yes
Online debate	yes	yes	yes	yes	no	yes
Number of opportunities to debate with leaders	1	1,026	2,664	1	0	5,342

Functions of the party websites

Information provision

As stated, information provision was the key function for all websites. The Labour manifesto was the first thing offered to visitors, with policies broken down into seven key pledges supported by fourteen bespoke issue pages. News was also prominent, with 480 unique items across 48 pages. The Conservative priority was also getting manifesto messages out, and so it was also offered in a range of electronic formats including bitesize podcasts for download. The Liberal Democrats mirrored the information-heavy approach, offering a large news archive and fifty-four discrete policy documents. The Green Party and UKIP sites were much more basic, mostly providing information and a news and media archive, which together constituted around 80 per cent and 100 per cent respectively of publicly viewable material. The BNP similarly offered vast amounts of information, though of the 9,432 informational items, only 419 items, all documents made available to read or download, offered no opportunities to comment. The BNP's news section and even the candidate profiles were all presented in a weblog format allowing comments, providing a co-produced feel reminiscent of the Obama site.

Campaigning

Campaigning messages equally predominated, but with a slightly different emphasis. Labour foregrounded volunteering, donating and joining on each page, as well as offering links to party campaigns that visitors could sign up to within their Membersnet area. The Conservative site had a donate function on each page, and led with messages persuading voters to elect the party and avoid the hung parliament; this included numerous fear appeals about the election outcome. The Liberal Democrat, Green and UKIP sites focused on persuading in a very traditional campaigning style. Persuasive campaigning is also emphasised across the BNP site, however it also evidenced a broad group of active campaigners at work, creating a greater sense of energy and community around their ideas. This was mirrored to an extent on the Conservative's Blue Blog and MyCons as well as LibDem Act, though it was not explicit across the site in the same way as for the BNP.

Negative campaigning

Negativity was also a clear feature of the campaigning of all the parties, though again there were divergences in strategy linked to the positions and stance of the parties. As the incumbent government, the Labour message was almost wholly promotional, yet two policy sites detailed 'The Conservative Risk' and 'The Liberal Democrat Risk', which compared Labour to their main opponents and were a very small percentage of the site (approximately 5 per cent). Some of the comments within the Membersnet and weblogs linked to by the party were more attacking of the Conservatives. The Conservative site offered a more mixed message, the campaign area being largely devoted to promoting Conservative policy but also stopping, for example, 'Gordon Brown's Death Tax'; referencing proposed reforms to inheritance tax. Videos also offer a negative tone at times, though messages were largely comparative as opposed to outright attacks, giving the site a positive tone overall. A similar tone was found on the Liberal Democrat site, and the Obama style of having an 'US' and creating a 'THEM' or 'OTHER', which is unnamed but is clearly the main competitor, overrides overt attacks (Lilleker and Scullion 2009). The Greens predominantly offered a similar comparative tone, but there are also significantly more named attacks on the record of the major three parties and their similarity on key issues, reinforcing the Greens' 'real alternative message'. UKIP launched most attacks against the EU generally, but the main UK parties also feature in their messages. There is also greater personalisation of the attacks; the two figures that receive most attacks are Brown as Prime Minister, but more prominent is House of Commons Speaker John Bercow, due to the fact that the former UKIP leader Nigel Farage was in the middle of a high-profile campaign to unseat Bercow in the seat of Buckingham. Given that the Speaker is usually unopposed by the main parties, this gave UKIP a platform for greater media coverage, though this did not translate into votes for Farage. The BNP made numerous attacks on the other parties and provided a coproduced section entitled 'Liars, Buggers and Thieves', which exposed spurious 'criminal' activities of various elected representatives of the three major parties. The site offered a highly negative tone against the notions of a multicultural society and tolerance of homosexuality, both of which included user-generated material which presented evidence, often highly anecdotal and hard to either refute or substantiate, to support the party's stance on both issues.

Resource generation

The situation was little different from 2005 (Jackson 2006b), with the sites of Labour, the Greens, the BNP and the Liberal Democrats all inviting donations from supporters, and seeking volunteers for the campaign and the promotion of the party via social networks. UKIP have no outward links to social networks so encouraged no sharing; they also did not explicitly seek volunteers, but the party did, however, invite donations via their site. The Conservative site offered a range of opportunities to donate and volunteer, and the MyCons network was geared solely to soliciting volunteering and donations. Additionally, the site included a social action page, which advertised local activities across constituencies working with the deprived as well as working abroad, including community projects in Srebrenica. Labour, Conservatives, Liberal Democrats and Greens also heavily promoted themselves on social networks as a way of drawing more online users to their sites, as well as gaining endorsements from online users across their social media presences. All parties also used email lists to solicit donations, as well as mobilising activists, and Labour and the Conservatives promoted iPhone applications, which aided the party to co-ordinate activism and linked their supporters and activists into a network.

Networking

The Conservatives, Liberal Democrats and BNP all created their own networks within their sites. This enabled them to have a loyal audience to communicate with, as well as encouraging the creation of a community around the party. The features were similar to many social networks and mirrored MyBO, if less user friendly. Labour's Membersnet offered a similar function but had the appearance of being a hub for members, built as it was onto the CLP intranet interface. Externally, Facebook emerged as a key networking tool used by Labour to create campaign-specific groups as well as having their own fan page (31,468 members). The Conservatives did similarly and gained 70,732 fans; the Liberal Democrats eventually boasted a 70,012 strong fan page, gaining 200 per cent more members following the first TV debate (Kimberley 2010). The Green Party was the first party to use Facebook to create events that promoted their campaigns and used it throughout the 2006–10 period, including the 2009 European Parliamentary election, yet they only gained 7,858 fans. UKIP were the losers on Facebook (21 fans), but their page was not promoted and, unlike the other parties, their posters were only for downloading, not sharing, across the Internet. UKIP's focus appeared to be on offline campaigning. The BNP did not promote their page as much, but still gained 19,394 fans; this was despite the fact that Facebook user groups campaigning against the BNP mobilised over 800,000 people across more than 20 groups. The BNP were perhaps most effective in creating a network outside of mainstream social networks, and embedded this within their site rather than having external links to Facebook. Their approach suggests a desire to have a private forum in public, one where people have to purposely go to engage as opposed to ones that are politically broad churches and where more liberal movements have been successful in mobilising activists.

Promoting participation

Apart from UKIP, all parties promoted participation beyond the simple act of voting, which was actually less explicit and more of an implicit aspect of their campaigning function. Every aspect of the BNP site offered a form of participation, be it promoting pages via sharing facilities, commenting or being more politically active within the site or the party. However, participation in the BNP campaign seemed to be more focused on the online modes of content generation than offline activism; to volunteer required training for which visitors had to sign up. The Liberal Democrats sought volunteers, as did the Green Party; the former created LibDem Act, an activism hub which was promoted across the site, as were their social networks presences. This campaign-oriented participation was mirrored on the Labour and Conservative sites, but in more sophisticated ways.

The Labour Doorstep campaign, which had a Twitter hashtag (#labourdoorstep) and fed directly to the main site, Membersnet campaign mini-sites, iPhone application interfaces and Facebook pages, were Labour's key modes for encouraging participation. These spoke largely to those who wished to publicly volunteer and contribute positively to the campaign either on the doorsteps or by uploading supportive content. The Membersnet, which anyone could join, did allow anyone to create a blog (548 were created) and comment on others; the party elite, however, did not take part and it functioned as a members community with light touch control. The Conservatives offered two participatory access points from the front page of the website. The Blue Blog, launched 26 September 2008, contained an average of fifty-four entries per month and these gained up to 271 comments (average 32), so immediately offering 1,026 points of access into a party website based public sphere to which key party figures regularly contributed. The second access point was myconservatives.com, a direct copy of Obama's social network MyBO. This contained six campaign-oriented blog posts which allowed comments, 330 local campaigns, which were mostly geared towards electing a candidate within a local constituency, and ten national campaigns. Each campaign provided a Wall space for members to comment. Activity on MyCons was low, however, with most Walls clean of posts and the more popular attracting an average of twelve to twenty contributions. Campaigns seemed to lack the proactive communication strategy that prevailed within MyBO and so, while innovative, MyCons seemed under-utilised and more of a cobweb than a vibrant hub for resource generation.

A 2.0 election

All the sites performed a range of campaigning features, some of which we have already noted feature Web 2.0 elements, though this does not necessarily suggest an adherence to the big ideas of Web 2.0. While UKIP eschewed all forms of participation, the others did not. This analysis will assess the parties' performance as compared to the use of Web 2.0 tools across the online user community.

The capacity for individual production and user-generated content

The Labour site offered the least opportunities for coproduction of site elements. Apart from the Twitter feeds to the home page, only the Membersnet area was co-created, but here there were multiple opportunities to upload material and create content. The Green Party site offered limited participatory opportunities, but allowed comments on all videos posted to YouTube, and also developed conversations with fans on Facebook, with leader Caroline Lucas an active participant. The LibDem Act area also encouraged participation and the supporting of a range of political campaigns, and offered real inclusivity. All 126 videos and 2,224 photographs uploaded allowed site members to comment direct to the site; the average comments per item was twenty-six. The Conservatives' Blue Blog and MyCons were explicitly about the creation of content, and while the original posts were largely authored by doyens of the party, both adhered to a 'they will come and build it' philosophy. Visitors could also create events and invite other members with links through to social networking sites and the iPhone applications. The BNP offered 4,680 news items in weblog format and overall, the average comments per item was sixty-eight, with some receiving over 200 individual comments; overall, the news area advertised 332,231 comments by 85,046 readers. The reply function on each post facilitated conversations, as do similar functions on the 286 videos within BNPtv, and these took place with a number of party candidates participating. In fact, all pages permitted some form of co-creation, be they comments, sharing or uploading material. However, generally, the parties sought to either minimise or control the level of coproduction of content, which is consistent with Jackson and Lilleker's (2009) 'peace time' findings.

Harnessing the power of the crowd

The volunteer resource generation function clearly drew lessons from Obama's harnessing of the crowd online. With Twitter tsar Kerry McCarthy leading by example, Labour's #labourdoorstep could be contributed to by anyone, and this was fed live to the Labour Doorstep page designed to mobilise supporters. Visitors to the site were also encouraged to sign up as fans of Facebook, and pictures of their friends appeared beneath the sign-up button to act as a further call to action. 'Why I am Labour' and 'Change we see' encouraged visitors to offer supportive comments, and these were fed into the site in various places including the home page. Labour also used a 'Word of Mouth' splash screen on Election Day, where visitors could enter their username and password for Twitter and Facebook and post the message 'I'm voting Labour'. The Conservative Party harnessed the power of the crowd to an extent in terms of using them to promote the party on the Wall, myriad opportunities to share across the Internet and download logos for personal sites; while the emphasis within the MyCons social network was on mobilising supporters and also encouraged sharing of pages. The Liberal Democrats promoted sharing within the Act network only, but there were no opportunities elsewhere on the main site, only from their Facebook page. Limited opportunities were offered by the Green Party, with a key tool being Facebook, which they used to promote campaign events and create groups that would act as supportive hubs for their candidates. The Greens also allowed visitors to personalise a video by name and two key policy areas, and send it to friends or share on their Facebook profiles in order to gain promotion from supporters. The BNP had the most active social network and encouraged their supporters to get involved within their site to maximise their reach. The site contained 295 issue-specific groups, and the twenty largest and most active were listed on the main group page and boasted between 492 and 1,405 members; the latter being the membership of the largest group, which campaigns on the premise that 'Immigrants, not the British, must adapt'. The network advertised the 140 most recently active members, so total membership is impossible to tell.

However, it worked on the same basic premise as Facebook in terms of having friends and sharing material, but as with MyBO and MyCons was more related to joining in campaign groups. Alongside this network, and the myriad opportunities to participate, the BNP also encouraged submissions to BNPtv that furthered the party's campaigns, which largely elicited material containing racist and homophobic overtones.

Access to data on an epic scale

Given the information-heavy focus, access to data was a key function of the sites. However, the majority of information was centred on the one contest rather than offering any historical material, the Liberal Democrats being unusual in this respect. The Labour and Green Party sites most evidenced this strategy, being lean and focused on the Manifesto. The Conservatives similarly focused on campaign-focused content and offered various versions of the manifesto, including for older people, the armed forces and public sector workers, and these could be downloaded in thirty-three issue-focused podcasts. Alongside the manifesto, policy statements and other campaign materials, the BNP offered a range of materials, all with a political bias and particularly reinforcing their anti-immigration agenda. Across all the sites, including UKIP, news archives represented a key data source, though most would only go back for a maximum of two years.

An architecture of participation

Election-related architectures of participation varied but overall were partially in place across the Internet, and this was mirrored on the party sites. Labour and the Liberal Democrats created, respectively, the Membersnet and LibDem Act areas which facilitated supporter networking within their sites. Both parties, like the Greens, also offered participatory potential on Facebook. The Conservative presences on social networks such as Facebook, Twitter, YouTube, the live feed, which allowed comments during debates, their blog site and MyCons were all geared towards encouraging participation, and presented a far more participatory experience for visitors. The BNP site was, largely, one single architecture of participation in which a community of right-wing activists shared opinions and ideas, many of which may well be deemed inappropriate and possibly illegal within a society that outlaws discrimination. The community, though open to be read by any member of the public, seems to have been used as a haven for marginalised voices.

The network effect

As with the networking campaign function, using the network was a sporadic activity. The Greens' use of Facebook and a number of sharing options seemed the most common strategy, their personalised video facility being their only innovation. Labour mainly encouraged promotional opportunities, and the contribution of positive comments via Twitter provided one co-created element on the home page. The creation of bespoke networks by the Conservatives, Liberal Democrats and BNP did see innovations in this area, though the BNP site was the only one that was not created for the 2010 election and had adopted this format for two years. These areas encouraged supporters to interact within the site and build relationships with one another and, importantly, with the party, and aided the party in recruitment online and offline. The BNP also had areas where activists could sign up for training. While all parties encouraged some element of sharing, none were of the scale of the BNP, where every page could be shared using Twitter, Facebook or Delicious. However, the sharing facility worked best for the Conservative Party with one viral, highly negative advertisement being the fifth most shared video by 5 May, according to New Media Age (www.nma.co.uk/resources/viral-brand-chart). The same chart for the week 6–13 May, which covered the final week of the campaign, had three Conservative videos 3rd, 6th and 7th, and two by Labour 4th and 5th; Labour's featured endorsements by celebrities (comedian Bill Bailey and actor Ross Kemp), two of the Conservatives were negative and one featured party leader David Cameron answering questions in a public forum. The mediation during transmission was not, however, always as intended. The Conservatives' negative video polarised opinion, and because of this seemed to elicit a range of negative as well as positive accompanying comments; in this way one can see that the network effect can be highly unpredictable and potentially act as a counter to campaign messages.

Openness

Openness is perceptual, and thus this brief discussion is perhaps the most subjective and qualitative in its approach to analysis. Openness links to transparency and accessibility, and thus not only how much data are available, but also the levels of interactivity allowed. Our assessment is that there was limited openness displayed by all parties. We posit this based on the following observations. The persuasive tone of the discourse of Labour, the Greens, the Liberal Democrats and UKIP suggests discussion was closed. While Labour and the Liberal Democrats allowed a degree of inclusivity within the networks created, these were geared towards marshalling volunteers and the promotion of the party rather than giving access to policy making. The LibDem Act area demonstrated clear openness and accessibility and encouraged political comments, and elsewhere the amount of information could be seen as desirous of appearing transparent, but inclusivity is limited. Similarly, the Conservatives gave an impression of openness, exemplified in the manifesto title 'Invitation to join the Government of Britain'. This perception of openness was reinforced through the provision of opportunities to contribute, but was mostly about overtly supporting and promoting the party. The BNP offered a curious series of perceptions in terms of openness. While there was the clear ideal of allowing anyone to participate, one feels that either heavy moderation took place or that only those who share the values and opinions of the community felt able to communicate within this highly ideological forum. The BNP site felt more like that of a private members-only club, targeted at its own internal audiences, than that of a political party.

Evaluating interactivity

Table 8.2 shows the number of items classified within each category of our interactivity model for each party. What we see clearly is a mixture of strategies which have few patterns in terms of ideology or size of party and resources available; instead, they seem to overtly link to the campaign goals of the individual parties.

The main parties have a mixed strategy, offering some degrees of interactivity, but combined with a large amount of information provision. There are also significant amounts of parasocial communication, where interaction is repackaged as persuasive communication to be presented back to their audience. Thus, these sites appear to be used as shopfronts for the brands, places where visitors can gain insights into policy packaged into the manifestos and promotional videos as well as becoming more involved in party activities. As visitors progress along the loyalty ladder (Christopher *et al.* 1991) there are greater opportunities for interacting with other users, but as first-time visitors seeking information, the only interactivity is a product of the site and the documents it holds. The Green Party and UKIP largely eschewed an interactive strategy; with the UKIP demographic this may be sensible, but in the case of the Greens it may be a resource issue and so they rely on the features freely available through Facebook. The BNP are an anomaly. Politically and ideologically they are consistent with studies of right-wing parties (Sudulich 2009), which suggests they are promotional, propagandistic and offer one single persuasive narrative. Conversely, the levels of sharing and content creation suggest that the site should offer a more diverse range of opinions and allow debate on policy. However, the site actually represented a co-created ideological narrative which lacked diversity in tone, tenor or content. The site presented itself as a space where individuals who possess highly right-wing views can vent their feelings, often their anger and frustration, at what they see as marginalisation within a multicultural society. As such, it was a hub of radicalisation and the cementing of views, both of which lead site members to be loyal adherents of the party. While highly interactive, this is a very limited public sphere which focuses on a core body of ideas with little diversity of opinion allowed by the discourse, and possibly reinforced through heavy moderation. In this sense, the BNP may be the most interactive, but it is not the most inclusive and one finds a broader range of views expressed on the lesser interactive sites of the Green Party, via their Facebook page, the Labour Membersnet and the larger networks offered by the LibDems or the Conservatives' Blue Blog. However, in terms of building a community around the party, the BNP are far more advanced, and have a far more active membership than any of the other parties.

Table 8.2 User-to-User interactivity: UK 2010

Level of receiver control	*Direction of communication*		
	One Way	*Two Way*	*Three Way*
10			BNP – 38851 CON – 7886 Green – 399 LAB – 569 LDEM – 11266
9			BNP – 295 CON – 51 Green – 129 LAB – 5 LDEM – 126
8			BNP – 1 CON – 1373 Green – 2 LAB – 4 LDEM – 2 UKIP – 1
7		BNP – 3 CON – 2 Green – 1 LAB – 2 LDEM – 2 UKIP – 1	
6			
5	BNP – 105 CON – 104 Green – 194 LAB – 624 LDEM – 1024 UKIP – 40	BNP – 10 CON – 41 Green – 7 LAB – 76 LDEM – 348 UKIP – 7	
4	BNP – 300 CON – 11688 Green – 2778 LAB – 505 LDEM – 2809 UKIP – 796	CON – 1 Green – 1 LAB – 2 LDEM – 2 UKIP – 1	
3	BNP – 2 CON – 1 Green – 2 LAB – 1 LDEM – 2 UKIP – 2	BNP – 1 CON – 1 LAB – 1	
2	BNP – 107 CON – 65 Green – 50 LAB – 31 LDEM – 155 UKIP – 112		
1			

Table 8.3 User-to-document interactivity: UK 2010 (number of items per category)

	BNP	*CON*	*Green*	*LAB*	*LDEM*	*UKIP*
Downward flows (Packaged)	419	11,698	2,831	536	2,956	904
Upward flows (Content on Demand)	7	7	4	6	4	3
Lateral flows (Content on Demand)	102	100	190	622	1,020	37
Asynchronous (Content Exchange)	302	149	145	94	495	16
Synchronous (Co-created Content)	38,851	7,886	399	568	11,266	0

When focusing on the number of items within each of the categories offered by Sarah McMillan (2002a), a similar pattern to that of interactivity is observed (Table 8.3). The BNP site is almost wholly co-created due to the use of a weblog to support news and the number of comments this receives; this gives the impression of a site similar to that of Obama, which essentially it is, albeit in a bastardised form. The BNP site was one co-created promotional and campaigning tool built to solidify support for the party. In fact, it conformed to Sunstein's (2007) definition of a cyber ghetto, where adherents could go to reinforce their existing prejudices. The Liberal Democrat site is divided into large news and informational sections, with the large LibDem Act network providing a space for participation, the area is not heavily promoted and appeared, like the Labour Membersnet, to be for insiders. This presents a difference to the co-created content appearing on the Conservative site, which was more integrated across the campaign, as opposed to on the periphery. The norm was to contain co-creation and participation within a bespoke area. Both Labour and the Green Party marshalled their feeds well to give a co-created impression at points, but this is limited as a part of the overall site. UKIP eschewed Web 2.0 and any aspect of interactivity and co-creation.

Mixed strategies: mixed approaches

Despite earlier hype, the Internet played a secondary role in the UK election campaign. The first ever televised leaders' debates dominated the campaign, relegating the Internet to playing the role of a niche communication tool. Undoubtedly, outward online communication by the parties and candidates played a much greater role than in previous campaigns, but its role was more informative to the wider public, as well as using the site to mobilise party supporters. In this sense there were incremental improvements on 2005 (Stanyer 2005; Jackson 2007), rather than a paradigm shift. It is unlikely the Internet helped parties and candidates reach floating voters as well as the leaders' debates, rather its focus was supporters. However, it is worth noting that there was a hybridisation in political communication. The leaders' debates may have dominated the campaign, but many people accessed them, or their perceptions of the debates were shaped by, Web 2.0 applications such as YouTube and Twitter.

It seems that the parties had two objectives that underpinned the functions their websites performed. First, was the overriding function of providing information for potential voters. This was the key purpose of all the UK party websites, and clearly the online environment is viewed by the parties as an opportunity to present complex arguments to persuade potential voters. This is a task they find hard, if not impossible, via the mass media. Thus, most websites are used as a means of talking directly to voters, and the content prioritised across the websites was persuasive communication presented in engaging and easily accessible ways. This is consistent with the earliest perspectives of the role of the Internet as acting as a direct communication channel from the party to potential voters (Morris 1999).

The second function, which complements the information provision but also diverges from a top-down communicative approach to some extent, is the harnessing of the power of the crowd, or more specifically the power of their supporters, within existing or bespoke networks. The ability to promote the party across the Internet is the most basic example, encouraged by all apart from UKIP. Using social networking sites to both promote the party directly and gain secondary promotion within the networks of those who befriend or become fans of the party, is equally seen as a key way of reaching potential voters. Beyond this, the encouragement to join the site and become involved in discussions adds a further development in terms of participation. This strategy is essentially a way of generating resources: donations, members and volunteers. However, there are divergent strategies for doing this. UKIP largely expect those sympathetic to the party's arguments to give them money and to join the party, while volunteering is handled at the local level. The Greens rely on Facebook as a tool for discussion and the management of events, both of which can draw supporters closer to the party; their site, however, also aims to mainly solicit funds. The Conservatives, Labour and the Liberal Democrats all target visitors with requests for donations, but they also try to create a more community atmosphere and shared ownership of the campaign. Their bespoke social networks, though very different, encourage a sense of community and so greater loyalty and activism through peer pressure. The BNP are outliers, and it seems they simply want a community to contribute opinions or money. The BNP's use of the Internet does not support Benkler's (2006) belief in the positive power of the network, rather it seems to support Sunstein's (2004) view of an echo chamber or cyber ghetto. For the BNP, their website appears to act as an online rally for the faithful; participants act as a chorus line for the party and its policies rather than a deliberative forum that shapes strategy. Therefore, overall it appears there is an emergent strategy for resource generation that explicitly uses interactivity as a way of building an online community to complement the offline, local organisations.

Unlike Germany, there is far less standardisation; rather, there is greater individualism in how parties use the Internet. Although the major parties employed American advisers before the election, there is limited evidence that the UK imported innovations wholesale from Obama. In part, this individualism reflects the fact that the size and representation of the six parties is not equal. The three larger parties were similar in their use of their Web 2.0 applications. With fewer resources, the three smaller non-parliamentary parties could not necessarily compete. However, size alone does not explain such individualism, and although UKIP have been reluctant at adopting Web 2.0 applications and interactivity, the BNP do not share their caution. Ideology does not appear to be relevant, with the least (UKIP) and most likely (BNP) to use Web 2.0 on the right. UK political parties, whilst being aware of the experience of Web 2.0 applications in other election campaigns, developed their own individual approaches driven by a combination of the nature of the electoral system, available resources and past experience. The party considered political pariahs, the BNP, were the most likely to adopt Web 2.0; but the second most likely, the Conservatives, had widespread access to a favourable offline media.

As a means of generating resources, all parties have developed some aspect of encouraging participation mirroring innovations developed by the Obama campaign. The Conservatives perhaps copied the Obama site design the most closely, but all the major parties created their own network for site members and encouraged differing levels of content creation. The BNP had their own network and forum in place prior to Obama, placing online communication onto the campaign agenda in a profound way. However, this was enhanced significantly since 2008 (Jackson and Lilleker 2009a), and allowing the creation of groups and encouraging uploading content reached a new level, with the party allowing its support network to advance their campaigns, an objective shared by all the parties studied to an extent. Participation was allowed in order to create a win-win zone for party and supporters, but the result was largely to create an ideologically closed public sphere. This was a marketing tool that aimed to influence the perceptions of site visitors. The participation allowed did not necessarily provide clear advances in political communication.

9 Elections 2.0

Interactivity, the Internet and political campaigning 2007–10

Our assessment of the data gathered across these four elections is that there is clear evidence that the Internet can be viewed as a mainstream channel for election campaigning by political parties and candidates, yet in none of the elections studied has the Internet become the primary campaigning tool for reaching voters. In terms of reaching and persuading voters, the Internet is still a useful supplementary, rather than the primary channel in the elections toolbox; though there is in reality no primary channel as each medium can perform a discrete function within a campaign, some channels have greater reach than others. Despite the view of Brian Eno outlined in our Introduction, and that of other commentators (Stirland 2008; Greengard 2009), we suggest that it is very unlikely that even in the US, the use of the Internet can claim to have determined the outcome of an election. Traditional 'modern' campaigning tools of mass media, especially television (Norris 2000), can still be considered to be the most important channels for reaching voters. Our four election campaigns do not offer proof that we have moved to postmodern campaigns, though the Internet is, as we would expect, progressively more important in this tranche of elections than the previous ones in each country. Politicians have made more of the Internet both qualitatively and quantitatively, and more citizens have access to the Internet. In engaging with non-partisan voters we see evidence for incremental, not revolutionary change. In terms of the 'holy grail' of delivering floating voters, the Internet is not a magic bullet.

We suggest that the impact of the Internet on election campaigns is more radical, and probably a greater medium to long-term impact, in the reaching of internal audiences. The evidence from the four election campaigns studied is that the Internet is fast-becoming the primary channel for internal marketing and communication. Rather than directly influencing voter behaviour, the Internet is much better at facilitating a revised two-step flow model of communication. Increasingly, candidates and parties have turned to the Internet as a means of mobilising resources, be they financial or volunteers; this is consistent with predictions that the Internet would be a viable direct communication channel for political communicators (Morris 1999). However, the revolutionary nature of the Internet is in developing more intimate relationships with those who already have an affinity with a party or candidate, and to encourage them to act as advocates on and offline. Supporters are drawn into partisan communities where they are free to express ideas consistent with party or candidate ideological tenets, and these can be strengthened and reinforced through interaction within the community. Thus, the Internet may nurture feelings of belonging for those seeking active membership of a political tribe, and there is the potential that the stronger the use of Web 2.0, as with Obama and the British BNP, then the stronger the sense of belonging. We find, in terms of internal marketing, there is evidence of postmodern campaigning. The increasing use, and effectiveness, of email, social networking sites and Twitter for mobilising supporters provides greater control to central professional campaigners. Therefore, the impact of the Internet is not uniform; to persuade voters it is incremental, but to mobilise existing support it is increasingly revolutionary.

We suggest that websites have increased in their functionality and that the features built into their architectures are used to potentiate win-win zones for a range of audiences; a point we will return to and explore in further depth later in this chapter. However, this increased functionality does not necessarily add to or amend recognised schematics for understanding the purpose of websites during election campaigns. To identify the overall lessons we have identified, this chapter will start to assess the impact of Web 2.0 on election campaigns by considering the extent to which the websites designed for elections 2007–10, across France, the US, Germany and the UK, adhere to the functions we outlined in Chapter 1 and operationalised in Chapter 4.

Functions of the party websites

Adapting the Gibson and Ward (2000b) methodology, we identified six key functions that websites have played historically in election campaigns up to 2005. In the four elections studied, we found all these functions again well served by the websites of all the candidates and parties. However, we also note new ways to fulfil these functions that are facilitated by Web 2.0 technologies, and so observe the evolution of campaign websites. We find that websites retain the same functional qualities, but they are built using a range of up-to-date and increasingly sophisticated features in order to provide a positive experience to visitors and offer potential electoral advantages to the host.

Information provision

Informing is a key function of any party or candidate website, as this is the single time that people may be drawn to seeking information about them to support their voter choices (Kitchens *et al.* 2003). Given the often subjective nature of media reporting, the Web offers a way of delivering information to more involved potential voters directly in formats that are engaging and accessible. All parties' and candidates' websites served this function well, and divergences are only in the delivery modes and techniques which perhaps relate to resources. Websites were content heavy in Germany and the UK, and the campaigns of Royal in France and McCain in the US. Video emerged as a key medium for some candidates, Obama particularly, and the UK Conservatives. File-sharing sites, such as YouTube, allowed candidates and parties to create profiles and extend the reach of their videos, with many being the most shared within specific and important periods of the campaign. Interestingly, we also find changes in the content of information. Rather than offering long histories or archived information, the websites tend to be trimmed down to focus on the contest, disseminating short, sharp key messages using a range of media devices. The anomaly here is the text-heavy news archives, which remain large sections of the websites. This suggests journalists, as well as bloggers, political researchers and 'anoraks', are for some a key audience. Information is now carefully packaged for consumption, with websites sometimes offering micro-sites with information tailored for very specific audience members (in Germany the Turkish community; Obama's targeting of Hillary Clinton supporters; the youth micro areas of Royal and many German and UK parties). With political campaigners increasingly recognising the relevance of marketing techniques such as segmentation and targeting, their websites are now designed so that a range of audiences are provided with bespoke areas from which they can each take away something of relevance.

Campaigning

Election websites have evolved from being fairly static entities containing a range of pieces of information (Sadow and James 1999), to being bespoke online presences designed for specific purposes. Despite taking over the main URLs of the party or candidate, the sites tended to exist as campaign micro-sites focused on the campaign itself and providing only information related to the manifestos, policy pledges and containing persuasive content designed to aid voter choices. The divergence from this was those parties that created areas designed for supporters which, while also having a campaigning function, broadened out the nature of content, as this combined party- or candidate-led aspects with user-generated materials. Perceptually, however, visitors gained impressions based on what they were able to view; therefore, publicly observable conversations between supporters who joined the site, and between the campaign staff and site members, served explicit campaign functions.

Negative campaigning

Much has been written on the consequences of 'going negative', the general rule being that overt attacks lead floating voters to disengage with messages, but if the attack has resonance it reinforces voter choices (Ansolabehere and Iyengar 1995; Lilleker and Scullion 2009). Taking a negative turn, therefore, can be a risky strategy and there are some interesting patterns which may be a consequence of strategic decision making. While the website is only one location for the placement of negative messages, if these represent the key direct, non-mediated communication medium, it can be used as a reference point for understanding what the campaign wishes to say to potential voters and their own supporters.

The sharpest contrast can be seen when looking at the campaigns of the presidential candidates within our sample. Analysing the sites of the four finalists, we find that Royal in France and Obama in the US offered only a minor level of negativity (0.4 per cent and less than 0.1 per cent respectively). In contrast, Sarkozy and McCain led with a predominantly attacking tone; 60 per cent of the Sarkozy site and 25 per cent of that of McCain is a significant level of content to devote to attacks. Clearly, negativity worked for Sarkozy, and his attacks seemed to have resonance among his supporters, perhaps obviously, as well as with enough floating voters to gain him just enough support to get over 50 per cent of the national vote; the reverse was the case with McCain by a wide margin, and few of his attacks worked and were often criticised for having negative overtones in the US media (Heilemann and Halperin 2009). However, it does not mean that neither Royal nor Obama eschewed material that attacked their opponent. The Segosphere network of blogs contained a significant amount of rebuttals to Sarkozy's argumentation, as well as direct attacks on Sarkozy as an individual and a politician. This once caused a problem, as an attack was deemed anti-Semitic and so damaged Royal's reputation (Vedel and Michalska 2007). Similarly, Obama's blog often gained comments that were nothing but attacks on McCain, and were often not even linked to the content of the original post. The fact that the community was self-regulating allowed Obama some degree of distance from this content, though none was highlighted as inappropriate by McCain or the US media, which would have been damaging. Thus, websites can be used overtly for negative campaigning, or to allow negativity through the backdoor where supporters narrowcast ideas within these areas which can reinforce existing prejudices and provide material for wider dissemination. This allows the candidates to distance themselves from the more negative material, while also offering a repository for attacks.

There is less divergence on the whole across party websites in Germany. The Left Party were slightly more negative and the SPD the least, the latter due to the inability to attack a government they had been a part of; but all offered a similar level of negative content. There were divergent strategies in the UK, with the BNP and UKIP being explicitly negative with around half of the parties' (50 per cent and 45 per cent respectively) websites focusing on attacks; the Green Party were slightly less so, devoting 30 per cent to overt attacks. These parties, however, together with the Liberal Democrats (whose website was 15 per cent negative), focused attacks on a constructed other. This could be all the other parties, in the case of the BNP, due to their support for liberal immigration and social policies. The pro-EU parties represent the other for UKIP; the Greens offer themselves as the alternative to soft environmentalist parties; in the Liberal Democrat case, the major parties are set up as a more direct 'other' linked to their positioning prior to joining a coalition. Interestingly, the two major combatants show very traditional approaches, with Labour mainly offering positive content defending their record and with two bespoke attack pages which constitute 5 per cent of the overall site. In contrast, the Conservatives led with an attack, devoting 20 per cent of the total site to attacks on competitors; mainly the Labour government. All UK parties except Labour are more negative than the German parties, suggesting this is a strategy seen to be more successful in the UK; McCain is seen as very balanced compared to UK parties and to Sarkozy. Thus we observe interesting combinations of patterns in website usage, and the way that online messages link to party positioning and their overall campaign strategy.

Resource generation

Traditionally, resource generation has been almost solely related to soliciting donations from supporters, and has been most evident in the campaigns of those standing for US president (Howard 2006; Anstead 2008). While seeking donations follows a range of strict rules in most other nations, it remains a key function of the websites of US presidential candidates. It is also featured across the sites of all German and UK parties, but the levels of success are lower. The French candidates did not seek donations online. However, resource generation has taken on new meanings within Web 2.0 environments. Supporters are a key target audience for candidate and party websites, and they are encouraged to climb the loyalty ladder (Christopher *et al.* 1991): from giving latent support to becoming active advocates. There are numerous ways supporters are encouraged to affiliate themselves with parties and candidates, in particular joining the website and the active member areas. There are also numerous means offered to those willing to act as overt supporters, downloading logos and badges to promote on social networking profiles, uploading supportive content to campaign areas and openly stating why they are supporting that party or candidate. This adapts the rules of offline campaigning, canvassing and getting out the vote to an online networked society. While Obama may have been carried to office through using social networking tools to mobilise new sets of activists, these tools were pioneered by Howard Dean in 2003 and it is perhaps a Dean model we are seeing evidenced as prevailing online. The Obama campaign was Dean Plus, with the functional use of the Internet being comparable, but the Plus being that Obama was a more credible candidate. The Segosphere, MyBO and the German StudiVZ, which often adopted the 'meine' possessive and personal epithet, and the counterparts created by some UK parties alongside the social networking fan pages, were all geared towards generating resources. Joining supplied the campaign with a bank of emails allowing them to contact an involved audience, and these were used to target them with personalised messages, recruit members, solicit donations and activate those who would connect to offline supporter networks. Thus, Web 2.0 facilitated a move towards a more personalised pre-modern style of campaigning, while also fitting perfectly with the notions of postmodern, strategic campaigning.

Networking

The creation of networks, discussed above, and the use of social networking sites by the US candidates and all the German and UK parties is integral to the networking function. Rather than being limited to being part of a network, networking has evolved so that it now means the creation of a network, facilitation and moderation of communication with and between the members of that network, and using that network to promote the candidate or party. Most candidates and parties sought to promote themselves across a range of networks and this was a key function that Web 2.0 applications have added. In particular, the harnessing of sharing and promotion facilities to encourage supporters to become advocates, replicating peer-to-peer persuasive communication within social networks, act as a key aspect of this function within the context of a campaign. While there is a virtual uniformity in adherence to the function, strategies diverged. Royal harnessed online supporters within the semi-autonomous Segosphere; Obama had a strategy to appear everywhere, which was a technique for drawing online community members into MyBO. McCain, and German and UK parties tended to replicate the Obama strategy by building spaces within popular public networks, and linking these to their own sites and networks, though to varying degrees. The UK BNP focused on building an internal network, the Greens external only. Only Sarkozy and the UKIP eschewed this approach to network building.

Promoting participation

Where Butler and Ranney (1992) previously suggested that participation in an election was limited to just voting, participation has now developed beyond this. Participation can include using a range of interactive tools to further campaigning objectives, such as utilising email contacts, chat rooms, opinion polls, digital petitions or customised subscription and feedback options. In addition, there are Web 2.0 applications including blogs, social networking sites, Twitter, video and photo sharing, which all facilitate interactivity as a process between supporters. There are equally a range of product-based features that allow more limited forms of participation, such as enmeshing, search options or online games that can combine entertainment and engagement, and make sites more attractive to users and so sticky through some form of participation. Interestingly, it seems that it was harnessing political participation that was the key objective for all parties and candidates to some extent. Limited use of participatory tools was evidenced in analysis of the UKIP, Sarkozy and McCain websites, but these are outliers in this respect and still offered ways to interact with the site, and all but UKIP also offered some, if limited, means to interact with others and the campaign in some way. Using the online audience as a potential resource can enhance a network effect, whereby material would be shared widely and the campaign's reach would be extended due to the participation of the online visitors to their sites. This implies that there is a 'ripple effect' on participation, which in turn has an impact on campaigning reach.

Website functions for campaigning online

We suggest there is an emergent hierarchy for functions of websites. Perhaps the most important is to generate resources and mobilise the internal audience of supporters and loyalists. Resources can be in the form of either donations or support and we find that this is constrained and governed by the electoral system, traditions of political engagement surrounding donating and participation, and rules imposed that constrain soliciting funding. However, the shift towards the hypermedia campaign (Howard 2006) is evident across all four nations, the key to which is collecting data on supporters and harnessing them to the campaign. These aspects sit at the heart of campaign-specific bespoke campaign sites, which will reflect the overall branding of the candidate or party. They promote party messages in ways that engage the casual visitor to the site, and so perform a shopfront function that presents policies and personalities in an attractive and persuasive way. Websites, thus, all offer an attractive experience for supporters designed to harness them to the campaign. This allows a number of takeaways: for information-seeking visitors, simply packaged content that can be tailored for a range of key audiences; for supporters, there are numerous ways to be active and so there is a range of participatory opportunities offered in order to tap into the behaviour of the online user. The candidates and parties have moved on from the Web 1.0 era one-size-fits-all website, and they now offer information in a more sophisticated and targeted way.

We visualise this in Figure 9.1, which shows a range of tasks that sets of features that commonly appear on election websites perform for the candidate or party. These are tied to specific functions which permit users to perform tasks they are seeking or willing to perform. This thus links to specific audiences and creates a win-win zone for both the user and the candidate or party. However, these all serve the overriding objectives of the campaign, and websites are rarely designed to facilitate participation surrounding message or policy development. Yet, what we do find is that this may be an unavoidable by-product of using supporters to enhance the campaign's communication reach, and that the greater level of participation encouraged, the greater the ownership over the campaign, candidate or party can be demanded.

A 2.0 election?

The above notes that the traditional functions of election campaign websites continue to be well served. Indeed, these have been enhanced and expanded upon through the capabilities of Web 2.0 technological innovations. The constraints imposed by organisation objectives (Stromer-Galley 2000; Jackson and Lilleker 2009a; Lilleker *et al.* 2010) may limit innovations in terms of functionality. Yet, there is clearly a shift towards adopting all the latest features, and use of the latest platforms and media forms, within election campaigning. Therefore, we argue that Web 2.0 technologies, tools and features have increasingly played a role within election campaigns 2007–10. It is possible that this reflects simply

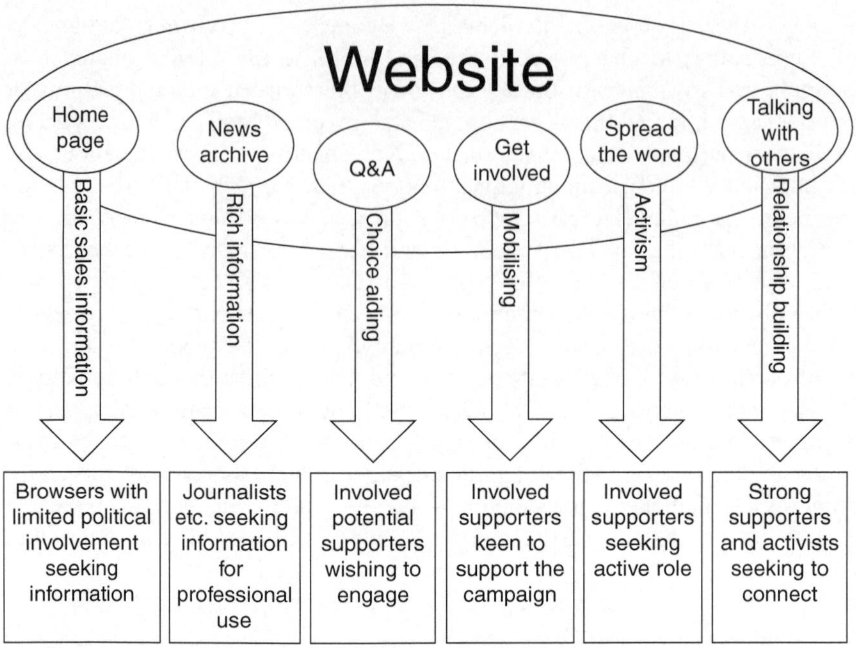

Figure 9.1 Functions, audiences and win-win zones potentiated in online communication strategies.

the sales side of the campaign and features can be selected to provide an impression of sophistication, or indeed accessibility, without adhering to the big ideas of Web 2.0 that could fundamentally change election campaigning. We provide an overview of the extent to which the candidates and parties philosophically adapted their communication to the rules of the Web 2.0 environment. In short, we try to address whether there is evidence for Anderson's (2006) big ideas.

Individual production and user-generated content

It is impossible to assess the extent to which user-generated content shapes the everyday experiences we all enjoy online. In fact, it is safe to say there is significant blurring between what is user-generated, and material created by organisations in the pursuit of an audience. Mash-ups, adaptations and user-uploaded content are the mainstay of many websites, and most social networks would have little or no content were it not for their user communities. The same is not as true for the online presences of most candidates or parties. While many encourage the contribution of content, this is within areas that are bracketed off from the main site and so the user only indirectly affects the experience of the browsing visitor. German parties demonstrate the most caution in allowing users to upload material, but hide this content behind passwords, so making these private areas that require a sign-up procedure. Royal, McCain and half of the UK parties allowed anyone to see user-generated content, but it was limited and retained within bespoke areas. These resembled user communities and the real innovation was their creation, and the fact that they were publicly viewable. The Obama approach was only really mirrored by the UK BNP, though with differing aims, modus operandi and results. Both websites allowed large amounts of user-generated content across wide areas of the sites that added a new dimension to all visitors' experiences. The UK Conservative Party made attempts to replicate this approach within their bespoke online community and on their blog, but with fewer contributions gained it appeared to be more of a cobweb than a hub of activism. Twitter feeds that allowed hashtag use, which fed main pages, was a key innovation in the UK that allowed users power to shape the campaign, something that replicated Royal's use of the Segosphere as one strand of message development.

On the whole, though, these represented ideologically homogenous communities, whose practice was geared more towards creating an echo chamber for ideas (Sunstein 2007) than offering space for public participation in politics. There was little sense of parties creating a broad political public sphere; rather, they were narrow public spheres which focused on the candidate or party and how to secure victory. Though perhaps there is a logic to this approach, given that the campaign and its supporters are obsessively focused on the contest. Many of Stromer-Galley's reasons for caution were evidenced by those who did encourage users to create and upload content online. Public contributions during the UK contest also highlight the threat of harnessing the produser. While in the US, produsers helped build MyBO and contributed positively to his campaign, often without direct requests; opportunities to contribute in the UK were as likely to be taken up by opponents as supporters. Although outside of the campaign period proper, and perhaps as a test initiative, the Conservative Party invited the online audience to complete the phrase 'I've never voted Conservative before but...' and then post both to the main site and their own web pages or social media profiles. Many were supportive, many were not, with some offering highly negative and defamatory remarks, and others, which were more likely to be shared, offering more satirical lines: apparently, 'I've never had a lobotomy either' was the most shared according to one insider. Perhaps unsurprisingly, it was www.mydavidcameron.com, a spoof home page for the Conservative leader, that was the most popular political website during the campaign.

Harnessing the power of the crowd

Linking to the observations above, the collective wisdom of the supporters was not harnessed in order to shape campaign messages or the campaign itself; perhaps the exception being Obama, who allowed his community to lead the way in creating events and messages. On the whole, though, it was the power of the crowd to extend the reach of the campaign that was harnessed. Parties sought to create an online network effect with their supporters, disseminating messages as widely as possibly within their own communities and networks. Sharing and promoting, on the whole, were the key functions awarded to those visiting websites who wished to have an active role. Obama did seek a greater depth of participation within his weblog and the MyBO community; as did Royal and the UK BNP. Royal was all about harnessing bloggers to spread the word and to position her at the head of the movement of activists; the BNP wanted to demonstrate they had strong support and also to use their supporters to build real-life examples to aid their campaigns. However, very few elements introduced across any of the websites created for these four contests fully link with the big ideas of harnessing the crowd to shape ideas or products; crowds were mainly sourced to act as megaphones for pre-existing ideas.

Access to data on an epic scale

Data provided on none of the websites could be described as being on an epic scale. Rather, it simply presented carefully packaged arguments, using a range of media, to disseminate core messages. The user of course could source a range of alternative data, but candidates and parties did not link to very much material that was in any way independent. External links were to overtly partisan sites that kept strictly on message; thus these sites cannot be seen as a gateway to anything except a homogenous set of ideas which may be presented in a polyphonic style, but essentially, at heart it was monologic communication built for an online audience of floating voters who were being targeted with persuasive communication.

Architecture of participation

Most candidates or parties created communities that acted as a participatory architecture, which encouraged visitors to contribute content. However, Sarkozy and UKIP eschewed this approach entirely, Royal bracketed this off outside of her site within the Segosphere or her small forum, German parties retained privacy over user-generated content, and Obama, the BNP and UK Conservatives tried with varying degrees of success to harness activism; thus cumulatively we see gradual increases in permitting participation if in a rather sporadic form. Again, this does not yet adhere to the idea of 'they will come and build it', even the Obama site would have had significant amounts of content without user contributions. However, few sites consisted entirely of text-heavy shovelware and retained only a top-down model of political communication. Therefore, we argue there was a balance struck between the rules of the Web 2.0 community of practice and the strictures of election campaigning; while participation was permitted, there were rules set by either the host, the community or both, and areas allowing participation were, on the whole, subsidiary areas of the site, and not central features which shaped the experience of every user and permitted anyone to participate.

The network effect

Parties and candidates attempted to create a network effect in two ways. First, all but the French candidates joined a vast array of social networks, so reaching into public and social spaces used by those with whom they needed to communicate. The main sites were Facebook and YouTube, but other bespoke communities were also utilised to reach out to specific communities. Second, candidates and parties attempted to create their own networks and encourage the members to filter out their messages to a wider audience. Rather than solely relying on the mass media as a broadcast tool, they harnessed the users of StudiVZ, Facebook, Twitter and YouTube to extend their reach and build a multi-step flow dissemination approach. Their supporters were encouraged to share material within their networks, and then the hope was that their friends would do likewise and messages would cascade out across social networks. While the results are hard to measure, there were clearly some successes in reaching this objective. Campaign videos going viral, the donating of Twitter and Facebook updates to parties and candidates; both are good examples of the network being employed and having a positive effect in meeting the objectives of a campaign by employing the power of the social ecosystem created around Web 2.0 features, tools and platforms.

Openness

Whether an election campaign, which is inherently persuasive, can also offer a degree of openness in terms of either transparency over its operation or accessibility to all is perhaps an interesting philosophical conundrum. Based on the evidence of these four contests, we would suggest that it is not the case. While sites did offer open access to a range of communities, these were geared towards furthering the campaign and not enhancing public engagement with the democratic process. True there may be some overlap between access potentiated and the self-efficacy of users; however, it appears that this would be a by-product as opposed to the core mission of the creation of these areas. This is similarly the case with most elements that promote some degree of participation. In terms of transparency, little can be evidenced at all. While there were some debates involving elite actors within the campaign across Obama's blog, and so a sense that communication was bottom-up, this was limited and the only example that can be found. Therefore, this big idea is not realised in the context of election campaigning.

Elections 2.0: adherence to the big ideas

Across all four contests we find Web 2.0 was adapted for the purposes of campaigning, and there is limited evidence that the reverse was the case. User-generated content was a feature of the elections on many party websites, but its appearance was controlled and heavily moderated; thus the power of the crowd was harnessed to act as a megaphone, reinforcing campaign messages, and not creating content that could be used widely without some form of control being exerted. Of course this does not mean users did not generate content independently of the candidates and parties, nor that this did not go viral. But it is only really within the US that users were shaping the campaign in a significant way, and these instances show this was heavily driven by the media and limited to individuals with specific skills and resources. Thus, participatory architectures were built only to advance campaigning objectives, and in an attempt to gain purchase within online user networks and communities. Parties and candidates limited which data could be accessed from their site as well as what could be added, and there was little sense that the campaigns were open affairs accessible to all. We did not get a sense of real insight into the organisations, their workings or that there was meaningful inclusion offered to those who joined their support networks. Obama is the outlier here in all senses. There is a sense of ebb and flow between the campaign team and those who acted on his behalf across the Internet (Harfoush 2009). Equally, the content contributed to his weblog did have an impact on the campaign in a fundamental way. Therefore, this single participatory architecture not only encouraged participation and content generation, but also harnessed a crowd of activists, and they would later be specific about the change they sought from his presidency. Despite these examples being set in 2008 and early 2009 as he entered the White House, there is little sense of an Obama effect that shifted the balance of power away from campaign teams to the wider public. Perhaps, though, this is not simply about the will of the organisations; the fact that Obama did indeed have people that came and built his site, possibly in their thousands, meant he had gained a community that would not be ignored. There is no sense that any of the parties in Germany or the UK had anything near the size of Obama's network, not even one proportionately smaller when compared to total electorates; thus they did not have the membership to extend their architectures, and the online aspect of the campaign remained on the margins of campaign strategy.

Elections and the Internet: the impact of Web 2.0

In the Introduction we set out four main aims of this book:

1 The meaning of Web 2.0 within the context of elections;
2 To consider the impact of Web 2.0 on elections;
3 To assess whether we have entered the era of Elections 2.0;
4 To identify common lessons which can be learnt from the four elections studied.

In considering these, we note that Web 2.0 has two meanings within the context of an election. First, Web 2.0 technologies and the features, tools and platforms that have been built independently of party campaigning offer a range of ways in which anyone can contribute to an information ecosystem relating to any event. Thus, we can argue that a big conversation is potentiated which can sprawl across a range of Web addresses drawing together wikis, forums, personal and organisation websites, and profiles across social networking and file sharing sites. Thus, as part of the rich browsing and creating experiences which Web 2.0 potentiates, anyone can be a political communicator. Second, this ecosystem represents enormous potential for any organisation or individual that wishes to speak directly and indirectly to, and interact with, a broad, possibly global, audience. The Web presences of political parties and candidates for election are on the periphery of the conversation, and their creators and the communication strategists working at the hub of election campaigns seek to enter this ecosystem in order for the message reach to be extended. At the same time, they would also seek to control the ways in which messages are disseminated. Thus, the impact of Web 2.0 at this point is to create numerous opportunities for conversations and contributions which relate to an election. These could be shaped by one or any of those seeking election; equally, they may be marginal voices within the online conversation. The task parties and candidates face is how to harness the online produser, in a way that both gain a sense of efficacy through the use of these technological features.

The contests we have analysed all drew in aspects of Web 2.0. The Sarkozy site relied on sharing facilities, while Royal sought to harness the blogosphere to amplify and extend the reach of her messages. McCain attempted to get some interaction on his weblog, but like Sarkozy sought sharing by his supporters, in particular getting the negative messages about Obama out online given that the offline and traditional media outlets were reluctant to be critical. Obama himself offered change, and that was represented through his website which stood as a metaphor for collaborative politics. His site used Web 2.0 features to involve and connect supporters and gain donations, but further than that he used Web 2.0 to allow conversations between his campaigners and supporters to the point where the lines between campaign elite and online supporter blurred. This is the watershed in Elections 2.0 thus far. German party websites were traditional with communities added on, but hidden behind passwords. In the UK, strategies were more mixed, but the Web 2.0 features that encourage participation were largely bracketed off from the main sites. Activists could shape the website of both Labour and the Conservatives, and fans could converse with Green Party leader Caroline Lucas on Facebook, or share and comment on nearly every page of the site of the BNP. But these are random examples which do not betray an emergent strategy.

While in France, Germany and the UK the Internet truly came of age, and in the US there were significant innovations, talk of an Internet election, never mind a Web 2.0 election, seemed a little trite. What emerges is a pattern in functionality of election websites. First, they provided a significant amount of information delivered using increasingly sophisticated and engaging formats and styles, utilising the most up-to-date technological features resources could afford. Second, they attempted to harness supporters and increase their levels of active promotion either online or offline. Online campaigns thus, we predict, will mirror offline messages and reflect the overall party strategy; in this way, they act as the shopfront for those standing for election. All functions will link to the objectives set out for campaigning, and it is unlikely that technological innovations will have a serious impact upon how campaigns are operationalised. The factor that may change this, and may well be the long- or short-term impact that Web 2.0 can have, may well be dependent upon the nature and scale of participation: here, we look to the Obama campaign. Obama was successful in drawing an unprecedented number to his campaign, both online and offline. Through adapting the Dean approach to Web campaigning, as well as drawing on his own experience as a community organiser, Obama facilitated interaction with and among a wide community in a similar way to the workings of a number of social networks: Meetup.org in the US or the UK's Netmums, for example. This drew in to the MyBO community significant numbers, and they used the facilities created for them. The levels of participation, in terms of creating events, supporting the campaign, donating, etc., gave them part ownership over his presidential challenge and so they expected to be heard. Comments to the blog post and internal discussions on policy needed an outlet, and thus the campaign developed a more co-created dimension. This may, though, have been driven by the community and not the campaign team, despite demonstrations of an ethos of openness and participation (Harfoush 2010). Thus, within a Web 2.0 election, we predict that the community of users will be not only co-creating content and shaping the experiences of all visitors, but also demanding the power to shape policy. No other candidate or party had this problem, yet no other candidate or party was able to harness the numbers Obama drew in to the campaign. Elections 2.0 appears to have huge potential, yet also represents a potential threat to a campaign.

In the Introduction we identified five factors which might act as mediating variables, and so shape the use of the Internet during elections: the political system; the electoral system; candidate or party systems; party size; and ideology. The political system appears to have very limited effect, with the US presidential election being the most likely to be influenced by Web 2.0 applications, and the French presidential election the least. The two parliamentary systems are fairly similar, with possibly Web 2.0 having more of an impact in the UK. Whilst the electoral system may influence the likelihood of strong party- or candidate-centred systems, in itself there is no strong evidence that a particular mechanism for choosing the political elite is critical for encouraging use of the Internet. There is some evidence that, as might be expected, candidate-centred systems use the Internet to inform voters, generate resources and mobilise supporters. Though, as Anstead and Chadwick (2008) note, this also reflects legal as well as political factors in the US. Yet, although Obama was the most likely to adopt Web 2.0 applications, McCain was not. Indeed, we note that rather than the Internet further enhancing the gap in campaigning between candidate- and party-centred systems, Web 2.0 applications may be closing this gap. The Internet may be slowly moving the party-centred systems outlined by Klingemann *et al.* (1994) towards the more individualist model highlighted by Miller and Stokes (1963). Candidates within parties are able to create their own public space, separate to the controls from their party hierarchies. Party size has an impact, but we note that it is associated with the political system. In the two Presidential elections, we are much more likely to find evidence of politics as normal (Margolis and Resnick 2000). Whereas, in the two parliamentary systems there is much more evidence for ebb and flow (Gibson *et al.* 2003) in that, whilst generally the bigger parties are more likely to use Web 2.0 applications, there is evidence that some smaller parties (though not all) use Web 2.0 applications to reach new audiences, and to build relationships with existing audiences. In terms of ideology there is a very mixed picture, and no clear support for either a left-wing interactive online strategy (Sudulich 2009) or one of the right (Copsey 2003; Jackson and Lilleker 2009a). For the major parties in our four elections, left, centre and right wing were just as likely to be employing a wide range of features, and potentiating a wide range of user experiences. Whilst the Greens in both the UK and Germany did make use of Web 2.0 applications, by and large the smaller left-wing parties did not follow suit. Similarly, we do not see evidence of the smaller right-wing parties adopting Web 2.0 as much, with the very notable exception of the BNP. There is no clear and absolute pattern suggested by these five factors, rather we need to look at very specific circumstances affecting the decisions of candidates and party leaders in each country.

Web 2.0 appears to have a limited effect on election campaign strategy. Of Rohrschneider's five 'trade-offs', Web 2.0 has a clear resonance with two. First, some candidates and parties used the website predominantly to focus on core voters, and some to reach out to new voters. The two clearest examples of Web 2.0 use, Obama and the BNP took different approaches, with Obama using the technology to reach out to new constituencies, and the BNP using it to deepen their relationship with existing supporters. Second, the evidence is that largely, candidates and parties focused on reaching voters, but a consequence of such activity, as we note above, was to inherently invite a higher level of interaction between voter and political actors than in previous elections. Similarly, in terms of the five different electoral strategies open to candidates and parties, not all apply to the use of Web 2.0 applications. If the use of negativity noted earlier indicates a differentiation between policies, then there is some evidence for a rational choice model in the two party-centred systems, the UK and Germany, as this implies that policy is communicated in a mode designed to persuade voters. But the two strategies with which the Internet is being used most are mobilisation and targeting. Mobilisation was particularly used when a party, such as Labour, was seeking to defend its previous election success, and targeting often manifested itself in greater weighting being awarded to internal audiences rather than the external search for new followers needing to be converted. As a strategic tool, Web 2.0 applications were used primarily conservatively to build on existing relationships.

Election 1.0, 1.5 or 2.0: mapping candidate and party strategies 2007–11

When we produce averages for our two dimensions: the direction of communication and extent of user control which are allowed by each of the website designers, we find a sense of the overall user experiences potentiated across the websites. While in some ways these are artificial, as the overall size of a site can skew them, for example, having a large area containing press releases can draw averages into that sector for the whole site, they are useful in suggesting to what extent Web 2.0 features are adopted and strategies incorporate a more conversational style of communication. The websites of both candidates for the French presidency were locked into a Web 1.0 mode of communication, with both averages being within the realm of one-way communication and user control being four; which is defined as permitting users to control read, video play and link options, and to download content. In the US presidential campaign, the Obama site was three-way and scoring nine out of ten for user control, showing the level of participation permitted. McCain shared the exact same average as his French counterparts, one way with user control scoring an average of four. The reason for this disparity was that, while the Obama site provided a range of policy documents, on-demand video and biographical and political information, the aspects that could not be shared or commented upon, constituted only 4 per cent of the total space occupied by his website. McCain clearly offered significant opportunities for online users to contribute to the site, but this was only across 6 per cent of the total pages. Thus, while the site experimented with weblogs, encouraged promotion through the online network and used social networks to reach out to US voters, it remained in-between Web 1.0 and Web 2.0. Architectures of participation appeared, but they were not core to the McCain site to the same extent as was the case for Obama. Despite Obama's innovations and their partial adoption, the German parties fell primarily into the one-way communication model with low to medium degrees of user control. As regards the latter, the Grüne scored lowest with an average of three, showing hyperlinks being the most common interactive feature; the FDP, CDU and CSU averaged five, which permits control over clicking and sending information, and the SPD six showing they allowed a greater amount of debate to take place. Linke, the Left Party, averaged within the two-way communication quadrant, and also gained six for the average level of user control. However, this is due to the overall size of the site and the paucity of features, which allows the weblog containing 100 posts to make it appear more interactive than the competitors, which in reality was not wholly the case. Overall, the UK parties offer stark contrasts internally. On average, Labour, the Green Party and UKIP all provided predominantly one-way communication across their sites; though the extent of usage of Web 2.0 differed strikingly between Labour and the other two parties. Average direction does not reflect this adequately due to the amount of information provided by Labour; neither do averages of user control scores. UKIP scored four, the Green Party and Labour five. The LibDem website on average reached 2.4 for direction due to the sheer scale of the LibDem Act area, and the Conservatives just topped that with 2.7 due to the opportunities to participate on the Blue Blog and the party-specific social network. However, the greater openness of the LibDem Act area, and larger amount of user-generated content, gives them eight for user control, reflecting the greater participatory experience that could be witnessed and joined; the Conservatives scored seven. The BNP site, as reported earlier, averages as three-way and scores nine for user control; the only party website to match the interactive levels offered by Obama.

Thus, we find that the campaigns of both Obama and the BNP most closely reflect the philosophy of Web 2.0, offering a high democratic structure where the community have significant control over communication, while also enabling participation across a large extent of the site rather than it being bracketed off within bespoke areas discrete and distinct from the overall site. The majority of parties are locked within the norms of Web 1.0 on average, retaining an information-heavy approach and marginalising participatory opportunities.

The use of Web 2.0 features by political parties

Reflecting on the UK party use of the Internet in 2008 (Jackson and Lilleker 2009a), we argued that parties were creating a hybrid experience which we termed Web 1.5. Figure 9.2 applies this model to our four election campaigns. With an architecture of participation locked within one single area, the UK Liberal Democrats prioritise participation less than other parties, but it is highly inclusive and widely used. The UK Conservatives and German Linke are divergent in style, but the size of both blogs, in addition to the MyConservatives network, means that while overall they remain two-way and retain significant

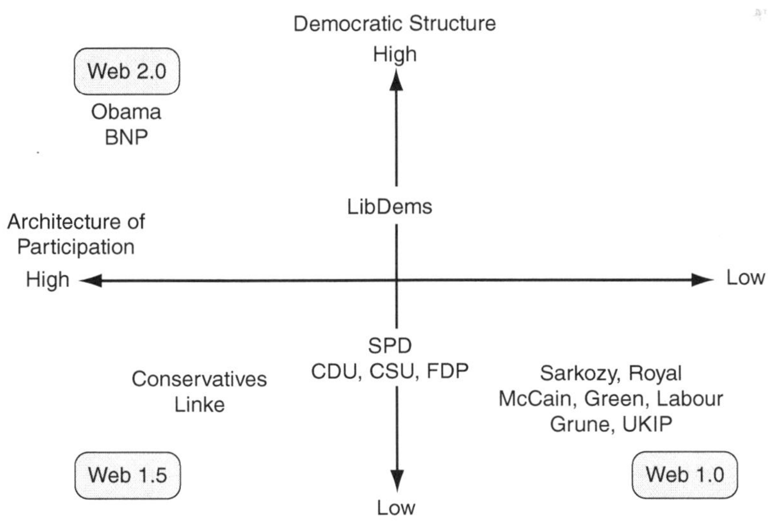

Figure 9.2 The use of Web 2.0 features by political parties.

control over communication, they offer a wider range of participatory opportunities while also retaining features consistent with a Web 1.0 approach. Hence we find a range of strategies; most fall within a Web 1.0 mode, two Web 2.0, but three parties offer hybrid forms where user experiences are mixed between receiving information while also being allowed to participate in a range of ways.

The impact of Web 2.0

One of the questions continually raised about new technologies, and in particular surrounding the introduction and evolution of the Internet, relates to the impact. We argue four potential impacts are currently evidenced by the use of the Internet, and the most recent innovations in Web 2.0: upon electioneering; candidates' and parties' standing; participation and democracy. We suggest there is a hierarchy of impacts beginning with the extent to which Web 2.0 influences the conduct of campaigning, and that this can enhance democracy to an extent. While evidence is patchy and not specific, trends can be identified as we speculate from elements of practice how impactful Web 2.0 might be within a political context.

Barack Obama's was perhaps the only campaign that demonstrated a wholly new approach to election campaigning. While he built on Howard Dean's innovations of four years previous, and the site functionality retained a clear link to the objectives of an election campaign, he harnessed his supporters in ways that none of his antecedents or contemporaries thought possible. While to an extent there was a desire to replicate Obama in Germany and the UK, quite simply neither country had a leader that was able to inspire a range of electoral segments in the same way as Obama. Hence, any replications of Obama's innovations attracted lower levels of engagement than the model which they copied. In many ways, the impact of Web 2.0 on electioneering could be argued to be limited, however this would actually negate a whole range of innovations that occurred over this four-year period. The key to understanding these is to situate the use of features by parties and site visitors within one of the key win-win zones identified earlier. Parties need supporters to actively spread the word and persuade others to join the campaign and pledge their support. In order to achieve this, supporters should feel involved emotionally and practically within the campaign. This, ceteris paribus, can be achieved by facilitating conversations across the party hierarchies, and allowing supporters to feel part of a community that is welcoming, empowering and encouraging.

As Table 9.1 shows, across nations there was a range of elements that allowed three-way participatory communication; this may have been a minority activity across many websites in many countries, but its presence suggests a shift in consideration of the role of bottom-up communication during elections. Web 2.0 allows a range of modes of participation, from open conversation through a range of opportunities to share, like, buzz and repost items. Harnessing these modes of participation to an election campaign suggests that campaigns will have, like to an extent that of Obama, a more co-created feel. That messages,

Table 9.1 Type of interactivity in each nation (in %)

	One-way	*Two-way*	*Three-way*
France 2007	**98.10**	0.90	1.00
USA 2008	6.13	0.03	**93.83**
Germany 2009	**88.54**	0.91	10.54
UK 2010	25.91	0.61	**73.47**
Total	*44.71*	*0.61*	*54.67*

Source: Table compiled with the assistance of Eva Schweitzer.

Notes
Bold numbers indicate the most prevalent type of interactivity in each country.

priorities, images and perhaps even policies may be created involving a wider mass of supporters. This could be in the process of field testing ideas within intranets, or opening up ideas to wider audiences with the attempt of gaining a larger engaged audience who will feel more supportive. While this is speculative, the Obama campaign suggests this is one future possibility and attempts to replicate this were not lost in either Germany or the UK; and whilst created beyond the period of the campaign and placed as an artefact of past collaboration on her website, Royal's *Notebooks of Hope* suggest such techniques may be more widely used as both a tool of electioneering and of shaping and presenting the brand. This suggests there may be some significant impact upon the way that candidates and parties behave in future elections.

While Margetts' (2001) cyberparties do not yet appear a reality, the online dimension of the party's or candidate's support network, which may have a fluid character across time, is clearly becoming very important. Currently, perhaps we are evidencing the importance of supporters as foot soldiers of the campaign, canvassing online and offline and acting as megaphones. Yet, if there are increased demands for involvement among supporters they may equally demand a more fundamental role in exchange for their efforts. While this does not suggest a shift towards a market orientation that places voter consumers at the heart of campaigns, it does suggest a more relational and long-term approach which overcomes the negative impacts of dealignment. Candidates and parties need to tie supporters to their campaigns, harness them as activists, but in order to achieve this they must create incentives. Given these individuals' levels of interest and involvement, it would seem that logically the only pay-off would be a greater sense of involvement, some sense of self-efficacy within driving the campaign and any resulting administration. In many ways this suggests a return to the mass party, but one with a very different character. This would not be a passive mass membership that will pay subscriptions and occasionally attend a local meeting; the cyberparty would use the online environment as a hub for community building and is likely to be as vocal in expressing distaste publicly as for pledging support. Thus, there is a range of challenges facing electoral organisations who seek to harness producers.

The factor underpinning many of these challenges is that participation cannot realistically be avoided, and if participation is not allowed within areas created by the campaign, the danger is these will be shunned in favour of unofficial areas which allow co-creation. Participation is at the heart of thinking about both Web 2.0 (O'Reilly 2005; Anderson 2007) but also about the future of politics and democracy. The work of Stephen Coleman in particular (Coleman and Ward 2005: Coleman and Blumler 2009) argues that the Internet needs to be used effectively within the democratic representative process to potentiate participation. Largely, none of those standing for election allowed open participation, Obama perhaps standing as the exception. This did not mean that participation elsewhere was disallowed; some level of participation was permitted by every candidate and party, most however were limited, many involved gatekeeping mechanisms and the outcomes were highly controlled. Instead, participation appeared to be taking place elsewhere online. The satirical sites, comments and debates on news sites (Thorsen 2010) gained more traffic than most party sites. Participation was largely limited to encouraging the strongest supporters to be more active within online environments; it is whether this is tenable long term that is the question.

Largely, all debates surrounding notions of e-democracy have ended with disillusionment. Politics online has represented a politics as usual, with power following offline patterns and behaviours showing little change from the traditions of top-down, elite-dominated propaganda. While we can say overall this pattern remains across most websites, the levels of co-creation are slowly increasing, participation is being allowed in more public ways and traditional hierarchies are to some extent being flattened. However, these are highly limited when considering how these can impact more broadly upon democracy.

Perhaps elections are the wrong times to seek evidence for an emergent model of e-democracy, however. They facilitate the expression of democratic choice, but elections, in themselves, are not times when public voices need most expression to ensure effective representation. The mass electorates are seeking cues for voting at elections, and thus the brand representations offered by candidates' and parties' communication are of ultimate importance alongside long-term perception-building exercises. However, elections are also times when those seeking election need to shape their manifestos for the future, design messages and seek modes and media for the transmission of messages. Core supporters play a key role in the latter two aspects, and perhaps desire a greater impact upon the former also. Thus, perhaps elections are a time for greater intraparty than extraparty democracy. We suggest that the changing nature of electioneering online facilitates changes within campaign hierarchies that necessitate a greater sense of inclusivity if Web 2.0 is to play a role within the election communication process. In turn, these developments will have an impact upon the nature of electoral participation for those sufficiently engaged to seek greater involvement. For this minority, which may well increase if successfully mobilised, there will be a greater sense of efficacy and involvement, and so their attachment to the democratic process may equally be enhanced through the use of Web 2.0.

Patterns across contests

Due to the lower levels of Internet penetration and adoption of social networking, France is in many ways acting as the control nation in our analysis. This represents the pre Web 2.0 mode of campaigning, despite the contest taking place well within the era of Web 2.0. It seems Obama has clearly changed the game in terms of use of the Internet within an electoral contest, and we see three broad innovations developed by the Barack Obama campaign which have become standard within professional campaigns. The most profound is the shift from private to public community areas for supporters. The MyBO model was replicated to an extent in Germany by the CDU and SPD, and in the UK by the Conservatives, who followed the model most closely, the BNP, Labour and the Liberal Democrats. The latter parties essentially opened what had previously been areas for party members only to public access. Second, the use of online social networks with existing penetration in society emerged as key communication tools. Obama used eighteen different networks including those for a range of ethnic groups and GLEE, for gays, lesbians and everyone else. In Germany, StudiVZ was used alongside Facebook (see also Jurgens and Jungherr 2010), which was also widely used by parties in the UK. Finally, and perhaps least innovative, was the use of weblogs. Obama and the BNP created the largest participatory networks by converting the presentation of news into a participatory forum; for the rest of the UK and all the German parties who used weblogs these were adjuncts to other forms of information that allowed varying degrees of user interaction.

That only two of our sample of sixteen political actors may have created, at least in some form, a non-hierarchical campaign raises some interesting questions. It would appear that the variables identified by Gibson and Ward (2000b) have little predictive value here, and perhaps reflect that adoption and use of the Internet is governed by a range of internal factors specific to parties as opposed to systemic effects. In terms of Web 2.0, there seem to be no specific differences that can be traced to the presidential or party system, nor indeed to the media environment. Resources clearly played a role and provided Obama with a huge advantage; yet this did not make him the only one to see Web 2.0 as offering electoral advantages. Ideology also failed to play a key role, though perhaps both Obama and the BNP sought to create the most active communities; the former focused on mobilisation, while the BNP wanted to build cohesion around its ideological and political stances. Organisational age, status or support also appear to lack any predictive power; this suggests that the ebb and flow model remains useful, and that we see this not only within each national context but may be also detecting an ebb and flow of innovations between nations. While regression would normally be used to identify the predictive power of national, systemic or political variables, the small overall sample with predominance of party sites reduces the reliability of results. We note, however, that the patterns we identify resonate with those of Kluver *et al.* (2007). Supporting the hypothesis of Foot and Schneider (2006), there are identifiable genres in Web production, and party and candidate sites conform, within this context, to the functions of election campaigning. Overall, however, it appears the only safe conclusion is that the more interactive use of the Internet is driven by idiosyncratic factors internal to the candidate or party and their strategy teams.

That said, we should note some extent of standardisation of practice. Activism is the key element supported by Web 2.0. The tools that allow simple conversations to take place allow supporters to network with each other within the party site and across social networks and Twitter. This network effect is harnessed to spread the word and acts as a form of crowd sourcing, encouraging latent supporters to get involved within a word-of-mouth campaign. Due to the constraints of the campaign, user-generated content is minimal and supportive only; this provides a perception of unity and community, though also appearing in some cases as an echo chamber around candidates or party leaders and their policies (Sunstein 2007). Thus, the openness and transparency synonymous with the Web 2.0 participatory architecture may appear limited due to the purpose of the sites. However, given that these sites are analysed in the final throes of an election campaign, perhaps the level of participation is quite surprising.

Clearly, electoral contestants are all adopting Web 2.0 to offer participatory opportunities, and it seems that for the parties in Germany and UK, despite the more limited resources available to them, Obama provided them with a direction for their Internet campaigning. Candidates and parties globally have tried to rework the Obama magic, with copycat sites created in such diverse polities as Israel (Lev-On 2010) and Portugal (Sebastiao 2010), and elections of the future may adopt a similar strategy of seeking to replicate Obama's ability to capture the imagination and enthusiasm of a mass of supporters. Web 2.0, however, was not the reason for this, being only one part of the Obama toolkit. However, the lessons he taught campaigners were adapted to the contexts of Germany and the UK, and one would expect the same to occur in the future. Thus, we predict that the tentative forays into Web 2.0 will evolve into further strategic adaptations, and that a greater role will be given to creating win-win zones where parties, supporters and politically interested Web browsers may observe one another's behaviour, chat and socialise and so create communities of interest around political candidates and party campaigns. This trend will see greater co-creation of campaigning, and thus elections may become one large architecture of participation where the lines between campaign team and some sections of the mass electorate become blurred as elections become dragged into conforming to the big ideas of Web 2.0.

The challenge for political candidates and parties, however, is not simply about what content they place upon their site but also how to drive traffic towards them. With the Internet being full of opportunities to join and interact with like-minded communities, there is no logic that suggests a party site will be prioritised as a destination for browsers. Given the perception of political communication as spin, unworthy of trust, that often underpins broader ratings of politicians, it would actually seem more logical to suggest party websites will gain very little traffic. As Web 2.0 evolves into Web 3.0, and the semantic and intuitive Web, this may be an even more complex issue. Browsers desire information delivered to them that is relevant and in tune with a range of their behaviours. Unless they search for the party or candidate name, it is unlikely the campaign website will be on the first page of Google, Yahoo or their search engine of choice; and even then it may not be the case. This suggests that election communication strategists need to consider how to optimise their site to meet trends in search behaviour. Issues of personal relevance to members of the online community may well be more important than names, slogans or key messages. Targeted emails can build a certain degree of connectedness between the organisation and the online network, yet these need to be sent with the permission of the receiver, as spamming is seen as a counterproductive enterprise. Furthermore, it may be that the produser is more likely to be the driver of Web users than the party, thus harnessing advocates and cheerleaders may supplement search engine optimisation strategies. Interestingly, this suggests that electoral candidates need to become closer to both their supporters and the mass online user, and as the latter become the critical mass in society, there may well be a more distinct trend towards treating them as representative. Thus, we may see a greater drift towards market-oriented behaviour as an adjunct of an online communication strategy. This leads to the big question for the future, hinted at earlier in this chapter, and relating to democracy. Currently, we do not see a conscious attempt to enhance democracy online; however, could the demands of the online user, familiar in Web 2.0 and Web 3.0 environments, begin to demand greater influence? Could democracy actually be driven not by constitutions or political ideals, but by a desire to reach audiences through effective political campaign communication adhering to the rules of online communities of practice? While it would seem to be an upside-down route to greater democratisation, it may just have possibilities to reverse the spin culture and create a communication environment that involves a wider mass community.

Notes

1 Introduction

1 For a more detailed discussion of these seven features see Anderson 2006 and Chadwick 2009.

2 E-campaigning and e-elections

1 Although the UK general election has to be held once every five years, the Prime Minister has the power within that timeframe of calling an election.

3 Web 2.0

1 Andrew Chadwick conducted a similar analysis based on O'Reilly's approach. Chadwick identified seven key themes: Internet as a platform for political discourse; the collective intelligence emergent from political Web use; the importance of data over particular software and hardware applications; perpetual experimentalism in the public domain; the creation of small-scale forms of political engagement through consumerism; the propagation of political content through multiple applications; and rich user experiences on political websites. Both Anderson's and Chadwick's models are similar, but we have applied Anderson's as we feel this is more applicable to election campaigns.

4 Measuring for a new style of campaigning

1 The method of downloading and saving websites and the sampling procedure varied slightly within the data collection process for the German chapter; this is detailed in a specific section within Chapter 7.

5 France 2007: tentative interactivity

1 By 2009, these figures have increased exponentially with France on 65.7 per cent, Germany 67 per cent, the UK 70.9 per cent and the US with 74.7 per cent penetration (www.internetworldstats.com/stats.htm)

8 The UK 2010: interacting with echo chambers

1 Respect was a party created by George Galloway MP after his expulsion from the Labour Party in October 2003 for his opposition to the Iraq War and defence of the regime of Saddam Hussein. Anti-war candidates stood in the 2005 UK General Election, but only Galloway was successful due to a high-profile campaign within the

strongly Muslim constituency of Bethnal Green and Bow in London. Interestingly, Galloway himself makes much use of the Internet as a campaigning tool and was found to be highly interactive in 2008 (Jackson and Lilleker 2009b), yet this was not sufficient for him to win in 2010 when he stood in a different constituency.

2 The main parties are the Scottish Nationalist Party, Welsh Nationalist Party Plaid Cymru and the Northern Irish Ulster Unionist Party who are aligned with the Conservatives. Additionally, the Northern Irish Democratic Unionist Party, Social and Democratic Labour Party and Sinn Fein have all gained some representation, though the latter refuse to take their seats in Westminster due to their campaign for a sovereign Northern Ireland.

Bibliography

Abbate, J. (1999) *Inventing the Internet*, Cambridge, MA: MIT.

Agre, P. E. (2002) 'Real-time politics: The Internet and the political process', *The Information Society*, 18 (5): 311–31.

Albrecht, S. (2007) 'Weblog campaigning in the German Bundestag Election 2005', *Social Science Computer Review*, 25 (4): 504–20.

Anderson, C. (2006) *The Long Tail: Why the Future of Business is Selling Less of More*, London: Hyperion.

Anderson, C., Blais, A., Bowler, S., Donovan, T. and Listhang, O. (2007) *Losers' Consent: Elections and Democratic Legitimacy*, Oxford: Oxford University Press.

Anderson, P. (2007) *What is Web 2.0? Ideas, technologies and implications for education*, JISC Technology and Standards Watch Report, February.

Ansolabehere, S. and Iyengar, S. (1995) *Going Negative: How Political Advertisements Shrink and Polarize the Electorate*, New York: Free Press, 1995.

Anstead, N. (2008) 'The Internet and campaign finance in the U.S. and the UK: An institutional comparison', *Journal of Information Technology and Politics*, 5 (3): 285–302.

Anstead, N. and Chadwick, A. (2008) 'Parties, election campaigning, and the Internet: Toward a comparative institutional approach', in A. Chadwick and P. Howard (eds) *Handbook of Internet Politics*, New York: Routledge.

Arterton, C. and Greener, W. (2009) 'Obama: Strategies and tactics in the general election', in D. Johnson (ed.) *Campaigning for President 2008: Strategy and Tactics, New Voices and New Techniques*, London: Routledge: 174–88.

Auty, C. and Nicholas, D. (1998) 'British political parties and their web pages', *Aslib Proceedings*, 50 (10): 283–6.

Backhouse, J. (2008) 'Election campaigning in the era of Web 2.0 and social media', in D. Remenyi (ed.) *Proceedings of 4th International Conference on e-Government*: 55–62.

Baines, P. R., Scheucher, C. and Plasser, F. (2001) 'The "Americanization" myth in European political markets: A focus on the United Kingdom', *European Journal of Marketing*, 35 (9/10): 1099–116.

Banwart, M. C. (2002) 'Videostyle and Webstyle in 2000: Comparing the gender differences of candidate presentations in political advertising and on the Internet', unpublished doctoral thesis, University of Oklahoma.

Barber, B. (1984) *Strong Democracy: Participatory Politics for a New Age*, London: University of California Press.

Barr, K. (2009) 'A perfect storm: The 2008 youth vote', in D. Johnson (ed.) *Campaigning for President 2008: Strategy and Tactics, New Voices and New Techniques*, London: Routledge: 105–25.

Barsky, E. (2006) 'Introducing Web 2.0: Weblogs and podcasting for health librarians', *Journal of the Canadian Health Librarians Association*, 27 (2): 33–4.

Barsky, E. and Purdon, M. (2006) 'Introducing Web 2.0: Social networking and social bookmarking for health librarians', *Journal of the Canadian Health Libraries Association*, 27 (3): 65–7.

Bay, L. (2008, 17 November) 'Krampf im www.ahlkampf' [Cramps in www.campaigning], *Focus*, 47: 54–6.

Belenky, A. (2005) 'Competitive strategies of U.S. presidential candidates in election campaigns', *Computer and Mathematics with Applications*, 49 (1): 53–71.

Bell, D. and Criddle, B. (2002) 'Presidentialism restored: The French elections of April–May and June 2002', *Parliamentary Affairs*, 55 (4): 643–63.

Benhold, K. (2007) 'French election strategies confound experts from America', *International Herald Tribune*, Saturday–Sunday, 14–15 April: 3.

Benkler, Y. (2006) *The Wealth of Networks: How Social Production Transforms Markets and Freedom*, New Haven: Yale University Press.

Bennett, W. L. (1998) 'The Uncivic Culture: Communication, identity, and the rise of lifestyle politics', *PS: Political Science and Politics*, 31 (4): 741–61.

Benoit, W. L. (1999) *Seeing Spots: A Functional Analysis of Presidential Television Advertisements, 1952–1996*, Westport, CT, USA: Greenwood Publishing Group.

Benoit, W. and Benoit, P. (2000) 'The virtual campaign: Presidential primary websites in Campaign 2000', *American Communication Journal*, 3 (3). Online. Available HTTP: http://acjournal.org/holdings/vol.3/Iss3/curtain.html#4 (accessed 10 May 2008).

Berelson, B., Lazarsfeld, P. and McPhee, W. (1954) *Voting: a study of opinion formation in a presidential campaign*, Chicago, IL: University of Chicago Press.

Bergs, A. (2006) 'Analyzing online communication from a social network point of view: Questions, problems, perspectives', *Language@Internet*, 3. Online. Available HTTP: www.languageinternet.de/articles/2006/371/index_html (accessed 12 June 2007).

Bernays, E. (1923) Crystallizing Public Opinion, Kessing Publishing (2004 issue).

Bernstein, J. (2009) The 2010 YouTube Election has just begun, *The Media Blog*, September 16. Available online at http://jonbernstein.wordpress.com/2009/09/16/youtube-conservative-home-gordon-brown-2010-election-has-just-begun/ accessed 14 March 2010.

Berry, L. (1983) 'Relationship marketing', in L. Berry, G. Shostack and G. Upak (eds) *Emerging Perspectives on Services Marketing*, Chicago: American Marketing Association: 25–8.

Bialek, C. (5 March 2009) *'Internetkampagnen: Herzstück oder Hysterie?'* [Internet campaigns: Centrepiece or hysteria?]. Online. Available HTTP: www.handelsblatt.com/unternehmen/strategie/internetkampagnen-herzstueck-oder-hysterie;2188153 (accessed 30 September 2009).

Bieber, C. (2000) *'Im digitalen Hinterzimmer'* [In the digital backroom], Politik-Digital. Available HTTP: http://politik-digital.de/archiv/hintergrund/hinter.shtml (accessed 30 September 2009).

Bieber, C. (2001) 'Information and political engagement in America: The search for effects of information technology at the individual level', *Political Research Quarterly*, 54 (1): 53–67.

Bimber, B. (1998) 'The Internet and political mobilisation', *Social Science Computer Review*, 16 (4): 391–401.

Bimber, B. (2003) *Information and American Democracy: Technology in the Evolution of Political Power*, Cambridge: Cambridge University Press.

Bimber, B. and Davis, R. (2003) *Campaigning Online: The Internet in U.S. Elections*, Oxford: Oxford University Press.

Bingener, R., Veser, R. and Wagner, M. K. (23 September 2009) 'Blitzmeuten im Spätwahlkampf: Jeder Satz der Kanzlerin wird mit "Yeah" – Rufen quittiert – "Flashmobs" hatten aber auch schon ihre Verdienste' [Sudden packs in the hot campaign phase: Every sentence of the chancellor is answered by sarcastic shouts of 'Yeah!' – but flashmobs also had their merits], *Frankfurter Allgemeine Zeitung*, 221: 7.

Blood, R. (2000) 'Weblogs: A history and perspective'. Online. Available HTTP: www.rebeccablood.net/essays weblog_history.html (accessed 9 March 2004).

Blumenthal, S. (1980) *The Permanent Campaign: Inside the World of Elite Political Operatives*, Boston: Beacon.

Blumler, J. and Gurevitch, M. (1995) *The Crisis of Public Communication*, Abingdon: Routledge.

Blumler, J. and Gurevitch, M. (2001) '"Americanization" reconsidered: UK–US campaign communication comparisons across time', in L. Bennett and R. Entman, (eds) *Mediated Politics*, Cambridge: Cambridge University Press, pp. 380–406.

Blumler, J. and Kavanagh, D. (1999) The third age of communication: Influences and features, *Political Communication*, 16 (3): 209–30.

Boardman, M. (2005) *The Language of Websites*, London: Routledge.

Bohman, J. (2004) 'Expanding dialogue: The Internet, the public sphere and prospects for transnational democracy', *The Editorial Board of Sociological Review*, 131–55.

Bondarouk, T. V. and Ruel, H. J. M. (2008) 'HRM systems for successful information technology implementation: Evidence from three case studies', *European Management Journal*, 26 (3): 153–65.

Boogers, M. and Voerman, G. (2002) 'Who visits political websites, and why? Results of an online survey among visitors of political websites during the Dutch 2002 General Elections Campaign', paper prepared for the Euricom Project: Electronic Networks and Democratic Engagement, Nijmegen 9–12 October 2002.

Bordewijk, J. and van Kaam, B. (1986) 'Towards a new classification of tele-information services', *Intermedia*, 14 (1): 16–21.

boyd, d. and Ellison, N. (2007) 'Social network sites: Definition, history and scholarship', *Journal of Computer-Mediated Communication*, 13 (1). Online. Available HTTP: http://jcmc.indiana.edu/vol.13/issue1/boyd.ellison.html (accessed 25 April 2008).

Brams, S. and Davis, M. (1974) 'The 3/2's Rule in presidential campaigning', *American Political Science Review*, 68 (1): 113–34.

Bratten, C. (2005) 'Online zealotry: La France du peuple virtuel', *New Media and Society*, 7 (4): 517–32.

Brauckmann, P. (15 April 2009) *'Webwahlkampf: Was die Parteien wollen – und können'* [Web campaigning: What the parties want – and can do], Politik-Digital. Available HTTP: www.politik-digital.de/soziale-netzwerke-im-deutschen-wahlkampf (accessed 4 June 2009).

Briscoe, B., Odlyzko, A. and Tilly, B. (2006) Metcalfe's Law is wrong, *IEEE Spectrum*, July. Online. Available HTTP: http://spectrum.ieee.org/jul06/4109 (accessed 20 October 2007).

Brosius, H.-B., Breinker, C. and Esser, F. (1991) 'Der "Immermehrismus": Journalistisches Stilmittel oder Realitätsverzerrung?' [The 'more and more'-ism: Rhetorical device in journalism or distortion of reality?], *Publizistik*, 36: 407–27.

Brownstein, R. (2009) 'Obama's global audience', *National Journal*, 11 July. Online.

Available HTTP: www.nationaljournal.com/njmagazine/nj_20090711_1014.php (accessed 20 July 2009).

Bruns, A. (2005) 'Anyone can edit: Understanding the produser, the Mojtaba Saminejad lecture'. Online. Available HTTP: http://snurb.info/files/AnyoneCanEdit.ppt (accessed 12 September 2007).

Bucy, E. P. (2004) 'Interactivity in society: Locating an elusive concept', *The Information Society*, 20 (5): 373–83.

Burgess, J. (2006) 'Hearing ordinary voices: Cultural studies, vernacular creativity and digital storytelling', *Continuum: Journal of Media and Cultural Studies*, 20 (2): 201–14.

Burgess, J., Foth, M. and Klaebe, H. (2006) 'Everyday creativity as civic engagement: A cultural citizenship view of new media', in *Proceedings Communications Policy and Research Forum*, Sydney. Online. Available HTTP: http://eprints.qut.edu.au (accessed 5 August 2008).

Busemann, K. and Gscheidle, C. (2009) 'Web 2.0: Communitys [sic] bei jungen Nutzern beliebt: Ergebnisse der ARD/ZDF-Onlinestudie' [Web 2.0: Communities popular among young users], *Media Perspektiven*, 7: 356–64.

Butler, D. and Pinto-Duschinsky, M. (1970) *The British General Election of 1970*, Basingstoke: Macmillan.

Butler, D. and Ranney, A. (1992) (eds) *Electioneering: A Comparative Study of Continuity and Change*, New York: Oxford University Press.

Butler, D. and Rose, R. (1960) *The British General Election of 1959*, London: St Martin's Press.

Butler, D. and Stokes, D. (1971) *Political Change in Britain: Forces Shaping Electoral Choice*, Harmondsworth: Penguin.

Cammaerts, B. (2008) 'Critiques on the participatory potentials of Web 2.0', *Communication, Culture and Critique*, 1 (4): 358–77.

Campbell, A., Converse, P. E., Miller, W. E. and Stokes, D. E. (1960) *The American Voter*, New York: Wiley.

Campbell, J. (2000) *The American Campaign: US Presidential Campaigns and the Vote*, College Station: Texas A&M University Press.

Canetti, E. (1978) *Crowds and Power*, New York: Seabury Press.

Card, S. K., Moran, T. P. and Newell, A. (1986) *The Psychology of Human–Computer Interaction*, Hillsdale, NJ: Lawrence Erlbaum.

Carlson, T. and Djupsund, G. (2001) 'Old wine in new bottles? The 1999 Finnish election campaign on the Internet', *The Harvard International Journal of Press/Politics*, 6 (1): 68–87.

Castells, M. (1996) *The Information Age: Economy, Society and Culture, Vol. 1: The Rise of the Network Society*, Oxford: Blackwell.

Castells, M. (2002) *The Internet Galaxy: Reflections on the Internet, Business, and Society*, New York: Oxford University Press.

Castells, M. (2007) 'Communication, power and counter-power in the network society', *International Journal of Communication*, 1: 238–66.

Cayrol, R. (1997) *Média et démocratie la derive*, Paris: Presses de Sciences Po.

Chadwick, A. (2006) *Internet Politics: States, Citizens, and New Communication Technologies*, Oxford: Oxford University Press.

Chadwick, A. (2007) 'Digital network repertoires and organizational hybridity, *Political Communication'*, 24 (3): 283–301.

Chadwick, A. (2009) 'Web 2.0: New challenges for the study of e-democracy in an era of informational exuberance', *I/S: Journal of Law and Policy for the Information Society*, 5 (1): 9–41.

Chadwick, A. and May, C. (2003) 'Interaction between states and citizens in the age of the Internet: "E-government" in the United States, Britain and the European Union', *Governance: International Journal of Policy, Administration and Institutions*, 16 (2): 271–300.

Chaffee, S. (ed.) (1975) *Political Communication: Issues and Strategies for Research*, Beverley Hills, CA: Sage.

Chaffee, S. and Hochheimer, J. (1985) 'The beginnings of political communication research in the United States: Origins of a limited effects model', in E. Rogers and F. Balle (eds) *The Media Revolution in America and Western Europe*, Norwood, NJ: Ablex: 60–95.

Chalaby, J. (2005) 'French political communication in a comparative perspective: The media and the issue of freedom', *Modern and Contemporary France*, 13 (3): 273–90.

Chatratichart, W. (2009) 'Attitudes towards political leaders amongst young people in Thailand and their influence on electoral choices', unpublished doctoral thesis, Bournemouth University.

Christopher, M., Payne, A. and Ballantyne, D. (1991) *Relationship Marketing*, Oxford: Butterworth-Heinemann.

City University (2 March 2010) The first new media election? Online. Available HTTP: www.city.ac.uk/whatson/2010/3-mar/02032010-newmediaelection.html (accessed 10 March 2010).

Clarke, H., Sanders, D., Stewart, M. C. and Whiteley, P. (2004) *Political Choice in Britain*, Oxford: Oxford University Press.

Cocciolo, A., Chae, H. S. and Natriello, G. (2007) 'using social network analysis to highlight an emerging online community of practice', paper to international conference on computer support for collaborative learning, July, New Brunswick, NJ.

Colantoni, C., Levesque, T. and Ordeshook, P. (1975) 'Campaign resource allocation under the Electoral College', *American Political Science Review*, 69 (1): 141–54.

Cole, A. (2002) 'A strange affair: The 2002 Presidential and Parliamentary Elections in France', *Government and Opposition*, 37 (3): 317–41.

Coleman, S. (2001) (ed.) *2001: Cyber Space Odyssey – the Internet at the UK election*, London: Hansard Society.

Coleman, S. and Blumler, J. (2009) *The Internet and Democratic Citizenship: Theory, Practice and Policy*, Cambridge: Cambridge University Press.

Coleman, S. and Ward, S. (eds) (2005) *Spinning the Web: Online Campaigning During the 2005 General Election*, London: Hansard Society.

Comscore (2006) Online. Available HTTP: www.comscore.com/press/release.asp?press=849 (accessed 16 August 2008).

Converse, P. (1966) 'The concept of a normal vote', in A. Campbell, P. Converse, W. Miller and D. Stokes (eds) *Elections and the Political Order*, New York: Free Press: 9–39.

Conway, M. and Dorner, D. G. (2004) 'An evaluation of New Zealand political party websites', *Information Research*, 9 (4): Online. Available HTTP: http://informationr.net/ir/9–4/paper196.html (accessed 2 September 2007).

Copsey, N. (2003) 'Extremism on the net: The extreme right and the value of the Internet', in R. Gibson, P. Nixon and S. Ward (eds) *Political Parties and the Internet: Net Gain?*, London: Routledge: 218–33.

Cornfield, M. (2004) *Politics Moves Online: Campaigning and the Internet*, New York: Century Foundation Press.

Corrado, A. and Corbett, M. (2009) 'Rewriting the playbook on presidential campaign financing', in D. Johnson (ed.) *Campaigning for President 2008: Strategy and Tactics, New Voices and New Techniques*, London: Routledge: 126–46.

Corrado, A. and Firestone, C. M. (eds) (1996) *Elections in Cyberspace: Toward a New Era in American Politics*, Washington, DC: Aspen Institute.

Cox, G. (1999) *The Digital Crowd: Some Questions on Globalization and Agency*, MA: MIT Press.

Criado, H. (2008) 'The effects of party mobilisation strategies on the vote: The PSOE and the PP in the 1996 Spanish Election', *European Journal of Political Research*, 47 (1): 80–100.

Crystal, D. (2006) 'The future starts here'. Online. Available HTTP: www.davidcrystal.com/DC_articles/Langdeath17.pdf (accessed 13 April 2007).

D'Alessio, D. (1997) 'Use of the World Wide Web in the 1996 US Election', *Election Studies*, 16 (4): 489–500.

Dahlgren, P. (2005) 'The Internet, public spheres, and political communication: dispersion and deliberation', *Political Communication*, 22 (2): 147–62.

Dale, I. (2010) 'General Election 2010: This was meant to be the Internet election. So what happened?', *The Daily Telegraph*, 27 April 2010. Online. Available HTTP: www.telegraph.co.uk/news/election-2010/7640143/General-Election-2010-This-was-meant-to-be-the-internet-election.-So-what-happened.html (accessed 4 June 2010).

Davis, B. H. and Brewer, J. P. (1997) *Electronic Discourse: Linguistic Individuals in Virtual Space*, Albany, NY: State University of New York Press.

Davis, R. (1999) *The Web of Politics: The Internet's Impact on the American Political System*, New York, Oxford University Press.

Davis, R. (2005) *Politics Online: Blogs, Chatrooms And Discussion Groups in American Democracy*, London: Routledge.

de Landtsheer, C., Krasnoboka, N. and Neuner, C. (1999) 'Participation friendliness of political websites in Eastern and Western Europe', paper presented at the expert meeting on Political Communication and Technological Innovation, University of Perugia, 2–4 December.

de Landtsheer, C., Krasnoboka, N. and Neuner, C. (2005) 'Participation friendliness of Political Websites in Eastern and Western Europe', in R. F. Farnen, H. Dekker, C. de Landtsheer, H. Sunker, D. B. German, W. Ehlert and G. Szell (eds) *Democratization. Europeanization and Globalization Trends*, Frankfurt am Main: Peter Lang: 325–60.

Delaney, C. (2006) 'Online politics 101: The tools and tactics of on-line political advocacy', Washington, DC; at: www.epolitics.com/ (accessed 12 December 2007).

Denver, D. (1998) 'The British Electorate in the 1990s', *West European Politics*, 21 (1): 197–217.

Denver, D. and Hands, G. (1992) 'Constituency campaigning', *Parliamentary Affairs*, 45 (4): 528–44.

Denver, D. and Hands, G. (1997) *Modern Constituency Electioneering*, London: Frank Cass.

Denver, D. and Hands, G. (1998) 'Triumph of targeting? Constituency campaigning in the 1997 election', in D. Denver, J. Fisher, P. Cowley and C. Pattie (eds) *British Elections and Parties Review 8*, London: Frank Cass: 171–90.

Desquinabo, N. (2008) 'Dynamiques et impacts des propositions politiques dans les web-forums partisans', *Réseaux*, 26 (150): 107–32.

Devine, T. (2009) 'Obama wins the nomination: How he did it', in D. Johnson (ed.) *Campaigning for President 2008: Strategy and Tactics, New Voices and New Techniques*, London: Routledge: 31–43.
De Vrees, P. (2007) 'Candidate image in Belgian politics', unpublished PhD thesis, Universiteit Antwerpen.
DiMaggio, P., Hargittai, E., Neuman, W. and Robinson, J. (2001) 'Social implications of the Internet', *Annual Review of Sociology*, 27: 307–36.
Downs, A. (1957) *An Economic Theory of Voting*, New York: Harper and Row.
Downes, E. and McMillan, S. (2000) 'Defining interactivity: A qualitative identification of key dimensions', *New Media Society*, 2 (2): 157–79.
Downes, L. and Mui, C. (2000) *Unleashing the Killer App*, Boston, MA: Harvard University Press.
Drezner, D. and Farrell, H. (2004) 'The power and politics of blogs', paper presented to the annual meeting of the American Political Science Association, August, Chicago.
Druckman, J. N., Kifer, M. and Parkin, M. (2010) 'Timeless strategy meets new medium: Going negative on congressional campaign websites, 2002–2006', *Political Communication*, 27 (1): 88–103.
Dulio, D., Goff, D. and Thurber, J. (1999) 'Untangled Web: Internet use during the 1998 election', *Political Science and Politics*, 32 (1): 53–9.
E-Marketer (2009) Psst! Here's some viral marketing news … Pass it on, 31 January. Online. Available HTTP: www.emarketer.com/Article.aspx?R=1003796 (accessed 2 March 2009).
Esser, F., Reineman, C. and Fan, D. (2001) 'Spin Doctors in the United States, Great Britain and Germany: Metacommunication about media manipulation', *The Harvard International Journal of Press/Politics*, 6 (1): 16–45.
Fairclough, N. (2000) 'Discourse, social theory, and social research: The discourse of welfare reform', *Journal of Sociolinguistics*, 4 (2): 163–95.
Fairclough, N. (2001) 'The discourse of New Labour: Critical discourse analysis', in M. Wetherell, S. Taylor and S. J. Yates (eds) *Discourse as Data: A Guide for Analysis*, London: Sage: 229–66.
Fairclough, N. (2003) *Analysing Discourse: Textual Analysis for Social Research*, London: Routledge.
Fairclough, N. and Wodak, R. (1997) 'Critical discourse analysis', in T. Van Dijk, (ed.) *Discourse as Social Interaction*, London: Sage: 258–84.
Farrell, D. (1997) *Comparing Electoral Systems*, London: Prentice Hall/Harvester Wheatsheaf.
Farrell, D., Kolodny, R. and Medvic, S. (2001) 'Parties and campaign professionals in a digital age', *The Harvard International Journal of Press/Politics*, 6 (4): 11–30.
Farrell, D. and Schmitt-Beck, R. (eds) (2002) *Do Political Campaigns Matter?*, London: Routledge.
Fauvelle-Aymar, C., Lafay, J-L. and Servais, M. (2000) 'The impact of turnout on electoral choices: An econometric analysis of the French case', *Electoral Studies*, 19 (2/3): 393–412.
Fenn, P. (2009) 'Communication wars: Television and new media', in D. Johnson (ed.) *Campaigning for President 2008: Strategy and Tactics, New Voices and New Techniques*, London: Routledge: 210–21.
Ferber, P., Foltz, F. and Pugliese, R. (2007) 'Cyberdemocracy and online politics: A new model of interactivity', *Bulletin of Science, Technology and Society*, 27 (5): 391–400.
Filzmaier, P. and Plasser, F. (2001) *Wahlkampf um das Weiße Haus: Presidential*

Elections in den USA [Campaigning for the White House: Presidential elections in the USA], Opladen: Leske + Budrich.

Fischer, K. and Voß, O. (24 August 2009) 'Stimmenjagd im Netz: Die Piratenpartei führt vor, wie Online-Wahlkampf vor allem junge Wähler mobilisiert' [Fighting for votes on the net: The Pirate Party shows how to mobilise young voters through online campaigning]. *Wirtschaftswoche*, 35: 96.

Flanders, L., Goldstein, R., Kuipers, D., Ridgeway, J., Sanders, E. and Savage, D. (2007) *The Contenders*, New York: Seven Stories.

Foot, K. A. and Schneider, S. M. (2002) 'Online action in Campaign 2000: An exploratory analysis of the U.S. political web sphere', *Journal of Broadcast and Electronic Media*, 46 (2): 222–44.

Foot, K. A. and Schneider, S. M. (2006) *Web Campaigning*, Cambridge, MA: MIT Press.

Footitt, H. (2004) 'In search of lost women: Alternative political maps in the Presidential Election of 2002', in J. Gaffney (ed.) *The French Presidential and Legislative Elections of 2002*, Aldershot: Ashgate: 222–37.

Fouetillou, G. (2006) Ecologie de la Ségosphère [online] Compiègne, France: RTGI. Online. Available HTTP: www.observatoire-presidentielle.fr/?pageid=12 (accessed 10 October 2007).

Fox, S., Anderson, J. Q. and Rainie, L. (2005) *The Future of the Internet*, Washington, DC: Pew Research.

Franklin, B. (1994) *Packaging Politics: Political Communications in Britain's Media Democracy*, London: Edward Arnold.

Freedman, P. and Goldstein, K. (1999) 'Measuring media exposure and the effects of negative campaign ads', *American Journal of Political Science*, 42 (4): 1189–208.

Gaffney, J. (2004) 'The 2002 Elections in institutional and comparative perspective', in J. Gaffney (ed.) *The French Presidential and Legislative Elections of 2002*, Farnham: Ashgate: 1–15.

Garramone, G. M., Atkin, C. K., Pinkleton, B. E. and Cole, R. T. (1990) 'Effects of negative political advertising on the political process', *Journal of Broadcasting and Electronic Media*, 34 (3): 299–311.

Geer, J. G. (2006) *In Defense of Negativity: Attack Ads in Presidential Campaigns*, Chicago: Chicago University Press.

Gellner, W. and Strohmeier, G. (2002) 'Cyber-Kampagnen' [Cyber-campaigns], in A. Dörner and L. Vogt (eds) *Wahl-Kämpfe: Betrachtungen über ein demokratisches Ritual*, Frankfurt am Main: Suhrkamp: 164–80.

George, C. (2005) 'Usability testing and design of a library website: An interactive approach', *OCLC Systems and Services: International Digital Library Perspectives*, 21 (3): 167–80.

Germany, J. B. (2009) 'The Online Revolution', in D. Johnson (ed.) *Campaigning for President 2008: Strategy and Tactics, New Voices and New Techniques*, London: Routledge: 147–60.

Gibson, R. (2003) 'Web campaigning from a global perspective', paper presented to The IT Revolution and the Transformation of Society Conference, Institute for International Policy Studies, Tokyo, Japan.

Gibson, R. (2004) 'Web campaigning from a global perspective', *Asia Pacific Review*, 11: 95–126.

Gibson R. and McAllister, I. (2003) 'Cybercampaigning and the vote: Online communication in the 2001 Australian Election', paper delivered to the American Political Science Association, Philadelphia, August.

Gibson, R., Margolis, M., Resnick, D. and Ward, S. (2003a) 'Election campaigning on the WWW in the US and the UK: A comparative analysis', *Party Politics*, 9 (1): 47–76.

Gibson, R., Newell, J. and Ward, S. (2000) 'New parties, new media: Italian party politics and the Internet', *South European Society and Politics*, 5 (1): 123–42.

Gibson, R. and Römmele, A. (2001) 'Changing campaign communications: A party-centred theory of professional campaigning', *Harvard International Journal of Press/Politics*, 6 (4): 31–43.

Gibson, R., Römmele, A. and Ward, S. (2003b) 'German parties and Internet campaigning in the 2002 Federal Election', *German Politics*, 12 (1): 79–104.

Gibson, R. and Ward, S. (1997) 'UK political parties and the Internet: Prospects for democracy', *Working Papers in Contemporary History and Politics 13*, European Studies Research Institute, University of Salford.

Gibson, R. and Ward, S. (1998) 'UK political parties and the Internet: Politics as usual in the new media', *Harvard International Journal of Press/Politics*, 3 (3): 14–38.

Gibson, R. and Ward, S. (1999) 'Party democracy online: UK parties and new ICTs', *Information, Communication and Society*, 2 (3): 240–67.

Gibson, R. and Ward, S. (2000a) 'British party activity in cyberspace', in R. Gibson and S. Ward (eds) *Reinvigorating Government? British Politics and the Internet*, Aldershot: Ashgate: 155–207.

Gibson, R. and Ward, S. (2000b) 'A proposed methodology for measuring the function and effectiveness of political websites', *Social Science Computer Review*, 18 (3): 301–19.

Gibson, R. and Ward, S. (2002) 'Virtual campaigning: Australian parties and the impact of the Internet', *Australian Journal of Political Science*, 37 (1): 99–130.

Gibson, R. and Ward, S. (2003) 'Online and on message? Candidates websites in the 2001 General Election', *British Journal of Politics and International Relations*, 5 (2): 188–205.

Gibson, R., Ward, S. and Lusoli, W. (2002) 'Online campaigning in the UK: The public respond', paper presented to the American Political Studies Association, Boston, 29 August – 1 September.

Gibson, R., Ward, S. and Lusoli, W. (2003c) 'The Internet and political campaigning: The new medium comes of age', *Representation*, 29 (3): 166–80.

Gillespie, M. and Toynbee, J. (2006) *Analysing Media Texts*, New York: McGraw-Hill.

Gillmann, B. (2 April 2009) 'Parteien im Web 2.0: Siegen wie Obama? – No we can't...' [Parties in Web 2.0: Winning like Obama? – No we can't...], *Handelsblatt Online*. Available HTTP: www.handelsblatt.com/politik/deutschland/siegen-wie-obama-no-we-can-t;2223741 (accessed 15 April 2009).

Gillmann, B., Delhaes, D. and Knüwer, T. (19 March 2009) 'Brüder zum Netze, zu Facebook. Siegen wie Obama: Der US-Onlinewahlkampf und seine Folgen. Heute: die Strategien der großen Parteien' [Brothers go to the nets, go to Facebook. Winning like Obama: The U.S. online campaign and its consequences. Today: The strategies of the major parties], *Handelsblatt*, 55: 19.

Global Reach (2006) Online: Available HTTP: www.glreach.com/gbc/fr/french.php3 (accessed 12 April 2008).

Gobry, P.-E. (2007) Le Internet Campaign, *tech-President*. Online. Available HTTP: http://techpresident.com/blog-entry/le-internet-campaign (accessed 14 October 2009).

Grant, A. (2005) Party election finance in Britain and America: A comparative analysis, *Parliamentary Affairs*, 58 (1): 71–88.

Greener, W. and Arterton, C. (2009) 'McCain: Strategies and tactics in the General Election', in D. Johnson (ed.) *Campaigning for President 2008: Strategy and Tactics, New Voices and New Techniques*, London: Routledge: 163–73.

Greengard, S. (2009) 'The first Internet president', *Communications of the ACM*, 52 (2): 16–18.

Greer, J. and LaPointe, M. (2004) 'Cyber-Campaigning grows up: A comparative content analysis of websites for US Senate and gubernatorial races 1998–2000', in R. Gibson, A. Rommele and S. Ward (eds) *E-Democracy: Mobilisation, Organisation and Participation Online*, London: Routledge: 116–32.

Groeling, T. (2008) 'Who's the fairest of them all? An empirical test for partisan bias on ABC, CBS, NBC, and Fox News', *Presidential Studies Quarterly*, 38 (4): 631–57.

Grunig, J. E. and Grunig, L. A. (1992) 'Models of public relations and communication', in J. Grunig (ed.) *Excellence in Public Relations and Communication Management*, Hillsdale, NJ: Lawrence Erlbaum Associates: 285–326.

Haiman, F. (1989) 'A tale of two countries: Media messages of the French and American Presidential Campaigns of 1988', Report for Northwestern University, Evanston, IL. Institute for Modern Communications.

Hanke, T. (9 July 2009) 'Internet-Wahlkampf: Piraten jagen Partei-Schnarchnasen' [Internet campaigning: Pirates are chasing laggard parties], *Handelsblatt.* Online. Available HTTP: www.handelsblatt.com/meinung/kommentar-politik/piraten-jagen-partei-schnarchnasen;2430408 (accessed 18 July 2009).

Harfoush, R. (2009) *Yes We Did: An Inside Look at How Social Media Built the Obama Brand*, Berkeley, CA: New Riders.

Harrop, M. (1986) 'Voting and the Electorate', in H. Drucker, P. Dunleavy, A. Gamble and G. Peele (eds) *Developments in British Politics*, London: Macmillan: 46–54.

Haspells, M. (2008) 'Will you be my Facebook friend?', *Proceedings: 4th Annual Symposium: Graduate Research and Scholarly Projects*, Wichita, KS: Wichita State University: 47–8.

Hassan, R. (2004) *Media, Politics and the Network Society*, Milton Keynes: Open University Press.

Heath, A. F., Jowell, R. M. and Curtice, J. K. (2001) *The Rise of New Labour*, Oxford: Oxford University Press.

Hebecker, E. (2002) 'Experimentieren für den Ernstfall: Der Online-Wahlkampf 2002' [Experimenting for an emergency: The 2002 online campaign], *Aus Politik und Zeitgeschichte*, B49–50: 48–54.

Heclo, H. (2000) 'Campaigns and governing: A conspectus', in N. Ornstein and T. Mann (eds) *The Permanent Campaign and Its Future*, Washington, DC: American Enterprise Institute and The Brookings Institution: 1–37.

Heilemann, J. and Halperin, M. (2010) *Game Change: Obama and the Clintons, McCain and Palin, and the Race of a Lifetime*, New York: Harper Collins.

Herring, S. C. (2004) 'Computer-mediated discourse analysis: An approach to researching online behaviour', in S. A. Barab, R. Kling and J. H. Gray (eds) *Designing for Virtual Communities in the Service of Learning*, New York: Cambridge University Press: 338–76.

Hill, K. and Hughes, J. (1998) *Cyber Politics: Citizen Activism in the Age of the Internet*, Oxford, UK: Rowman and Littlefield.

Hirsch-Weber, W. and Schutz, K. (1953) *Wdhler und Gewahlte: Eine Unterscuchung der Bundestagswahlen 1953* (Schriften des Instituts fur Politische Wissenschaft Band 7).

Holbrook, R. (1996) *Do Campaigns Matter?* Thousand Oaks: Sage.

Holtz-Bacha, C. (2001) 'Negative campaigning: In Deutschland negativ aufgenommen' [Negative campaigning: Negatively perceived in Germany], *Zeitschrift für Parlamentsfragen*, 32: 669–77.

Holtz-Bacha, C. (2002) Massenmedian und Wahlen: Die Professionalisierung der Kampagnen, *Aus Politik und Zeitgeschichte*, 15–16: 23–8.

Holtz-Bacha, C. (2006) 'Political advertising in Germany', in L. L. Kaid and C. Holtz-Bacha (eds) *The Sage Handbook of Political Advertising*, Thousand Oaks, CA: Sage.

Holtz-Bacha, C., Kaid, L. L. and Johnston, A. (1994) 'Political television advertising in Western democracies: A comparison of campaign broadcasts in the United States, Germany and France', *Political Communication*, 11 (1): 67–80.

Hook, J. (2008) 'Obama has cash advantage over McCain', *Los Angeles Times*, 8 June. Online. Available HTTP: http://articles.latimes.com/2008/jun/05/nation/na-money5 (accessed 11 September 2008).

Horrigan, J. B. (2004) *How Americans get in touch with Government*, Washington, DC: Pew Research.

Horton, D. and Wohl, R. R. (1956) 'Mass communication and para-social interaction: Observations on intimacy at a distance', *Psychiatry*, 19 (3): 215–29.

Howard, P. N. (2006) *New Media Campaigns and the Managed Citizen*, New York: Cambridge University Press.

Institute for Politics, Democracy and the Internet (2002) *Online Campaigning 2002: A primer*, Graduate School of Political Management, The George Washington University.

Institute for Politics, Democracy and the Internet (2004) *Political Influentials Online in the 2004 Presidential Election*, Graduate School of Political Management, The George Washington University.

Internet Worlds Stats (undated). Online. Available HTTP: www.internetworldstats.com/stats.htm (accessed 20 July 2009).

Iyengar, S. and Simon, A. (2000) 'New perspectives and evidence on political communication and campaign effects', *Annual Review of Psychology*, 2000, 51: 149–69.

Jackson, D. (2008) 'Citizens, consumers and the demands of market-driven news', in D. G. Lilleker and R. Scullion (eds) *Voters or Consumers: Imagining the Contemporary Electorate*, Newcastle: Cambridge Scholarly Press: 141–61.

Jackson, N. (2003) 'MPs and web technologies: An untapped opportunity?', *Journal of Public Affairs*, 3 (2): 124–37.

Jackson, N. (2006a) 'An MP's role in the Internet era – the impact of e-newsletters', *Journal of Legislative Studies*, 12 (2): 223–42.

Jackson, N. (2006b) 'Banking online: The use of the Internet by political parties to build relationships with voters', in D. Lilleker, N. Jackson and R. Scullion (2006) *The Marketing of British Politics: Political marketing at the 2005 General Election*, Manchester: Manchester University Press.

Jackson, N. (2007) 'Political parties, the Internet and the 2005 General Election: Third time lucky?', *Internet Research*, 17 (3): 249–71.

Jackson, N. (2008a) 'MPs and their e-newsletters: Winning votes by promoting constituency service', *Journal of Legislative Studies*, 14 (4): 488–99.

Jackson, N. (2008b) '"Scattergun" or "Rifle" approach to communication: MPs in the blogosphere', *Information Polity*, 13 (1/2): 57–70.

Jackson, N. and Lilleker, D. G. (2004) 'Just public relations or an attempt at interaction?', *European Journal of Communication*, 19 (4): 507–33.

Jackson, N. and Lilleker, D. G. (2007) 'Information, input and the desire to find out what the opposition is doing: The uses and gratifications of political parties' e-newsletters', *Information, Communication and Society*, 10 (2): 242–64.

Jackson, N. and Lilleker, D. G. (2009a) 'Building an architecture of participation? Political parties and Web 2.0 in Britain', *Journal of Information Technology and Politics*, 6 (3/4): 232–50.

Jackson, N. and Lilleker, D. G. (2009b) 'MPs and e-representation: Me, MySpace and I', *British Politics*, 4 (2): 236–64.

Jackson, N. and Lilleker, D. G. (2010) Tentative steps towards interaction: The use of the Internet in the British European Parliament Election 2009, *Internet Research*.

Jackson, N. and Lilleker, D. G. (2011) 'Tweeting, constituency service and impression management – UK MPs and the use of Twitter', *Journal of Legislative Studies*, 17 (2).

Jacobsen, G. (1978) 'The effects of campaign spending in Congressional Elections', *The American Political Science Review*, 72 (2): 469–91.

Jacobsen, G. (1990) 'The effects of campaign spending in House Elections: New evidence for old arguments', *American Journal of Political Science*, 34 (2): 334–62.

Jagoda, K. (2002) *E-voter 2002 Study*, E-voter Institute.

James, M. G. (1991) *PRODUSER: PROcess for Developing USER Interfaces*, San Diego, CA: Academic Press Professional.

Jamieson, K. H. (1996) *Packaging the Presidency: A History and Criticism of Presidential Campaign Advertising*, Oxford: Oxford University Press.

Jandura, O. (2008) *Kleinparteien in der Mediendemokratie* [Minor parties in media democracy], Wiesbaden: VS Verlag für Sozialwissenschaften.

Jankowski, N. W., Foot, K., Kluver, R. and Schneider, S. (2005) 'The Web and the 2004 EP election: Comparing political actor websites in 11 EU Member States', *Information Polity: The International Journal of Government and Democracy in the Information Age*, 10 (3/4): 165–76.

Jansen, R. M. (2006) 'The medium is the message: The effects of new Web 2.0 technologies on knowledge management and learning', unpublished thesis of MA in Information Science, Universteit van Amsterdam.

Johnson, D. (2009) 'An election like no other?', in D. Johnson (ed.) *Campaigning for President 2008: Strategy and Tactics, New Voices and New Techniques*, London: Routledge: 1–28.

Johnson, L. (2007) 'John Edwards is Twittering personal democracy forum', Online. Available HTTP: http://techpresident.com/blog-entry/john-edwards-twittering (accessed 11 August 20007).

Johnson, T. J. and Kaye, B. K. (2004) 'Wag the blog: How reliance on traditional media and the Internet influence credibility perceptions of weblogs among blog users', *J and MC Quarterly*, 81 (3): 622–42.

Joinson, A. (2003) *Understanding the Psychology of Internet Behaviour: Virtual Worlds, Real Lives*, Basingstoke: Palgrave Macmillan.

Jones, C. (2000) 'Preparing to govern in 2001: Lessons from the Clinton presidency', in N. Ornstein and T. Mann, *The Permanent Campaign and Its Future*, Washington, DC: American Enterprise Institute and The Brookings Institution: 185–218.

Jones, L. (2007) 'Member of the Twittering classes', *The Guardian* 15 May 2007. Online. Available HTPP: www.guardian.co.uk/technology/2007/may/17/guardianweeklytechnologysection.socialnetworking (accessed 10 July 2009).

Jürgens, P. and Jungherr, A. (2010) 'Breaking the barrier: interactive election campaign communication on Twitter during the German General Election 2009', in M. Welker,

H. Geißler, L. Kaczmirek and O. Wenzel (eds), 12th General Online Research Conference, GOR 10: Proceedings, Pforzheim.

Kaid, L. L. (1991) 'Ethical dimensions of political advertising', in R. E. Denton Jr. (ed.) *Ethical Dimensions of Political Communication*, New York: Praeger.

Kaltenthaler, H. (2000) '"Negative Campaigning" in den USA: (K)ein Szenario für Deutschland?' [Negative campaigning in the USA: A (non-)scenario for Germany?], *Forschungsjournal Neue Soziale Bewegungen*, 13: 25–36.

Kamarck, E. C. (1999) 'Campaigning on the Internet in the Elections of 1998', in E. C. Kamarck and J. S. Nye Jr. (eds) *Democracy.com? Governance in a network world*, Hollis, NH: Hollis Publishing: 99–123.

Kanuka, H. and Anderson, T. (1998) 'Online social interchange, discord, and knowledge construction', *The Journal of Distance Education/Revue de l'Éducation à Distance*, 13 (1). Online. Available HTTP: www.jofde.ca/index.php/jde/article/view/137/412 (accessed 12 August 2008).

Katz, R. (1997) *Democracy and Elections*, New York: Oxford University Press.

Kavanagh, D. (1995) *Election Campaigning: The New Marketing of Politics*, Oxford: Blackwell.

Kennedy, R. (2004) 'Weblogs, social software and new interactivity on the Web', *Psychiatric Services*, 55 (3): 247–9.

Kenny, C. and McBurnett, M. (1994) 'An individual-level multi-equation model of expenditure effects in contested House elections', *American Political Science Review*, 88 (3): 699–707.

Kerbel, M. and Bloom, J. (2005) 'Blog for America and civic involvement', *Harvard International Journal of Press/Politics*, 10 (4): 3–27.

Ketchum (2008) *Media Myths and Realities*, London: Ketchum PR.

Key, V. (1966) *Responsible Electorate: Rationality in Presidential Voting 1936–60*, New York: Vintage Books.

Kim, J. and Margolis, M. (2005) 'Deploying email lists in the 2004 Presidential Campaign: Simple enhancements or new necessities', paper presented to The State of the Parties: 2004 and Beyond Conference, University of Akron, 5–7 October.

Kimberley, S. (2010) 'TV debate attracts 9.4m viewers and creates online frenzy', MediaWeek, 16 April. Online. Available HTTP: www.mediaweek.co.uk/news/997226/TV-debate-attracts-94m-viewers-creates-online-frenzy/ (accessed 20 April 2010).

King, T. (2007) 'Royal and Sarkozy tiptoe around the Internet', *Prospect*, 19 October 2007.

Kiousis, S. (2002) 'Interactivity: A concept explication', *New Media and Society*, 4 (3): 355–83.

Kiss, J. (2008) 'Why everyone's a winner', *The Guardian*, 10 November. Online. Available HTTP: www.guardian.co.uk/media/2008/nov/10/obama-online-strategy (accessed 10 November 2008).

Kitchens, J., Powell, L. and Williams, G. (2003) 'Information, please? Information seeking, mass media and the undecided voter', *Communication Research Reports*, 20 (1): 73–80.

Klapper, J. (1960) *The Effects of Mass Communication*, Glencoe, IL: Free Press.

Klemperer, P. (2006) 'Network effects and switching costs: Two short essays for the new', New Palgrave, *Economics Papers 2006-W06*, Economics Group, Nuffield College, University of Oxford.

Kline, D. and Burnstein, D. (2005) *Blog! How the Newest Media Revolution is Changing Politics, Business and Culture*, New York: CDS Books.

Klingemann, H-D., Hofferbert, R. and Budge, I. (1994) *Parties, Policies and Democracy*, Boulder: Westview Press.

Klotz, R. (1998) 'Virtual criticism: Negative advertising on the Internet in the 1996 Senate races', *Political Communication*, 15 (3): 347–65.

Klotz, R. (2004) *The Politics of Internet Communication*, Lanham, MD: Rowman and Littlefield.

Kluver, R., Jankowski, N. W., Foot, K. A. and Schneider, S. M. (2007) *The Internet and National Election: A Comparative Study of Web Campaigning*, London: Routledge.

Korte, K-R. (2006) 'Model or deterrence? The United States presidential election campaigns and the Bundestag election campaigns', *German Politics*, 15 (2): 153–65.

Kristol, W. (2008) 'The mask slips', *New York Times*, 14 April. Online. Available HTTP: www.nytimes.com/2008/04/14/opinion/14kristol.html (accessed 20 April 2008).

Krol, C. (1999) 'Finds real success in virtual world', *Advertising Age*, March.

Ku, G., Kaid, L. L. and Pfau, M. (2003) 'The impact of website campaigning on traditional news media and public information processing', *Journalism and Mass Communication Quarterly*, 80 (3): 528–47.

Kuhn, R. (2002) 'The French Presidential and Parliamentary Elections 2002', *Representation*, 39 (1): 44–56.

Kuhn, R. (2004) 'The media and the elections', in J. Gaffney (ed.) *The French Presidential and Legislative Elections of 2002*, Aldershot: Ashgate: 83–116.

Kuhn, R. (2005) 'Where's the spin? The executive and news management in France', *Modern and Contemporary France*, 13 (3): 307–22.

Kumar, N., Scheer, L. and Kotler, P. (2000) 'From market driven to market driving', *European Management Journal*, 18 (2): 129–42.

Kumar, R., Novak, J., Raghevan, P. and Tomkus, A. (2005) 'On the bursty evolution of blogspace', *World Wide Web: Internet and Web Information Systems*, 8 (2): 159–78.

Kyricau, G. (2007) 'The public face of Madame Royal', *Communication Director*, 1, 2007: 6–8.

Lasswell, H. (1927) *Propaganda Technique in the World War*, New York: Knofp.

Lau, R. R. (1982) 'Negativity in political perception', *Political Behavior*, 4 (4): 353–77.

Lau, R. and Pomper, G. (2004) *Negative Campaigning: An Analysis of U.S. Senate Elections*, Lanham, MD: Rowman and Littlefield.

Laufer, S. (18 July, 2009) '"Das Fernsehen hat als Leitmedium abgedankt". Scholz & Friends: Das Abendblatt im Gespräch mit dem Deutschland-Chef der Hamburger Werbeagentur' ['It's the end of television as prime medium.' Scholz & Friends: The newspaper 'Abendblatt' in a conversation with the head of the German advertising agency], *Hamburger Abendblatt*, 165: 24.

Laver, M., Benoit, K. and Sauger, N. (2006) 'Policy competition in the 2002 French Legislative and Presidential Elections', *European Journal of Political Research*, 45 (4): 669–99.

Lazarsfeld, P. F., Berelson, B. and Gaudet, H. (1944) *The People's Choice: How the Voter Makes Up His Mind in a Presidential Campaign*, New York: Columbia University Press.

Leadbeater, C. (2008) *We Think: The Power of Mass Creativity*, London: Profile.

Lees, C. (2005) 'Political Marketing in Germany: The case of the Social Democratic party', in D. Lilleker and J. Lees-Marshment (eds) *Political Marketing: A Comparative Perspective*, Manchester: Manchester University Press: 114–31.

Lees-Marshment, J. (2001) *Political Marketing and British Political Parties: The Party's Just Begun*, Manchester: Manchester University Press.

Lees-Marshment, J. (2008) *Political Marketing and British Political Parties*, 2nd edn, Manchester: Manchester University Press.

Lees-Marshment, J., Rudd, C. and Stromback, J. (2009) *Global Political Marketing*, Abingdon: Routledge.

Lemke, J. L. (1999) 'Multimedia demands of the scientific curriculum', *Linguistics and Education*, 10 (3): 1–25.

Le Monde (2007) Editorial, 23 April: 1.

Levine, P. and Lopez, M. H. (2002) *Factsheet: Youth Voter Turnout Has Declined, By Any Measure*, New York: The Center for Information and Research on Civic Learning and Engagement.

Lev-On, A. (2010) 'Internet use in election campaigns: The municipal angle', paper presented at the Communication and Citizenship IAMCR Conference, Braga, Portugal, 20 July.

Lewis-Beck, M. S. (2004) *The French Voter: Before and After the 2002 Elections*. Houndmills, Basingstoke: Palgrave Macmillan.

Lilleker, D. and Lees-Marshment J. (2005) *Political Marketing: A Comparative Perspective*, Manchester: Manchester University Press.

Lilleker, D. and Malagon, C. (2010) 'Making elections interactive: Online discourse during the 2006 French Presidential Election', *European Journal of Communication*, 25 (1): 25–42.

Lilleker, D., Pack, M. and Jackson, N. (2010) 'Political parties and Web 2.0: The Liberal Democrat perspective', *Politics*, 30 (2), 105–12.

Lilleker, D. G. (2002) 'Whose Left? Working-class political allegiances in post-industrial Britain, *International Review of Social History*, 47 (supplement 10): 65–86.

Lilleker, D. G. (2003) 'Interviewing the political elite: Navigating a potential minefield', *Politics*, 23 (3): 207–14.

Lilleker, D. G. (2006) *Key Concepts in Political Communication*, London: Sage.

Lilleker, D. G., Jackson, N. and Scullion, R. (2006) 'Conclusion: Was 2005 the year political marketing came of age?', in D. G. Lilleker, N. Jackson and R. Scullion *The Marketing of Political Parties: The UK 2005 General Election*, Manchester: Manchester University Press: 251–64.

Lilleker, D. G. and Negrine, R. (2002) 'Professionalisation: of what? since when? by whom?', *Harvard International Journal of Press/Politics*, 7 (4): 98–103.

Lilleker, D. G. and Negrine, R. 'Not big brand names but corner shops: Marketing politics to a disengaged electorate', *Journal of Political Marketing*, 2 (1): 55–76.

Lilleker, D. G. and Negrine, R. (2006) 'Mapping a market orientation: Can we detect political marketing only through the lens of hindsight?' in P. J. Davies and B. I. Newman (eds) *Winning Elections with Political Marketing*, Binghamton, NY: Haworth Press: 33–56.

Lilleker, D. G. and Scullion, R. (2008), *Voters or Consumers: Re-imagining the Postmodern Electorate*, Newcastle: Cambridge Scholarly Press.

Lilleker, D. G. and Scullion, R. (2009) 'Political Advertising', in H. Powell, J. Hardy, S. Hawkins and I. MacCrury (eds) *The Handbook of Advertising*, London: Routledge: 187–97.

Lincoln, Y. S. and Guba, E. G. (1985) *Naturalistic Inquiry*, Beverly Hills, CA: Sage.

Lippmann, W. (1922) *Public Opinion.* Online. Available HTTP: www.gutenberg.org/etext/6456 (accessed 12 November 2009).

Lusoli, W. (2005) 'The Internet and the European Parliament elections: Theoretical perspectives, empirical investigations and proposals for research', *Information Polity: The*

International Journal of Government and Democracy in the Information Age, 10 (3/4): 153–63.

Lusoli, W. and Ward, S. (2004) 'Country report for the Internet and Election project, 2004 European Parliament election – UK component'. Online. Available HTTP: www.esri.salford.ac.uk/ESRCResearchproject/ww/files/UK_report_Lusoli%20and%20Ward.pdf (accessed 10 June 2007).

Lusoli, W. and Ward, S. (2005) 'Logging on or switching off?', in S. Coleman and S. Ward (eds) (2005) *Spinning the Web: Online Campaigning During the 2005 General Election*, London: Hansard Society: 13–21.

Maarek, P. (1995) *Political Marketing and Communication*, London: John Libbey.

Maarek, P. (1997) 'New trends in French political communication: The 1995 French Presidential Elections', *Media, Culture and Society*, 19 (3): 357–68.

Maarek, P. (2002) 'Political communication and the unexpected outcome of the 2002 French Presidential Elections', *Journal of Political Marketing*, 2 (2): 13–24.

Machill, M. and Beiler, M. (2009) 'The importance of the Internet for journalistic research: A multi-method study of the research performed by journalists working for daily newspapers, radio, television and online', *Journalism Studies*, 10: 178–203.

MacManus, R. (2006) 'Top ten German apps', *ReadWriteWeb* 28 July. Online. Available HTTP: www.readwriteweb.com/archives/top_ten_german.php (accessed 10 December 2009).

McMillan, S. J. (2000a) 'Interactivity is in the eye of the beholder: Function, perception, involvement, and attitude toward the website', in M. A. Shaver (ed.) *Proceedings of the 2000 Conference of the American Academy of Advertising*: 71–8, East Lansing, MI: Michigan State University.

McMillan, S. J. (2000b) 'What is interactivity and what does it do?', paper presented at the Association of Education in Journalism and Mass Communication Conference, Phoenix, AZ., August.

McMillan, S. J. (2002a) 'A four-part model of cyber-interactivity: Some places are more interactive than others', *New Media and Society*, 14 (2): 271–91.

McMillan, S. J. (2002b) 'Exploring models of interactivity from multiple research traditions: Users, documents, and systems', in S. Livingstone (ed.) *The Handbook of New Media*, Thousand Oaks, CA: Sage: 163–82.

McMillan, S. J. and Downes, E. J. (2000) 'Defining interactivity: A qualitative identification of key dimensions', *New Media and Society*, 2 (2): 157–79.

McNair, B. (1995) *An Introduction to Political Communication*, London: Routledge.

MacNamara, J. (2008) 'Emergent media and what they mean for society, politics and organisations', public lecture, University of Technology, Sydney, 11 June. Online. Available HTTP: www.uts.edu.au/new/speaks/2008/June/resources/1106-talk.pdf (accessed 1 February 2009).

McStay, A. (2009) *Digital Advertising*, Basingstoke: Palgrave Macmillan.

Margetts, H. (2001) 'The cyber party', paper to workshop 'The causes and consequences of organisational innovation in European political parties', ECPR Joint Sessions of Workshops, Grenoble, 6–11 April 2001.

Margolis, M. and Resnick, D. (2000) *Politics as Usual: The Cyberspace Revolution*, Walnut Creek, CA: AltaMira.

Marnette, S. (2005) *Speech and Thought Presentation in French: Concepts and Strategies*, Philadelphia, PA: John Benjamins Publishing Company.

Matear, S., Osborne, P., Garrett, T. and Gray, B. J. (2002) 'How does market orientation contribute to service firm performance? An examination of alternative mechanisms', *European Journal of Marketing*, 36 (9/10): 1058–75.

Matsuno, K. and Mentzer, J. T. (2000) 'The effects of strategy type on the market orientation–performance relationship', *Journal of Marketing*, 64 (4): 1–16.

Mauser, G. (1983) *Political Marketing: An Approach to Campaign Strategy*, New York, NY: Praeger.

Mautner, G. (2005) 'Time to get wired: Using Web-based corpora in critical discourse analysis', *Discourse and Society*, 16 (6): 809–28.

Mayer, P. (1998) 'Computer-mediated interactivity: A socio-semiotic perspective', *Convergence*, 4 (3): 40–58.

McKenna, R. (1985) *The Regis Touch*, Reading, MA: Addison-Wesley.

McLuhan, M. (1964) *Understanding Media*, New York: New American Library.

Melber, A. (2008) 'Online activists keep the pressure on Obama', *The Nation*, 7 July. Online. Available HTTP: www.thenation.com/doc/20080721/melber (accessed 10 July 2008).

Meraz, S. S. (2004) 'Candidate websites and candidate press releases: Setting the media agenda in the 2002 Texas gubernatorial election', paper presented at the 54th Annual Conference of the International Communication Association, New Orleans, LA, USA, May 2004.

Michel, F. (2001) 'Diverted tautological political communication in French presidential elections: The case of Lionel Jospin in 1995', *The Web Journal of French Media Studies*, Volume 4 (1). Online. Available HTTP: http://eprints.ncl.ac.uk/file_store/nclep_971197381319.html (accessed 20 August 2008).

Miguet, A. (2002) 'The French Elections of 2002: After the earthquake, the deluge', *West European Politics*, 25 (4): 207–20.

Miller, W. and Stokes, D. (1963) 'Constituency influence in Congress', *American Political Science Review*, 57 (2): 45–56.

Morris, D. (1999) *Vote.com: How Big-money Lobbyists and the Media are Losing Their Influence, and the Internet is Giving Power Back to the People*, Los Angeles: Renaissance Books.

Moscovici, P. (2003) *Un an après*, Paris: Grasset.

Müller, A. (1999) *Von der Parteiendemokratie zur Mediendemokratie: Beobachtungen zum Bundestagswahlkampf 1998 im Spiegel früherer Erfahrungen* [From party to media democracy: Observations on the 1998 German national election campaign in the light of earlier experiences], Opladen: Leske + Budrich.

National Journal (2007) 'What de Vellis? Obama Consulting Firm Employee Made The Act', 21 March. Online. Available HTTP: http://hotlineoncall.nationaljournal.com/archives/2007/03/what_de_vellis.php (accessed 1 April 2007).

Negrine, R. (1996) *The Communication of Politics*, London: Sage.

Negrine, R. (2007) 'The professionalisation of political communication in Europe', in R. Negrine, C. Holtz-Bacha and P. Mancini (eds) *The Professionalisation of Political Communication*, Bristol: Intellect: 27–46.

Negrine, R. and Papathanassopoulos, S. (1996) 'The "Americanization" of political communication: A critique', *The Harvard International Journal of Press/Politics*, 1: 45–62.

Negroponte, N. (1995) *Being Digital*, New York: Free Press.

Neven, E. (1998) 'Media and politics in French political science', *European Journal of Political Research*, 33 (4): 439–58.

Newell, J., Gibson, R. and Ward, S. (2000) 'New parties, new media: Italian party politics and the Internet', *South European Society And Politics*, 5 (1): 123–42.

Newhagen, J. E. and Reeves, B. (1991) 'Emotion and memory responses for negative political advertising: A study of television commercials used in the 1988 Presidential Election', in F. Biocca (ed.) *Television and Political Advertising. Volume 1: Psychological Processes*, Hillsdale, NJ: Lawrence Erlbaum: 197–220.

Newman, B. (1994) *The Marketing of the President: Political Marketing as Campaign Strategy*, New York: Sage.

Newman, B. (1999) *The Mass Marketing of Politics: Democracy in an Age of Manufactured Images*, New York: Sage.

Nielsen, J. (2004) *Designing Web Usability: The Practice of Simplicity*, Indianapolis: New Riders Publishing.

Nimmo, D. (1999) 'The permanent campaign marketing as a governing tool', in B. Newman (ed.) *Handbook of Political Marketing*, Thousand Oaks, CA: Sage, 73–86.

Nimmo, D. and Sanders, K. (eds) (1981) *Handbook of Political Communication*, Beverly Hills: Sage.

Norris, P. (2000) *A Virtuous Circle: Political Communication in Post-industrial Societies*, New York: Cambridge University Press.

Norris, P. (2001a) *Digital Divide? Civic Engagement, Information Poverty and the Internet Worldwide*, Cambridge: Cambridge University Press.

Norris, P. (2001b) 'Do campaign communications matter for civic engagement? American elections from Eisenhower to G. W. Bush', in D. Farrell and R. Schmitt-Beck (eds) *Do Political Campaigns Matter?* London: Routledge: 127–44.

Norris, P. (2003) Preaching to the converted? Pluralism, participation and party websites, *Party Politics*, 9 (1): 21–45.

Norris, P. and Curtice, J. (2007) 'Getting the message out: A two-step model of the role of the Internet in campaign communication flows during the 2005 British General Election', *Journal of Information Technology and Politics*, 4: 3–13.

Norris, P., Curtice, J., Sanders, J., Scammell, M. and Semetko, H. (1999) *On Message: Communicating the Campaign*, London: Sage.

Obama, B. (2008) *Dreams From My Father*, New York: Three Rivers.

O'Grady, G. (2007) 'Telepresence to omnipresence'. Online. Available HTTP: www.videolinq.tafe.qld.gov.au/learningtechnologies2007/files/greg_ogrady.pdf (accessed 12 December 2008).

O'Keefe, G. J. and Atwood, L. E. (1981) 'Communication and election campaigns', in D. Nimmo and K. R. Sandars (eds) *Handbook of Political Communication*, Beverly Hills: Sage: 329–57.

O'Neill, D. and Harcup, T. (2009) 'News values and selectivity', in K. Wahl-Jorgensen and T. Hanitzsch (eds) *The Handbook of Journalism Studies*, New York: Routledge.

O'Reilly, T. (2005) 'What is Web 2.0: Design patterns and business models for the next generation of software'. Online. Available HTTP: www.oreillynet.com/pub/a/oreilly/tim/news/2005/09/30/what-is-web-20.html (accessed 1 October 2007 and 17 September 2009).

Ornstein, N. and Mann, T. (2000) *The Permanent Campaign and Its Future*, Washington, DC: American Enterprise Institute and The Brookings Institution.

Osel, J. (23 September 2009) 'Jubel, der fertigmacht. "Flashmob": Im Internet organisieren sich Wahlkampf-Störer' [Cheers that hurt you. 'Flashmob': Campaign disturbers get organised on the Internet], *Süddeutsche Zeitung*, 219: 1.

Panagopoulos, C. (2009) *Politicking Online: The Transformation of Election Campaign Communications*, Toronto: Rutgers University Press.

Papachrissi, Z. (2002) 'The virtual sphere: The Internet as a public sphere', *New Media and Society*, 4 (1): 9–27.

Patalong, F. (8 January, 2009) 'Die Roten sind jetzt blau: SPD-Wahlkampf im Web' [The reds are blue now: The SPD campaign on the Web], *Spiegel Online*. Available HTTP: www.spiegel.de/netzwelt/web/0,1518,600181,00.html (accessed 8 January 2009).

Pène, S. (2007) *Bloguer la politique, Communication et langage*, Paris: Armand Colin, 151: 39–89.

Perloff, R. M. and Kinsey, D. (1992) 'Political advertising as seen by consultants and journalists', *Journal of Advertising Research*, 32 (3): 53–60.

Perrier, F. (2007) 'How Web 2.0 impacted the French presidential campaign and helped Sarkozy enter Elysees 1.0?'., Online. Available HTTP: www.franckperrier.com/2007/05/07/how-the-web20-impacted-the-french-presidential-election-camapign-and-helped-sarkozy-enter-elyees-10/ (accessed 7 June 2007).

Peters, R. (2002) 'Congress and the permanent campaign', *Extensions*, Spring. Online. Available HTTP: www.ou.edu/special/albertctr/extensions/spring2002/Intro.html (accessed 11 August 2003).

Pew Research Center (2006) *The 2004 Political Landscape*, Washington: Pew Research.

Pfannenmüller, J. (2009) 'Wahlkampf im Zeichen der Krise' [Campaigning in times of crisis], *Werben and Verkaufen*, 4: 28–31.

Pfetsch, B. (1998) 'Government news management', in D. Graber, D. McQuail, and P. Norris (eds) *The Politics of News, The News of Politics*, Washington DC: Congressional Quarterly Press: 70–93.

Pfetsch, B. (2001) 'Political communication culture in Germany and the US', *Harvard International Journal of Press/Politics*, 6 (1): 46–67.

Phillips, C. (2007) 'Spanners for the virtual ego: An evaluation of facilities for online communities on the World Wide Web', paper presented to the 8th Annual Multimedia Systems, Electronics and Computer Science Conference, University of Southampton.

Pierce, R. (2005) 'Candidate evaluations and presidential electoral choices in France', in A. King (ed.) *Leaders' Personalities and the Outcomes of Democratic Elections*, Oxford: Oxford University Press: 96–126.

Plasser, F. (2002) *Global Political Campaigning*, Westport CT: Praeger.

Plehwe, K. (2009) *Von der Botschaft zur Bewegung: Die 10 Erfolgsstrategien des Barack Obama*, Hamburg: Hanseatic Lighthouse.

Pollach, I. (2003) 'Communicating corporate ethics on the World Wide Web: A discourse analysis of selected company websites', *Business and Society*, 42 (2): 277–87.

Powell, B. (2000) *Elections as Instruments of Democracy: Majoritarian and Proportional Visions*, New Haven, CT: Yale University Press.

Pullin, A. (2010) 'Internet will influence UK General Election', *TechEye*, March 11. Available online at www.techeye.net/internet/internet-will-influence-uk-generalelection accessed 14 March 2010.

Quan-Haase, A., Wellman, B., Witte, J. and Hampton, K. (2002) 'Capitalising on the net: Social context, civic engagement and sense of community', in B. Wellman and C. Haythornwaite (eds) *The Internet in Everyday Life*, Oxford: Blackwell: 291–324.

Rafaeli, S. (1988) 'Interactivity: From new media to communication', in R. P. Hawkins, J. M. Wiemann and S. Pingree (eds) *Sage Annual Review of Communication Research: Advancing Communication Science* Vol. 16, Beverly Hills, CA: Sage: 110–34.

Rainie, L., Fox, S. and Fallows, D. (2005) *The Internet and the Iraq War*, Washington, DC: Pew Research.

Rainie, L. and Horrigan, J. (2007) *Election 2006 Online*, Washington, DC: Pew Research.

Rash, W. (1997) *Politics on the net: Wiring the political process*, New York: W. H. Freeman & Co.

Reichart, M. (20 January 2009) 'Politik 2.0: Die Macht des Internets' [Politics 2.0: The power of the Internet], *Focus Online.* Available HTTP: www.focus.de/digital/multimedia/dld-2009/tid-13155/politik-2–0-die-macht-des-internets_aid_363558.html (accessed 28 September 2009).

Reichheld, F. F. and Schefter, P. (2000) 'E-loyalty: Your secret weapon on the Web', *Harvard Business Review*, July–August: 105–14.

Reinemann, C. and Eichholz, M. (2006) 'What's news in Germany?', in P. Shoemaker and A. Cohen (eds) *News Around the World: Content, Practitioners, and the Public*, New York: Routledge: 165–88.

Resnick, D. (1998) 'Politics on the Internet: The normalization of cyberspace', in C. Toulouse and T. W. Luke (eds) *The Politics of Cyberspace*, New York: Routledge: 48–69.

Rheingold, H. (1993) *The Virtual Community: Homesteading on the Electronic Frontier*, New York: Harper.

Rheingold, H. (1995) *The Virtual Community: Finding Connection in a Computerised World*, London: Minerva.

Richards, B. (2007) *Emotional Governance: Politics, Media and Terror*, Basingstoke: Palgrave Macmillan.

Ridout, T. N. and Smith, G. R. (2008) 'Free advertising. How the media amplify campaign messages', *Political Research Quarterly*, 63 (4): 598–608.

Roberts Frith, C. (2005) 'Candidates on the stump online: Framing the Internet in the early stages of the 2004 Presidential Election', paper presented at the 55th Annual Conference of the International Communication Association, New York, NY, USA, May 2005.

Rodgers, J. (2005) *Spatializing International Politics: Analysing Activism on the Internet*, London: Routledge.

Roggenkamp, K. (4 June 2009) 'Kolumne "Wahlkampf virtuell": Wie Wahlkampf im Netz gut funktionieren kann' [Column 'Virtual Campaigning': How campaigning works well on the net], *Welt Online.* Available HTTP: www.welt.de/politik/wahlkampf-virtuell/article3850277/Wie-Wahlkampf-im-Netz-gut-funktionieren-kann.html (accessed 18 July 2009).

Rohrschneider, R. (2002) 'Mobilising versus chasing: How do your parties target voters in election campaigns?', *Electoral Studies*, 21 (3): 367–82.

Romano, A. (2008) 'Obama's official blog is boring. McCain's is enjoyable. Why that's bad news for the GOP', *Newsweek*, 9 June. Online. Available HTTP: http://blog.newsweek.com/blogs/stumper/archive/2008/06/09/mccain-obama-blog.aspx (accessed 12 June 2008).

Rosenstone, S. and Hansen, J. (1993) *Mobilization, Participation, and Democracy in America*, New York: Macmillan.

Rössler, P. (2001) 'Between online heaven and cyberhell: The framing of "the Internet" by traditional media coverage in Germany', *New Media and Society*, 3: 49–66.

Rybarczyk, C. (7 September 2009) 'Irrtümer im Online-Wahlkampf: "Die Parteien haben die Internetgemeinde nicht verstanden"' [Fallacies in online campaigning: Parties don't understand the Internet community], *Hamburger Abendblatt Online*. Available HTTP: www.abendblatt.de/politik/deutschland/article1171855/Die-Parteien-verstehen-die-Internetgemeinde-nicht.html (accessed 30 September 2009).

Sadow, J. and James, K. (1999) 'Virtual billboards? Candidate websites and campaigning in 1998?', paper presented to American Political Studies Association, Atlanta, September.

Sarcinelli, U. (1998) 'Parteien und Politikvermittlung: Von der Parteien – zur Mediendemokratie?' [Parties and the communication of politics: From party to media democracy?], in U. Sarcinelli (ed.) *Politikvermittlung und Demokratie in der Mediengesellschaft: Beiträge zur politischen Kommunikationskultur*, Bonn: Bundeszentrale für politische Bildung.

Sauger, N. (2007) 'The French Legislative and Presidential Elections of 2007', *West European Politics*, 30 (5): 1166–75.

Scammell, M. (1995) *Designer Politics: How Elections Are Won*, London: Palgrave.

Scarrow, S. E. (2004) 'Embracing dealignment, combating realignment: German parties respond', in P. Maier, W. C. Müller and F. Plasser (eds) *Political Parties and the Electoral Change: Party Responses to Electoral Markets*, London: Sage.

Schemel, B. (2004) 'Das Internet im Bundestagswahlkampf 2002: Anlass und Instrument der Parteienmodernisierung' [The Internet in the 2002 German National Election: Cause and tool of party modernisation], in A. Siedschlag and A. Bilgeri (eds) *Kursbuch Internet und Politik 2003: Politische Kommunikation im Netz*, Wiesbaden: VS Verlag für Sozialwissenschaften.

Schmitt-Beck, R. and Faas, T. (2006) 'The campaign and its dynamics at the 2005 German General Election', *German Politics*, 15 (4): 393–419.

Schmitt-Beck, R. and Farrell, D. (2002) 'Studying political campaigns and their effects', in D. M. Farrell and R. Schmitt-Beck (eds) *Do Political Campaigns Matter? Campaign Effects in Elections and Referenda*, London: Routledge: 1–21.

Schneider, S. and Foot, K. (2002) 'Online structure for political action: Exploring presidential campaign websites from the 2000 American Election', *Javnost/The Public*, 9 (2): 43–60.

Schneider, S. and Foot, K. (2004) 'The Web as an object of study', *New Media and Society*, 6 (1): 94–102.

Schneider, S. and Foot, K. (2006) 'Web campaigning by U.S. presidential primary candidates in 2000 and 2004', in A. P. Williams and J. C. Tedesco (eds) *The Internet Election: Perspectives on the Web in Campaign 2004*, Lanham, MD: Rowman and Littlefield: 21–36.

Schoenbach, K. (1996) 'The "Americanisation" of German Election Campaigns: Any impact on votes', in D. Swanson and P. Mancini (eds) *Politics, Media and Democracy: An International Study of Innovations in Electoral Campaigning and their Consequences*, London: Praeger: 91–104.

Schultz, W., Zeh, R. and Quiring, O. (2005) 'Voters in a changing media environment: A data-based retrospective or consequences of media change in Germany', *European Journal of Communication*, 20 (1): 55–88.

Schweitzer, E. J. (2005) 'Election campaigning online: German party websites in the 2002 National Elections', *European Journal of Communication*, 20 (3): 327–51.

Schweitzer, E. J. (2008a) 'Germany: Online campaign professionalism in the 2002 and 2005 National Elections', in S. Ward, D. Owen, R. Davis and D. Taras (eds) *Making a Difference: A Comparative View of the Role of the Internet in Election Politics*, Lanham, MD: Lexington Books: 235–56.

Schweitzer, E. J. (2008b) 'Innovation or normalisation in e-campaigning? A longitudinal content and structural analysis of German Party websites in the 2002 and 2005 National Elections, *European Journal of Communication*, 23 (4): 449–70.

Schweitzer, E. J. (2010a, in print) 'Global patterns of virtual mudslinging? Comparing the use of attacks on German party websites in state, national, and European parliamentary elections', *German Politics*, 19 (2).

Schweitzer, E. J. (2010b, in print) 'Normalisierung 2.0: Die Online-Wahlkämpfe deutscher Parteien zu den Bundestagswahlen 2002–2009' [Normalization 2.0: The online campaigns of German parties in the national elections 2002–2009], in C. Holtz-Bacha (ed.) *Die Massenmedien im Wahlkampf: Analysen zum Super-Wahljahr 2009*, Wiesbaden: VS Verlag für Sozialwissenschaften.

Scott, D. M. (2010) *The New Rules of Marketing and Public Relations*, London: John Wiley.

Scott, J. W. (2006) 'La difference comme categorie utile d'analyse historique', *Raisons Politiques*, 31 (3): 105–13.

Sebastiao, S. P. (2010) 'Social media and user-generated content: An example of e-participation in the Portuguese Parliament Political Campaign', paper presented at the Communication and Citizenship IAMCR Conference, Braga, Portugal, 22 July.

Sednow, G. (1998) *Electronic Whistle Stops: The Impact of the Internet on American Politics*, Westport CT: Praeger.

Shah, D., Cho, J., Eveland, W. and Kwak, N. (2005) 'Information and expression in a digital age: Modelling Internet effects on civic participation', *Communication Research*, 35 (5): 531–65.

Shah, D. V., McLeod, D. M., Kim, E., Lee, S. Y., Gotlieb, M. R., Ho, S. S. and Brvik, H. (2007) 'Political consumerism: How communication and consumption orientations drive "lifestyle politics"', *Annals of the American Academy of Political and Social Science*, 611: 217–35.

Shama, A. (1976) 'The marketing of political candidates', *Journal of the Academy of Marketing Science*, 4 (4): 767–77.

Sharratt, M. and Usoro, A. (2003) 'Understanding knowledge-sharing in online communities of practice', *Electronic Journal on Knowledge Management*, 1 (2): 187–96.

Shaw, D. (1999) 'The methods behind the madness: Presidential Electoral College strategies 1988–1996', *The Journal of Politics*, 61 (4): 893–913.

Slevin, J. (2000) *The Internet and Society*, Oxford: Polity.

Soufron, J.-B. (2007) 'Internet politics in France', *Dissent Magazine*, Fall. Online. Available HTTP: www.dissentmagazine.org/article/?articel=938 (accessed 3 May 2008).

Stanyer, J. (2005) 'Political parties, the Internet and the 2005 General Election: From Web presence to e-campaigning?' *Journal of Marketing Management*, 21 (9/10): 1049–65.

Stanyer, J. (2006) 'Online campaign communication and the phenomenon of blogging: An analysis of weblogs during the 2005 British General Election Campaign', *Aslib Proceedings*, 58 (5): 404–15.

Starke, F. C. (1993) *Krise ohne Ende? Parteiendemokratie vor neuen Herausforderungen* [Crisis without an end? Party democracy under challenge], Köln: Bund-Verlag.

Steger, W. (1999) 'The permanent campaign – marketing from the hill', in B. Newman (ed.) *Handbook of Political Marketing*, London: Sage Publications: 661–84.

Steger, W., Kelly, S. and Wrighton, J. (2006) *Campaigns and Political Marketing*, Binghampton, NY: Haworth Press.

Stein, D. (2006a) 'Introduction', in B. Ben-Israel, M. Bensoussan and D. Stein (eds) *Language@Internet Special Volume 1*, NRW 'Centre of University Libraries', Cologne, Germany. Online. Available HTTP: www.languageatinternet.de/articles/LangInternet-SpecialVolume1 (accessed 12 April 2007).

Stein, D. (2006b) 'The website as a domain-specific genre', in B. Ben-Israel, M. Bensoussan and D. Stein (eds) *Language@Internet Special Volume 1*, NRW 'Centre of University Libraries', Cologne, Germany. Online. Available HTTP: www.languageatinternet.de/articles/LangInternetSpecialVolume1 (accessed 12 April 2007).

Stirland, S. (2008) 'Propelled by Internet, Barack Obama wins presidency', *Wired Magazine* 4 November 2008. Online. Available HTTP: www.wired.com/threatlevel/2008/11/propelled-by-in/ (accessed 16 June 2009).

Stoker, G. (2006) *Why Politics Matters*, Basingstoke: Palgrave.

Strandberg, K. (2006) *Parties, Candidates and Citizens On-Line: Studies of Politics on the Internet*, Abo Academy University Press: Abo, Finland.

Strandberg, K. and Carlson, T. (2005) 'The 2004 European Parliament Election on the Web: Finnish actor strategies and voter responses', *Information Polity*, 10 (3/4): 189–204.

Street, J. (2001) *Mass Media, Politics and Democracy*, Basingstoke: Palgrave.

Stromer-Galley, J. (2000) 'Online interaction and why candidates avoid it', *Journal of Communication*, 50 (4): 111–32.

Stromer-Galley, J. (2002) 'New voices in the public sphere: A comparative analysis of interpersonal and online political talk', *Javnost – The Public*, 9 (2): 23–42.

Stromer-Galley, J. (2004) 'Interactivity-as-product and interactivity-as-process', *The Information Society*, 20 (5): 391–4.

Sudulich, M. (2009) Do ethos, ideology, country and electoral strength make a difference in cyberspace? Testing an explanatory model of parties' websites, paper to ECPR Joint Session, April, Lisbon.

Sundar Shyam, S. (2004) 'Theorizing interactivity's effects', *The Information Society*, 20 (5): 385–9.

Sunstein, C. (2004) 'Democracy and filtering', *Communications of ACM*, 47 (12): 57–9.

Sunstein, C. (2007) *Republic.com*, Princeton, NJ: Princeton University Press.

Suroweiki, J. (2004) *The Wisdom of Crowds: Why the Many are Smarter than the Few and How Collective Wisdom Shapes Business, Economies, Societies and Nations*, New York: Anchor.

Suroweiki, J. and Silverman, M. P. (2007) 'The wisdom of crowds', *American Journal of Physics*, 75 (2): 190–2.

Swanson, D. and Mancini, P. (1996) *Politics, Media and Modern Democracy: An International Study of Innovations in Electoral Campaigning and Their Consequences*, Westport: Praeger.

Swanson, D. and Nimmo, D. (eds) (1990) *New Directions in Political Communication: A Resource Book*, London: Sage.

Taylor, S. (2001) 'Evaluating and applying discourse analytic research', in M. Wetherell, S. Taylor and S. Yates (eds) *Discourse as Data: A Guide for Analysis*, London: Sage: 311–30.

Tedesco, J. C. (2005) 'Intercandidate agenda setting in the 2004 Democratic Presidential Primary', *American Behavioral Scientist*, 49: 92–113.

Tedesco, J. C. (2007) 'Examining Internet interactivity effects on young adult political information efficacy', *American Behavioral Scientist*, 50 (9): 1183–94.

Tedesco, J., Miller, J. and Spiker, J. (1999) 'Presidential campaigning on the information superhighway: An exploration of content and form', in L. Kaid and D. Bystrom (eds) *The Electronic Election: Perspectives on the 1996 Campaign Communication*, Mahwah, NJ: Lawrence Erlbaum: 51–63.

Thies, S. (31 May 2009) 'Polit-Generation 2.0: Online-Netzwerke wie "Twitter" und "Facebook" werden immer beliebter' [Political generation 2.0: Online networks like 'Twitter' and 'Facebook' get more and more popular], *Welt am Sonntag*, 22: NRW2.

Thomas, S. (2005) 'pervasive, persuasive e-learning: Modelling the pervasive learning space', *Proceedings of the Third IEEE International Conference on Pervasive Computing and Communications Workshops* (PERCOMW'05): 332–6.

Thorsen, E. (2010) 'BBC Newsroom convergence, online journalism and citizenship during the 2005 and 2010 UK General Elections', paper presented at the Communication and Citizenship IAMCR Conference, Braga, Portugal, 22 July.

Thurber, J. (2002) 'Is the permanent campaign alive and well after 9/11?', Online. Available HTTP: www.american.edu/spa/ccps/pdffiles/permanent.pdf (accessed 11 August 2003).

Tillmann, S. (13 August 2009) 'Die Internet-Lüge: Die Parteien eifern Barack Obama nach und verlagern den Bundestagswahlkampf mehr ins Netz' [The Internet deception: Parties imitate Obama and shift the national election campaign to the net]. *Financial Times Deutschland*, 10.

Titscher, S., Meyer, M., Wodak, R. and Vetter, E. (2000) *Methods of Text and Discourse Analysis*, London: Sage.

Tkach-Kawasaki, L. (2003) 'Politics@Japan: Party competition on the Internet in Japan', *Party Politics*, 9 (1): 105–23.

Tolbert, C. and McNeal, R. (2003) 'Unravelling the effects of the Internet on political participation', *Political Research Quarterly*, 56 (2): 175–85.

Trammell, K. (2006) 'Blog offensive: An exploratory analysis of attacks published on campaign blog posts from a political public relations perspective', *Public Relations Review*, 32 (4): 402–6.

Trammel, K. D., Williams, A. P., Postelnicu, M. and Landreville, K. D. (2006) 'Evolution of online campaigning: Increasing interactivity in candidate websites and blogs through text and technical features', *Mass Communication*, 9 (1): 21–44.

Trent, J. and Friedenberg, R. (1991) *Political Campaign Communication: Principles and Practices*, 2nd edn, Westport, CT: Praeger.

Trippi, J. (2004) *The Revolution Will Not be Televised: Democracy, the Internet and the Overthrow of Everything*, New York: Harper Collins.

Ulrich, K. and Eppinger, S. (1999) *Product Design and Development*, London: McGraw-Hill.

US Census Bureau (2006) *Voting and Registration in the Election of November 2004*, Washington, DC: U.S. Census Bureau.

Uther, P. (2007) Ségolène Royal s'invite dans Second Life, *Jeuxonline*. Online. Available HTTP: www.jeuxonline.info/actualite/13341/segolene-royal-invite-second-life (accessed 11 January 2008).

Utter, D. (2007) 'French politics goes to the blogs', 10 January. Online. Available HTTP: www.webpronewsfrance.com/2007/0110.html (accessed 12 January 2007).

Vaccari, C. (2008) 'Surfing to the Élysée: The Internet in the 2007 French Elections', *French Politics*, 6 (1): 1–22.

Van Dijk, J. (2006) *The Network Society*, London: Sage.

Van Eimeren, B. and Frees, B. (2009) 'Der Internetnutzer 2009 – multimedial und total vernetzt? Ergebnisse der ARD/ZDF-Onlinestudie 2009' [The 2009 Internet user – multimedia and totally connected?], *Media Perspektiven*, 7: 334–48.

Van Os, R. (2005) 'Framing Europe Online: French political parties and the European Election of 2004', *Information Polity*, 10 (3/4): 205–18.

Vasterman, P. L. M. (2005) 'Media-hype: Self-reinforcing news waves, journalistic standards and the construction of social problems', *European Journal of Communication*, 20: 508–30.

Vedel, T. (2000) 'L'Internet el les villes: trois approaches de la citoyennete', *Hermes*, 26–27: 247–62.

Vedel, T. (2003) 'Political communication in the age of the Internet', in P. J. Maarek and

G. Wolfsfeld (eds), *Political Communication in a New Era*, London: Routledge: 41–59.

Vedel, T. (2007) 'Les électuers et la champagne électorale: une vision désenchantée des candidats? Le panel Électoral Français 2007', vague 2, CEVIPOF. Online. Available HTTP: www.cevopof.msh-paris.fr (accessed 1 February 2008).

Vedel, T. and Michalska, K. K. (2007) 'Political participation and the Internet: Evidence from the 2007 French Presidential Election', paper presented at the 3rd International Conference on e-Government, University of Montreal, Canada, 26/28 September.

Verna, P. (2009) 'User-generated content: more popular than profitable', *E-marketer*, Online. Available HTTP: www.emarketer.com/Report.aspx?code=emarketer_2000549 (accessed 10 September 2009).

Villalba, B. (2003) 'Moving towards an evolution in political mediation? French political parties and the new ICTs', in R. Gibson, P. Nixon and S. Ward (eds) *Political Parties and the Internet. Net gain?* London: Routledge: 120–38.

Vitzthum, T. (1 April 2008) 'Die Blogisierung der Politik: Wie und warum Merkel, Westerwelle und Co. ihre Botschaften immer häufiger per Internet unters Volk bringen' [The blogisation of politics: How and why Merkel, Westerwelle and others turn to the Internet to deliver their messages in the public], *Welt Online*. Available HTTP: www.welt.de/welt_print/article1858079/Die_Blogisierung_der_Politik.html (accessed 5 May 2008).

Volkery, C. (26 August 2008) 'Twittern im Obama-Rausch: SPD-Generalsekretär Heil in Denver' [Tweeting like Obama: SPD general secretary Heil in Denver], *Spiegel Online*. Available HTTP: www.spiegel.de/politik/deutschland/0,1518,574521,00.html (accessed 2 October 2009).

Von Baeyer, H. C. (2003) *Information: The new language of science*, London: Phoenix.

Von Marschall, C. (23 August 2009) 'Online zum Sieg: Wie Obama den Wahlkampf revolutionierte – und warum das in Deutschland anders funktioniert' [Winning online: How Obama revolutionised the campaign – and why it works differently in Germany], *Der Tagesspiegel Online*. Available HTTP: www.tagesspiegel.de/politik/online-zum-sieg/1585868.html (accessed 30 September 2009).

Walsh, K. T. (2008) 'Massive turnout and desire for change give Barack Obama the presidency', *US News and World Report*. Online. Available HTTP: www.usnews.com/articles/news/campaign-2008/2008/11/05/massive-turnout-and-desire-for-change-give-barack-obama-the-presidency.html (accessed 5 November 2008).

Walther, J. B. (2004) 'Language and communication technology: Introduction to the special issue', *Journal of Language and Social Psychology*, 23 (4): 384–96.

Ward, S. (2008) 'Introduction: Parties and election campaigning online. A new era?', in S. Ward, D. Owen, R. Davis and D. Taras (eds) *Making a Difference: A Comparative View of the Role of the Internet in Election Politics*, Lanham, MD: Lexington Books: 1–14.

Ward, S. and Gibson, R. (1998) 'UK political parties on the Internet: Politics as usual in the new media?', *Harvard International Journal of Press Politics*, 3 (3): 14–38.

Ward, S. and Gibson, R. (2000) 'The politics of the future? UK parties and the Internet', in S. Coleman (ed.) *Elections in the Age of the Internet: Lessons from the United States*, London: Hansard Society: 29–36.

Ward, S. and Gibson, R. (2003) 'Online and on message?: Candidates' websites in the 2001 General Election', *British Journal of Politics and International Relations*, 5 (2): 188–205.

Ward, S., Gibson, R. and Lusoli, W. (2005) 'Old politics, new media: Parliament, the public and the Internet', paper presented to the Political Studies Association Conference, University of Leeds, 5–7 April.

Ward, S. and Lusoli, W. (2005) 'From weird to wired: MPs, the Internet and representative politics in the UK', *The Journal of Legislative Studies*, 11 (1): 57–81.

Ward, S., Owen, D., Davis, R. and Taras, D. (eds) (2008) *Making a Difference: A Comparative View of the Role of the Internet in Election Politics*, Lanham, MD: Lexington Books.

Watts, D. (1997) *Political Communications Today*, Manchester: Manchester University Press.

Webber, R. (2006) 'How parties used segmentation in the 2005 British General Election', *Journal of Direct Data and Digital Marketing Practice*, 7 (3): 239–52.

Weber, L., Loumakis, A. and Bergman, J. (2003) 'Who participates and why? An analysis of citizens on the Internet and the mass public', *Social Science Computer Review*, 21 (1): 26–42.

Weinberger, D. (2007) *Everything is Miscellaneous: The Power of the New Digital Disorder*, New York: Times Books.

Welch, E. W. and Hinnant, C. C. (2003) 'Internet use, transparency, and interactivity effects on trust in government', *System Sciences, 2003, Proceedings of the 36th Annual Hawaii International Conference*.

Wenger, E. (1999) *Communities of Practice: Learning, Meaning and Identity*, London: Cambridge University Press.

Wenger, E., McDermott, R. and Snyder, W. (2005) *Cultivating Communities of Practice: A Guide to Managing Knowledge*, New York: Harvard Business School Press.

Wetherell, M., Taylor, S. and Yates, S. (2001) *Discourse as Data: A Guide for Analysis*, London: Sage.

Wicks, R. H. and Souley, B. (2003) 'Going negative: Candidate usage of Internet websites during the 2000 Presidential Campaign', *Journalism and Mass Communication Quarterly*, 80 (1): 128–44.

Wiesendahl, E. (2001) 'Die Zukunft der Parteien' [The future of parties], in O. W. Gabriel, O. Niedermayer and R. Stöss (eds) *Parteiendemokratie in Deutschland*, Bonn: Bundeszentrale für politische Bildung.

Williams, A. P., Trammell, K. D., Postelnicu, M., Landreville, K. D. and Martin, J. D. (2005) 'Blogging and hyperlinking: Use of the Web to enhance viability during the 2004 US Campaign', *Journalism Studies*, 6 (2): 177–86.

Williams, R. (1997) 'The social shaping of information and communications technologies', in H. Kubicek, W. H. Dutton and R. Williams (eds) *The Social Shaping of Information Superhighways: European and American Roads to the Information Society*, Frankfurt: Campus Verlag: 299–338.

Winston, B. (1998) *Media Technology and Society: A History From the Telegraph to the Internet*, London: Routledge.

Wolf, G. (2004) 'How the Internet invented Howard Dean', *Wired Magazine*, Issue 12/01. Online. Available HTTP: www.wired.com/wired/archive/12.01/dean.html?pg=1&topic=&topic_set= (accessed 12 June 2008).

Wood, J. (2007) 'French politics go virtual', *Soft32*, 26 March. Online. Available HTTP: http://news/soft32.com/surreal-campaigns-as-french-go virtal_3786.html (accessed 11 December 2007).

Wood, L. (2009) 'Research and markets: By 2013, 155 million of US Internet users will consume some form of user-created content, up from 116 million in 2008', Reuters,

26 February. Online. Available HTTP: www.reuters.com/article/pressRelease/idUS144011+26-Feb-2009+BW20090226 (accessed 1 March 2009).

Wood, L. A. and Kroger, R. O. (2000) *Doing Discourse Analysis: Methods for Studying Action in Talk and Text*, Thousand Oaks, CA: Sage.

Wright, G. C. and Berkham M. B. (1986) 'Candidates and policy in United States Senate Elections', *The American Political Science Review*, 80 (2): 567–88.

Wring, D. (1996) 'Political marketing and party development in Britain: A "secret" history', *European Journal of Marketing*, 30 (10–11): 92–103.

Wring, D. (1999) 'The marketing colonisation of political campaigning', in B. Newman (ed.) *A Handbook of Political Marketing*, London: Sage: 41–53.

Wroe, A. and Herbert, J. (2008) *Assessing the Bush Presidency: A Tale of Two Terms*, Edinburgh: Edinburgh University Press.

Wu, T. (2006) 'Does YouTube really have legal problems?', *SLATE*, 26 October. Online. Available HTTP: www.slate.com/id/2152264 (accessed 12 September 2007).

Xenos, M. and Foot, K. (2005) 'Politics as usual or politics unusual? Position taking and dialogue on campaign websites in the 2002 U.S. elections', *Journal of Communication*, 55 (1): 169–85.

XiTi Monitor (2007a) 'Presidential election: The subjects of most interest to Internet users concerning the 4 candidates leading the polls', *XiTi Current Events Article*, 3 June. Online. Available HTTP: www.atinternet-institute.com/en-us/focus-on-current-events/the-2007-presidential-elections-february-2007/index-1–2–1–75.html (accessed 19 September 2007).

XiTi Monitor (2007b) '2nd round of the Presidential Election 2007: S. Royal and N. Sarkozy neck to neck on the Web', *XiTi Current Events Article*, 5 September. Online. Available HTTP: www.atinternet-institute.com/en-us/focus-on-current-events/the-2007-presidential-elections-may-9–2007/index-1–2–1–92.html (accessed 19 September 2007).

Zaller, J. (2002) 'The statistical power of election studies to detect media exposure effects in political campaigns', *Electoral Studies*, 21 (2): 297–329.

Zelle, C. (1995) 'Social dealignment versus political frustration: Contrasting explanations of the floating vote in Germany', *European Journal of Political Research*, 27 (3): 319–45.

Zillmann, D. and Brosius, H.-B. (2000) *Exemplification in Communication: The Influence of Case Reports on the Perception of Issues*, Mahwah, NJ: Lawrence Erlbaum.

Index

Page numbers in **bold** denote figures.